Political Philosophy versus History?
Contextualism and Real Politics in Contemporary Political Thought

Is the way in which political philosophy is conducted today too ahistorical? Does such ahistoricism render political philosophy too abstract? Is political philosophy thus incapable of dealing with the realities of political life? This volume brings together some of the world's leading political philosophers to address these crucial questions. The contributors focus especially on political philosophy's pretensions to universality, and on its strained relationship with the world of real politics. Some chapters argue that political philosophers should not be cowed by the accusations levied against them from outside of their own field. Others insist that these accusations require a dramatic reshaping of normative political thought. The volume will spark controversy across political philosophy and beyond.

Jonathan Floyd is British Academy Post-Doctoral Fellow in the Department of Politics and International Relations, University of Oxford, and Research Fellow in Political Theory at St Hilda's College, Oxford. He is currently working on a book on methodology in political philosophy, as well as a book on the same topic as the present volume.

Marc Stears is Fellow in Politics at University College, Oxford, and University Lecturer in Political Theory in the Department of Politics and International Relations, University of Oxford. His most recent book is *Demanding Democracy: American Radicals in Search of a New Politics* (2010).

T0384522

Political Philosophy versus History?

Contextualism and Real Politics in Contemporary Political Thought

Edited by

JONATHAN FLOYD AND MARC STEARS

CAMBRIDGE
UNIVERSITY PRESS

CAMBRIDGE
UNIVERSITY PRESS

University Printing House, Cambridge CB2 8BS, United Kingdom

Cambridge University Press is part of the University of Cambridge.

It furthers the University's mission by disseminating knowledge in the pursuit of education, learning and research at the highest international levels of excellence.

www.cambridge.org
Information on this title: www.cambridge.org/9780521146883

First published 2011

A catalogue record for this publication is available from the British Library

Library of Congress Cataloguing in Publication data
Political philosophy versus history : contextualism and real politics in contemporary political thought / edited by Jonathan Floyd, Marc Stears.
   p.   cm.
ISBN 978-0-521-19715-1 (hardback)
1. Political science – Philosophy.   I. Floyd, Jonathan, 1980–   II. Stears, Marc.   III. Title.
JA78.P53   2011
320.01–dc22

                                                          2011005953

ISBN 978-0-521-19715-1 Hardback
ISBN 978-0-521-14688-3 Paperback

Contents

    BONNIE HONIG AND MARC STEARS

    Relative value and assorted historical lessons: an afterword   206
    JONATHAN FLOYD

    Index   226

Note on the contributors

Jonathan Floyd is British Academy Post-Doctoral Fellow in the Department of Politics and International Relations, University of Oxford, and Research Fellow in Political Theory at St Hilda's College, Oxford. He is currently working on a book on methodology in political philosophy, as well as a book on the same topic as the present volume.

Gordon Graham is Henry Luce III Professor of Philosophy and the Arts at Princeton Theological Seminary. His recent publications include *The Re-enchantment of the World: Art versus Religion* (2007) and *Ethics and International Relations* (2008).

Bruce Haddock is Professor of Modern European Social and Political Thought at Cardiff University. His recent publications include *A History of Political Thought: From Antiquity to the Present* (2008) and *A History of Political Thought: 1789 to the Present* (2005).

Iain Hampsher-Monk is Professor of Political Theory at the University of Exeter. His recent publications include: 'Democracy and federation in the federalist papers', in M. Burgess and M. Gagnon (eds.), *Federal Democracies* (2009) and (with Andrew Hindmoor) 'Rational choice and interpretive evidence: caught between a rock and a hard place?', *Political Studies*, 58: 1 (2010).

Bonnie Honig is the Sarah Rebecca Roland Professor of Political Science at Northwestern University and a senior research professor at the American Bar Foundation. Her books include *Political Theory and the Displacement of Politics* (1993), *Democracy and the Foreigner* (2001) and *Emergency Politics: Paradox, Law, Democracy* (2009).

Paul Kelly is Professor of Political Theory and Head of the Government Department at LSE. His recent publications include *Locke's Second Treatise of Government* (2007) and *British Political Theory in the Twentieth Century* (2010).

Melissa Lane is Professor of Politics at Princeton University. Her books include *Method and Politics in Plato's Statesman* (1998) and *Plato's Progeny: How Plato and Socrates still Captivate the Modern Mind* (2001).

Andrew Sabl is Associate Professor of Public Policy and Political Science at the University of California, Los Angeles. He is the author of *Ruling Passions: Political Offices and Democratic Ethics* (2002) and is currently completing a book for Princeton University Press on the political theory of David Hume's *History of England*.

Marc Stears is Fellow in Politics at University College, Oxford, and University Lecturer in Political Theory in the Department of Politics and International Relations, University of Oxford. His most recent book is *Demanding Democracy: American Radicals in Search of a New Politics* (2010).

Acknowledgements

This book first emerged from a one-day workshop organised by Jonathan Floyd and hosted at University College, Oxford in the summer of 2007. We are extremely grateful to everyone who participated in that initial event, including Michael Freeden, Benjamin Jackson, Mark Philp, Alan Ryan, Quentin Skinner and Adam Swift. We are also grateful to the participants at two further events, one held at the American Political Science Association annual convention in Boston in 2008, and the other, in 2009, again at University College, Oxford. These participants included Annabel Brett, Christopher Brooke, Jeremy Farris, Jeremy Jennings, David Leopold, Lois McNay and Reidar Maliks. Generous financial support for these events came from Oxford's Centre for Political Ideologies, where we warmly thank the Centre's Director, Michael Freeden, for his invaluable assistance, and from University College, Oxford, where we equally warmly thank the Senior Tutor, Anne Knowland. We also greatly appreciated the work of the excellent team at Cambridge University Press who helped us transform the conversations at these events into a book. John Haslam was the ideal editor, generous and demanding in exactly the right measure, and Josephine Lane offered superb support throughout the final process.

We have both learnt an enormous amount from colleagues and friends as we have considered how best to develop this book. Jonathan Floyd would like to thank, in particular, Rita Floyd. She was the first to hear of the idea for this endeavour, and has encouraged him along every step of the way. Marc Stears would also like to thank Elizabeth Frazer, Bonnie Honig, Desmond King, David Leopold, Lois McNay, Lizzy Pellicano, Stuart White and Lea Ypi for extremely stimulating and insightful conversations on questions at the heart of our project. The support of all of these people has been invaluable. Finally, we would also like to thank each other. Marc Stears has nothing but admiration for the energy, determination and thoughtfulness with which Jonathan has shaped this project throughout. Jonathan Floyd also has a great deal of admiration for Marc – in this case not just for being an excellent co-editor, but also for supporting the project back when it was just an idea and he was just one pesky graduate student amongst many. We hope very much that our readers enjoy the results.

Introduction

JONATHAN FLOYD AND MARC STEARS

Political philosophy is a peculiarly self-reflective discipline. Even more than their colleagues in other subjects throughout the humanities and social sciences, political philosophers regularly question the means and purpose of their practice.

In this volume we carve out a new approach to the identity of political philosophy by exploring a problem that is central to such disciplinary soul-searching: the problem of political philosophy's relationship with history. We do this in part because, according to whether they describe their approach to political philosophy as analytic, continental, Rawlsian, post-Rawlsian, pluralist, realist, post-structural, or indeed, outright historical, political philosophers of different stripes tend, amongst other things, to hold very different positions on this relationship, and that is a very curious pattern. We also do it because, as evinced by the following chapters, reflecting upon the significance of history for political philosophy soon leads to a host of new insights about the nature of our subject. But we also do it for another reason. We do it because, of the many accusations made of political philosophy over the last forty or so years, the claim that it is carried out in too 'ahistorical' a fashion has been not just one of the most prominent,[1] but also, interestingly enough, one of the least scrutinised.[2]

---

[1] Amongst other places, it can be found in the works of Isaiah Berlin, John Dunn, Raymond Geuss, John Gray, Charles Larmore, Alasdair MacIntyre, Richard Rorty, Judith Shklar, Quentin Skinner, James Tully and Bernard Williams.

[2] Instead, one generally finds in the literature engagements either with those individual thinkers who have levelled this accusation, or with questions pertaining more to matters of methodology in the history of political thought, e.g. G. Graham, 'Macintyre's fusion of history and philosophy', in J. Horton and S. Mendus (eds.), *After Macintyre* (Cambridge: Polity, 1994), 161–75; M. Philp, 'Political theory and history', in D. Leopold and M. Stears, *Political Theory: Methods and Approaches* (Oxford: Oxford University Press, 2008); and R. Tuck, 'History', in R. E. Goodin and P. Pettit (eds.), *A Companion to Contemporary Political Philosophy* (Oxford: Wiley-Blackwell, 1993).

The variation in content given to this charge against political philosophy – the charge that it somehow is or at least tries to be too ahistorical – is also a most curious thing. Sometimes, for instance, it involves the grand claim that we cannot know what political principles to follow until we know what universal human values underpin them, and cannot know those until we know first just what values have, as a matter of fact, been adhered to in all known historical periods. History, on this account, is invaluable because it gives us access to timeless moral knowledge. Alternatively, it might involve the more modest suggestion that even if the search for 'timeless' values is hopeless, history can nevertheless reveal the political principles upon which, it just so happens, humanity is steadily converging. History, in this case, might divine for us the *telos* towards which we are proceeding. A third suggestion, more modest still, would be that even if there is no such convergence, perhaps the historical record reveals that all but one set of principles, when politically enacted, end in disaster. History, in this case, would identify for us the only set of political principles worth implementing.

These are not, of course, the most plausible of all possible suggestions, although they have all been advanced, in various forms, by notable political thinkers down the ages.[3] The authors gathered in this volume, by contrast, have much more subtle and striking visions of the history-political-philosophy relationship in their sights. Yet what is really striking is that a clear set of shared concerns have emerged from their work. When we, as editors, first approached our authors, we asked them straightforwardly to write on the potential significance of history for political philosophy. Yet without exception, and without further prompting, they each homed in on either one or other of two themes: the first of which concerns the place of *universalism* in political philosophy, and the second of which concerns the place of *realism*. On the basis of these chapters, then, it has become clear to us that the best way to think about our subject is in response to these two challenges.

First is the challenge of – and to – universalism. Here political philosophers are required to find the right balance between understanding political principles as timeless prescriptions, applicable and determinate in all times and all places, and understanding them instead as theoretical

---

[3] For sustained discussion of both these and other possibilities, see J. Floyd, 'Is political philosophy too ahistorical?', *Critical Review of International Social and Political Philosophy*, 12: 4 (2009).

distillations of whatever moral culture it is that we happen to find ourselves a part of. This presents a spectrum which ranges from understanding morality as a universal and singular blueprint to seeing it as composed of an incommensurable plurality of local codes; between understanding political concepts such as tolerance and justice as timeless and universally significant theoretical phenomena and understanding them as temporarily useful tools made available solely for the purpose of solving contingent and local problems; and between understanding values such as liberty and happiness as transcendent, intuitively knowable entities and understanding them as both by-products of contingent historical processes and as items which only interpretive historical enquiry will be able to discern. Here, in short, our task is to situate political philosophy between the potentially strident demands of universalism and contextualism.

The second challenge is that of – and to – *realism*. Here the demand is to situate political philosophy between utopianism and pessimism. Drawing less on the history of ethics and intellectual enquiry and more on the history of political practice, political philosophers are required to work out just how ambitious political philosophy ought to be in its prescriptions. In order to do this, we shall need to gain a better understanding both of the timeless features of politics – if any such exist – and of those features which are peculiar to politics in the here and now. With Raymond Geuss, for instance, we shall want to identify the ways in which the necessities of power always permeate and influence political possibilities, whilst with John Dunn we shall want to know just what trends and obstacles have to be particularly attended to in the face of the modern state, modern capitalism and democratic societies.[4] History, in this case, tells us both of those enduring and permanently problematic features of political life – such that political philosophy must take account of them or render itself irrelevant – and of those particular features of political life as it exists today, which, again, any political philosophy worthy of the name will have to come to terms with if it is to function as a guide to practical action.

We might further consider here that, when properly understood, the task of positioning ourselves in response to this second challenge

---

[4] See R. Geuss, *Philosophy and Real Politics* (Princeton, NJ: Princeton University Press, 2008) and J. Dunn, *The Cunning of Unreason* (London: HarperCollins, 2000).

requires not one choice but two, for what we shall have to do in this case is render political philosophy more realistic not just in terms of *what* it tells us to aim for but also in terms of *how* it tells us to achieve it. What we shall have to decide, in the light of what history tells us, is not just whether we ought to aim for something like Plato's *Kallipolis* or settle for a workable peace, but also whether we ought to try to achieve either of these things by violent or by peaceful means, by way of a permanent revolution or in accordance with the dictates of public reason, in support of a Malcolm X or a Martin Luther King, a Mao or a Gandhi. And the point now, to be clear, is not simply that there is an ethics of war and an ethics of peace, an ethics of good circumstances and an ethics of bad; it is instead that people will often need to act in morally regrettable yet politically necessary ways in the course of forging and preserving whatever forms of society they take to be desirable. Our task here, therefore, will be to frame the relationship between politics and political philosophy in just the right way, which means working with just the right kind of realism – neither too ambitious nor too pessimistic. We shall need to study what history tells us of the ineluctable necessities of political life, and then work out just what those necessities entail for the kinds of political prescriptions issued by political philosophers.

So, as political philosophers challenged by history we shall have on the one hand to locate ourselves on a spectrum between universal morality and a local ethics of context, whilst on the other on a spectrum between utopian idealism and political pessimism. It is with both of these tasks that the following chapters help us. Responding either to the suggestion that history tells us how *universalistic* political philosophy ought to try and be, or to the suggestion that it tells us how politically *realistic* it ought to become, the shared ambition of all of our authors is to see how, if at all, history may be used to get these balances right. Does history tell us something of what morality is? Does it tell us something of what politics permits? This is what we hope to find out.

The challenge of universalism

The chapters that follow begin by tackling history's challenge to universalism. Paul Kelly appropriately opens our volume with a history of the contextualist challenge to abstract universalism in political philosophy. His chapter begins by tracing the influence of R. G. Collingwood's claim that 'philosophers must be historians, or at least historians of thought' on a generation of political philosophers, many of whom worked for long periods in Cambridge, including John Dunn, Raymond Geuss, Quentin Skinner and Bernard Williams. Kelly shows the ways in which this generation pushed Collingwood's arguments to new levels, moving beyond the claim that history usefully informs political philosophy to the far bolder assertion that historical investigation demonstrates the essential error in all efforts to transcend the 'particularities of our own experience' and discern a more objective, transcendental idea of 'political reason'. Having surveyed the scene with an admirable generosity of spirit, Kelly then mounts a spirited, even fierce, defence of the aspiration to objectivism in political philosophy. Finding an initially unlikely ally in the hermeneutic theorist Hans-Georg Gadamer, Kelly insists that the Cambridge School's critique is over-stated, deriving substantive conclusions that do not in fact follow from its persuasive premises. While it is important for political philosophers to be alert to the contingencies of time and place, Kelly thus concludes, such attention as they pay need not distract them from the deeper philosophical tasks of assessing the 'objectivity or rightness' of first-order claims about politics.

In our second chapter, Jonathan Floyd, like Kelly, considers and rejects a number of suggestions made in recent times regarding the significance of historical context to political philosophy. Instead, he argues, we ought to examine the historical context, not of our contingently produced moral culture, but rather of political philosophy itself. His suggestion is that if political philosophers do find it difficult to produce plausible justifications for their particular proposed principles, then perhaps that difficulty derives not so much from their universalistic ambitions, as contextualists might think, but rather from certain aspects of the inherited method of enquiry they invariably adopt. This method Floyd calls 'mentalism', the defining assumption of which is that political principles, if they are to be justified, must be done so by reference to patterns in the way that we – that is, all human beings – think. As he points out, the suggestion that normative enquiry ought always to begin by reflecting upon how we think or feel about a simple and abstract situation – say, a boy drowning in a pond whom you could easily help if you chose to – before then moving on to consider just what our 'thinking' about that situation then 'means' for more complex and contested dilemmas, is one that is so established in our subject that it is hardly even noticed *as* a method at all. For Floyd, however, this method not only exists but is deeply flawed, a point he then explains by providing a brief demonstration of its inability to perform the task required of it. Instead, he thinks, political philosophers should be more concerned with patterns in the way that we behave than patterns in the way that we think – a point which, interestingly enough, puts him on shared ground with much of the 'realism' discussed in the later part of this book.

This then takes us to our third chapter, in which Bruce Haddock both continues this focus on the role of context in political philosophy and reaches very different conclusions from those drawn by either Kelly or Floyd. For Haddock, as humans living with others, we constantly enquire as to how we can establish terms of co-operation with others. The precise terms of that question change through time and space, Haddock insists – hence contingency – even whilst the general approach to providing an answer – what Haddock calls 'hard thinking' – does not. And we think best, he continues, when we are able to draw on our historical experience and the historical experience of others. Seen this way, the study of the history of political thought, of political philosophy, and even of political action itself, are divided not so much by their metaphysical or methodological underpinnings but rather by their relative distance to the necessities of action; by, as Haddock puts it, their 'urgency'. Other attempts to divide these forms of thinking from each other are always mistaken, Haddock concludes. Try as we might, we cannot but be substantive philosophers, historians and political actors all at the same time.

Gordon Graham's final chapter of Part I also draws our attention to the tension between universalism and contextualism in political philosophy. Insisting that the study of this subject must be clearly distinguished from the practices of the sciences, social or otherwise, Graham points out that whereas the sciences seek explanations and causal patterns – drawing on data, testing hypotheses and establishing 'results' as they do so – philosophy, and especially political philosophy, is concerned instead with a different kind of pursuit of truth. There is no 'progress' as such in philosophy, he argues; no movement towards 'demonstrably right answers'. Instead, there are questions that are posed differently by different generations, to which we sometimes return and from which we sometimes depart. On this account, we return to history in the form of studying the great texts of the past, at least when it can help us think about the questions that currently trouble us. The texts that we examine, and the way that we do so, are thus driven by our recognition of them as potential repositories of wisdom and sources of inspiration, even though we accept that the task of translating their arguments from their authors' time to ours is always a difficult one. Difficulty is not the same as impossibility, though, and Graham implores political philosophers to remember that.

The challenge of realism

In the wake of this final call to attend to the texts of the past, whilst not leaving them to fester in their own contexts, our chapters shift from the challenge of universalism to the challenge of realism. The problem now becomes that of identifying the extent to which history determines the level of optimism or pessimism that informs our political philosophising. Iain Hampsher-Monk's chapter opens this section and relates it directly back to the earlier debate. For Hampsher-Monk, it is vitally important for scholars and practitioners to distinguish between three separate endeavours: first, political philosophy, which rightly seeks to discern 'truths about the political realm'; second, the history of political thought, which tells the story of how such philosophising has changed across time; and, third, rhetoric, which is the practice of shaping political attitudes and actions through the use of argument. Rhetoricians, he concludes, are intimately concerned with ascertaining the limits of the 'actually possible' in political attitude and action, whilst political philosophers are not. It is not the task of the philosopher, on this account, to try to change the world, just to understand it, and, as long as we understand this distinction, then political philosophy should best proceed in ignorance of the limits that actually existing political beliefs might bring to bear in the hurly-burly world of 'real politics'.

Andrew Sabl, in Chapter 7, disputes exactly this separation. For Sabl, the very best kind of political philosophy is that which bridges the distinction between 'is and ought', and which employs subtle historical understanding in order to do so. Political philosophy, on this reading, should strive to be 'realist', and will be most realistic when it becomes most historical. In developing this argument, Sabl draws heavily on the Harvard School of realist political philosophers, led most notably by Judith Shklar. Such realists, he notes, are often criticised for being too conservative or pragmatic, with their attentiveness to the contingencies of time and place leading them to be too willing to cut their philosophical coat according to their historical cloth. This, Sabl insists, is an error because it relies upon the assumption that a philosophy that is attentive to the limitations of actual times and places is incapable of advancing convincing political arguments. Such is simply not the case, Sabl argues. Rather, if philosophers are really to make persuasive arguments, then they must be open to refutation, and the set of refutations that one can draw on must include claims derived from historically informed accounts of the realistic limits of political possibility. The fear that such refutations will limit the scope and ambition of our philosophising is natural, Sabl concludes, but does not make that fact avoidable.

Whereas Sabl emphasises the constraining role that realistic historical understanding should play in political philosophising, Melissa Lane's chapter emphasises instead its potential liberating characteristics. Although she agrees with Sabl that the very best of political philosophy is informed by realistic assessments of the politically possible, she also insists that such assessments can sometimes provoke more, rather than less, ambitious forms of political thinking. Historical reflection on actual politics can, she argues, provide exemplars of particular forms of behaviour, both good and bad, and can also lead philosophers to consider recommendations that they would otherwise have either rejected or failed to consider. John Rawls, she suggests, became far more open to the role of religion in public argumentation after he had spent time considering the actual practices of the anti-slavery movement in the nineteenth-century United States. Far from being solely a constraint, then, or an invitation to pessimism, well-informed historical reflection might actually make political philosophers bolder in their aspirations, perhaps even more utopian.

This theme is taken up further in Bonnie Honig and Marc Stears's closing chapter. Tracing the development of realist political philosophy over the last two decades, Honig and Stears detect both pessimistic and optimistic strands in this development, just as exemplified by Sabl and Lane in this volume. Neither of these strands, they go on to insist, deserves the name of 'realism', for their invocation of the 'real' is necessarily always partial, informed as much by their substantive political positions and by their own constructed narratives as by any observation of the rich and complex historical record of which realists claim to be so attentive. The solution, however, Honig and Stears conclude, is not to abandon the attempt to embed political philosophising in history and its stories of the politically possible, but instead to accept that such efforts will never overcome the complexities and dilemmas with which political philosophers are always faced. It is crucial, therefore, that political philosophy be 'real', yet also vital that we recognise that this reality will always itself be contested.

Conclusion

The chapters assembled in this volume offer new insights into the questions both of whether political philosophy is too ahistorical and of what would happen if it were to cease to be so. It is no surprise that our contributors disagree, sometimes ferociously so. Yet what we hope is clear from all of them is that these questions are far from trivial, far from being merely of 'methodological interest', and far from being tied irrevocably to the future of the Cambridge School and its approach to the history of political thought. They are instead crucial to the endeavour in which all political philosophers are engaged. We can, of course, never expect complete agreement on whether political philosophy should pursue universal truths or local knowledge, or on whether it should be constrained or liberated by assessments of political possibility. What we can expect is that those who read the following chapters will be much better informed in their decisions about such things than they would have been had they not done so.

PART I

The challenge of contextualism

1 Rescuing political theory from the tyranny of history

PAUL KELLY

... the only way to make discernible progress in political philosophy is by studying history, social and economic institutions and the real world of politics in a reflective way. This is not incompatible with "doing philosophy"; rather, in this area, it is the only sensible way to proceed. After all, a major danger in using highly abstractive methods in political philosophy is that one will succeed in merely generalising one's own local prejudices and repackaging them as demands of reason. The study of history can help us to counteract this natural human bias.[1]

Raymond Geuss's warning against excessive abstraction in political philosophy is well taken and familiar. Similarly, the claim that attention to history is also important for progress in political theory and philosophy is also eminently sensible (as far as it goes), and unlikely to be denied by any but the most uncompromising of rationalists: the late Robert Nozick and more recently the late Gerry Cohen might perhaps come to mind.[2] Most contemporary political philosophers acknowledge the importance of history and contingent circumstances in thinking about politics and moral life.[3] What is at issue is how far we should push this acknowledgement of the claims of history for any viable political philosophy. This is the issue I wish to address in this chapter. For despite the superficial good sense of Geuss's claims in the opening epigraph, he goes on in most of his work to make a much stronger assault on the possibility of a political philosophy that does not give pride of place to history, and he uses an appeal to history to support his scepticism about the claims of reason in political theory. In that respect

---

[1] R. Geuss, *Outside Ethics* (Princeton, NJ: Princeton University Press, 2005), 38–9.
[2] R. Nozick, *Anarchy, State and Utopia* (Oxford: Basil Blackwell, 1974) and G. A. Cohen, *Rescuing Justice and Equality* (Cambridge, MA: Harvard University Press, 2008), chs. 6 and 7.
[3] Even Geuss's *bête noire*, John Rawls, acknowledges the significance of contingency and history, in *Political Liberalism*, 2nd edn (New York: Columbia University Press, 2005).

Geuss is only one of a number of political philosophers and theorists who have made much stronger claims for the normative dominance of history in political philosophy and political theory. These thinkers, who deploy what I shall call a Collingwoodian paradigm[4] of the normativity of history, wish to subordinate the exercise of critical practical reason in politics to the contingencies of historical experience and practice. The point of this challenge is not merely to encourage a greater sensitivity to historical diversity[5] but rather the stronger claim that history undermines or limits the scope and aspiration of normative political philosophy. The turn to history that has developed within political theory over the last few decades has attempted to undermine the authority and claims of political theory or philosophy and displace what it considers the hubristic universalism of what has come to be called political moralism. By political moralism is meant the approach to normative political theory that begins with the primacy of ethical or moral claims and which uses these to construct theories about the fundamental structure of rightly ordered politics. The most important example of this approach to political theory is John Rawls's *A Theory of Justice* and similar theories inspired by Rawls's example.[6]

The realist assault on political moralism advanced by Stuart Hampshire, Bernard Williams, Raymond Geuss and Glen Newey[7]

---

[4] In identifying and criticising this Collingwoodian paradigm, I make no claim about the historical metaphysics of R. G. Collingwood. Other contributors to this volume are better placed to assess how far Collingwood is fairly described or caricatured by this epithet – see the chapter by Bruce Haddock in this volume. That said, a number of contemporary advocates of the subordination of political philosophy to history do indeed cite Collingwood as an authority, and it is that which I am precisely concerned with; see especially A. MacIntyre, *A Short History of Ethics* (London: Routledge & Kegan Paul, 1966), Q. Skinner, *Visions of Politics, Vol. I: Regarding Method* (Cambridge: Cambridge University Press, 2002) *passim*, and B. Williams, *In the Beginning was the Deed: Realism and Moralism in Political Argument* (Princeton, NJ: Princeton University Press, 2005), *passim*.

[5] For a recent critical assessment of the argument that political theory needs to be more historical, see J. Floyd, 'Is political philosophy too ahistorical?' *Critical Review of International Social and Political Philosophy*, 12 (2009), 513–33.

[6] J. Rawls, *A Theory of Justice* (Oxford: Oxford University Press, 1971).

[7] S. Hampshire, *Innocence and Experience* (Stanford: Stanford University Press, 1989); B. Williams, *In the Beginning was the Deed* (Princeton, NJ: Princeton University Press, 2005); R. Geuss, *Philosophy and Real Politics* (Princeton, NJ: Princeton University Press, 2008); and G. Newey, *After Politics* (Basingstoke: Palgrave, 2001).

amongst others is merely the latest variant of the historian's attack on the pretensions of political philosophy. Williams and by implication Geuss fall within the Collingwoodian paradigm and other 'realists' such as Hampshire and Newey, whilst not necessarily retreating to a historical metaphysics, have also deflated the claims of political philosophy in the face of the claims of history.

My concern in this chapter will be to contest the bold claims for history as a constraint upon normative political philosophy – what one might call the tyranny of history over political philosophy. The argument will begin with an outline of what I call the Collingwoodian paradigm and its subordination of political philosophy to history. In the latter part of the chapter I will challenge the pessimistic conclusion that the turn to history undermines the possibility of normative political philosophy. I intend to argue that contrary to the claims of MacIntyre, Skinner, Williams and Geuss, the turn to history must be subordinate to the demands of philosophical justification. Consequently, rather than making a case against the possibility and value of historical construction, the acknowledgement of history of the sort claimed by Geuss provides only useful supplementary material to a proper political philosophy.

The Collingwoodian paradigm – the problem

Although an influential historian and philosopher in his own lifetime,[8] R. G. Collingwood cultivated the impression of being a philosophical outsider through his autobiography and by his disdain for the dominant English philosophical schools of logical realism and logical positivism.[9] He remains a difficult philosopher to summarise and to fit into any of the standard schools of twentieth-century British philosophy, as he was equally uncomfortable with being described as an Idealist. Since his death, his philosophical reputation has been eclipsed by the linguistic turn associated with the later Wittgenstein at Cambridge and with Austin and Ryle at Oxford, so that his philosophy is considered as of merely historical interest outside the specialist field of the philosophy of

---

[8] He was after all elected to the Waynefleet Professorship of Metaphysical Philosophy at Oxford and a Fellowship of the British Academy, two of the signs of membership of the English philosophical elite.
[9] R. G. Collingwood, *An Autobiography* (Oxford: Oxford University Press, 1939).

history, which has itself become a marginal field in post-war British and American philosophy. Yet in recent political philosophy, where his major work has been systematically neglected by all but specialists,[10] Collingwood's ideas have begun to enjoy something of a renaissance, at least if we are to trust those who claim to be influenced by his reduction of philosophy to history. This return to Collingwood for inspiration is hardly an attempt to resurrect his defence of liberal civility from *The New Leviathan* and to offer it as an alternative to the liberal egalitarian philosophies that have emerged from post-war analytical philosophy. Yet in the work of Alasdair MacIntyre, Quentin Skinner, and to a degree in the work of a realist liberal such as Bernard Williams, we can see the explicit acknowledgement of Collingwood's equation of philosophy with history as a source of the turn to history in contemporary political philosophy and ethics. One can also argue that there is a considerable debt to Collingwood in Isaiah Berlin's amalgamation of political philosophy and the history of ideas, although in Berlin's case any philosophical metaphysic remains resolutely immanent.[11] In this respect Collingwood serves more as a signpost marking the correct direction for political philosophy to follow than as a teacher of specific doctrines.[12]

The turn to history amongst political philosophers and theorists has complex roots in the rise of positivism in American and British political science in the post-war period and the rejection of grand meta-narratives by post-war political theorists as diverse as Karl Popper, Isaiah Berlin and John Rawls. Popper's political writings are a complex extension of his path-breaking work in the philosophy of science. By criticising the pseudo-scientific claims of teleological theories of history (by which he primarily means Marxism, although National Socialism is also criticised) Popper rejects grand political speculation and replaces it with a form of what he calls 'piece-meal social engineering' in which all the problems of politics are reduced to technical questions, rather than grand questions about the nature of the good life or man's place in the

---

[10] R. G. Collingwood, *The New Leviathan* (Oxford: Clarendon Press, 1942). For the best discussion of Collingwood's philosophy see D. Boucher, *The Social and Political Thought of R. G. Collingwood* (New York: Cambridge University Press, 1989).

[11] See the essays in I. Berlin, *The Proper Study of Mankind* (London: Pimlico, 1998).

[12] This is actually how Collingwood wished to be read; see Collingwood, *An Autobiography*, 118–19. See also P. Johnson, *R. G. Collingwood: An Introduction* (Bristol: Thoemmes Press, 1998).

universe.[13] Subsequent liberals such as Berlin and Rawls can be seen to follow in this tradition by rejecting the claims of history as a teleological process and furthermore attempting to remain neutral on questions about ultimate political truths and values. This fact coupled, in Rawls's case, with a style of philosophy owing much, at least superficially, to the analytical approach of linguistic philosophy, led many to see contemporary political philosophy and ethics as dangerously abstract and consequently narrowly constrained to repeat as universal or conceptual truths the political prejudices of contemporary liberal societies.

Mid to late twentieth-century political philosophy has abandoned grand metaphysical claims and targeted more modest goals, but it has retained a belief in the role of reason and rejected the idea that a turn to history undermines the claims of political reason by reducing them to local prejudices. Isaiah Berlin, for example, acknowledges the claims of history and the contingency of human experience, but spends much of his later writings denying that this commits him to relativism or the view that his liberalism is little more than a local prejudice that cannot be defended by appeal to reason.[14]

Yet it is precisely this claim – that the historical vindication of reason undermines the point of normative political theory – that is advanced directly or indirectly by the likes of Skinner, MacIntyre and Williams on the basis of their own reading of Collingwood, and it is for this reason that I have characterised this Anglophone variant of contextualism as the Collingwoodian paradigm.

Skinner, MacIntyre and Williams all in different ways acknowledge the influence of Collingwood on their rejection of abstract normative political philosophy and their turn to history, and all three endorse some version of the authentically Collingwoodian claim that philosophers must be historians, or at least historians of thought.[15] One of the principal reactions against the emergence of an analytical political

---

[13] K. Popper, *Conjectures and Refutations* (London: Routledge & Kegan Paul, 1963).

[14] See 'The pursuit of the ideal' and 'Alleged relativism in eighteenth-century European thought', in I. Berlin, *The Crooked Timber of Humanity* (London: HarperCollins, 1991), 1–19 and 70–90. In a curious way Berlin is perhaps the most authentically Collingwoodian figure in late twentieth-century political philosophy, in no small part as a consequence of their shared interest in Vico.

[15] R. G. Collingwood, in R. Martin (ed.), *An Essay on Metaphysics* (Oxford: Clarendon Press, 2002).

philosophy in the post-war English-speaking world was the turn to history and the history of ideas that is associated with Cambridge historians such as John Pocock, Quentin Skinner and John Dunn[16] and their many students. Although describing themselves as disinterested historians free from the unhistorical concerns of normative theorists, they contributed an important voice that challenges the pretensions of political theory by asserting the historical specificity of political utterances and contextually bound speech-acts. This has had the consequence of asserting the disciplinary priority of historians over the ideas of political thinkers from the past, with the concomitant diminution of the value of reading such philosophers for wider philosophical insight. They endorse the prejudice that philosophical approaches to the thought of past thinkers is either 'history or humbug' – and philosophers and other theorists are regularly ridiculed for their naive handling of the thought of past thinkers, or their deployment of what Quentin Skinner describes as the 'fallacies' of doctrines, prolepsis or coherence. (What precisely is fallacious about these 'fallacies' is never clearly explained.) These 'historians' have always, rather disingenuously, denied that they are interested in deflating the claims of political theorists and instead asserted that they are only interested in the historian's proper business of recovering the past in its own terms.[17]

[16] See J. G. A. Pocock, 'The history of political thought: a methodological enquiry', in P. Laslett and W. G. Runciman (eds.), *Philosophy, Politics and Society, Series II* (Oxford: Basil Blackwell, 1962), 183–202; *Politics, Language and Time* (London: Methuen, 1972); and *The Machiavellian Moment* (Princeton, NJ: Princeton University Press, 1975); Q. Skinner, 'Meaning and understanding in the history of ideas', *History and Theory*, 8 (1960), 199–215; Q. Skinner, 'Conventions and the understanding of speech acts', *Philosophical Quarterly*, 20 (1970), 118–38; and Q. Skinner, 'Some problems in the analysis of thought and action', *Political Theory*, 2 (1974), 277–303. For a comprehensive review of Skinner's methodological position, together with critical essays and Skinner's response, see J. Tully (ed.), *Meaning and Context: Quentin Skinner and his Critics* (Cambridge: Polity Press, 1988); J. Dunn, 'The identity of the history of ideas', reprinted in J. Dunn, *Political Obligation and its Historical Context* (Cambridge: Cambridge University Press, 1980), 13–28; J. Dunn, 'What is living and what is dead in the political theory of John Locke?', in J. Dunn, *Interpreting Political Responsibility* (Cambridge: Polity Press, 1990), 9–25; and J. Dunn, *The History of Political Thought and Other Essays* (Cambridge: Cambridge University Press, 1996).

[17] This is most clear in Skinner's contribution to the Republican theory of freedom in the 1990s. See Q. Skinner, 'Machiavelli and the maintenance of liberty', *Politics*, 18 (1983), 3–15; Q. Skinner, 'The idea of negative liberty', in R. Rorty,

However, the Cambridge historians of ideas have lent support both directly and indirectly to others such as Geuss who are much more explicitly hostile to what he describes as the moralism of political philosophy.

Alasdair MacIntyre also criticises abstract normative political philosophy on putative Collingwoodian grounds when he argues that moral philosophy is the result of a history of particular answers to particular questions thrown up by different societies at different times. There is clearly a residual Marxian element in MacIntyre's thought, but he also explicitly acknowledges Collingwood's logic of question and answer in the structure of his history of ethics.[18] The logic of question and answer is transformed in Skinner's work in his analysis of speech-acts and linguistic actions as the primary object of the history of political thought. He claims that the history of political thought should only be concerned (if it is to be historical) with the linguistic actions of authors in particular contexts. Hence Skinner's concern to draw the attention of political theorists to such neglected topics as the deployment of rhetorical strategies and devices by great political thinkers such as Thomas Hobbes.[19] Neither MacIntyre nor Skinner explicitly states that the logic of question and answer undermines the claims of normative political realism, but the implication is clear. If all thought is always practical in addressing specific problems and answering specific questions then there is neither any possibility of universal political reason nor any universal problems of politics for such a political theory to address. Skinner is indifferent to this consequence, as he is ultimately a historian not a political philosopher, but his assault on perennial questions does raise a question about the status of any universal defence of justice, freedom or right. Similarly MacIntyre does not abandon the idea of

J. B. Schneewind and Q. Skinner (eds.), *Philosophy in History* (Cambridge: Cambridge University Press, 1984); and Q. Skinner, 'Pre-Humanist Origins of Republican Ideas', in G. Bock, Q. Skinner and M. Viroli (eds.), *Machiavelli and Republicanism* (Cambridge: Cambridge University Press, 1990). For the influence of Skinner's recovery of Civic Republicanism, see P. Pettit, *Republicanism* (Oxford: Clarendon Press, 1997).

[18] *A Short History of Ethics*. The argument is developed in a more sophisticated fashion in his later *Whose Justice? Which Rationality?* (London: Duckworth, 1988).

[19] See Skinner's *Reason and Rhetoric in the Philosophy of Hobbes* (Cambridge: Cambridge University Press, 1996), where he uses an analysis of Hobbes's complex rhetorical strategies to critique reductionist game-theoretical interpretations of Hobbes's arguments.

normative theory but claims that this must be internal to pre-given conceptual schemes or moral visions. There can be no possibility of breaking out of our moral frameworks and engaging across moral frameworks from the perspective of universal reason. The limits of reason to vindicate any universal ethical vision lead him to accept the primacy of faith over reason in his later philosophical Thomism.

Bernard Williams might seem to have least in common with this overt Collingwoodianism of Skinner and MacIntyre, but his views on normative political philosophy as a species of moralism also reflect this recognition of the historical contingency and specificity of our moral practices and therefore of the inability of ethics or morality to provide an ultimate guide to political judgement. This is illustrated most clearly in his claims about the relativism of distance, where the absence of real moral confrontation enables us to recognise the limits and specificity of our moral principles and values.[20] The richer our historical understandings, the less likely are we to make facile judgements that range across historically distinct world views and practices. Alongside the relativism of distance, Williams's realist turn, which emphasises the priority of the 'basic legitimation demand', denies that we are able to authentically accept forms of life and institutional arrangements that might well have been recognised as legitimate by others in different times and places. Yet the 'basic legitimation demand' and its current broadly liberal content is for Williams a fact of modernity, rather than a conclusion of reason. In this respect it is more like an absolute presupposition, rather than a conclusion of reason or the deliverance of a theory of justice.[21]

With the exception of Skinner's historical methodology, where the rejection of normative argument can be explained by the academic division of labour, the proponents of the Collingwoodian paradigm do not explicitly deny the possibility of philosophical rationalism and abstract normative political theory. But they do cast doubt on its value and interest as a way of addressing politics. It is precisely this point that is taken up by philosophers like Geuss who wish to make the further claim that the attempt to construct an abstract political philosophy must fail, because it can only be the local prejudices of a particular society. The turn to history has the consequence of sapping the confidence of normative political philosophy in the face of charges such as

---

[20] B. Williams, *Ethics and the Limits of Philosophy* (London: Fontana, 1985), 162.
[21] Williams, *In the Beginning was the Deed*, 18–29.

those of Geuss or Williams. The historical turn has left us with a choice of acknowledging the claims of history which dominates and exhausts the terrain of political thinking, or a search for an Archimedean perspective which is free from the corrosive effects of historical context. Faced with scepticism about an Archimedean perspective, political theory confronts the prospect of a retreat to history where the only viable activity seems to be the disinterested understanding of the ideas and actions of others. In the absence of a grand metaphysics of history of the sort challenged by Popper amongst others, we have history as a manifold of contingency. At best, we can say that the recognition of diversity gives us a reason to be open to contingency.[22] But this is a very poor reason for the recognition of normative obligations to others, as the assertion of historical contingency can just as easily leave the terrain of political action open to arbitrary moments of irrational decision. One of the central objections raised by critics about the turn to history of realist political philosophers such as Williams and Geuss is that it liberates the assertion of political will from the need to justify itself. If all political judgement is local and contingent, then either it is the expression of will, and therefore free of rational discipline, or else it is subject to the contingent discipline of historically arbitrary distributions of power. This might seem on the face of it an unduly strident claim, and one that misrepresents Williams and Geuss. Yet the crucial point is the distinction between justification and legitimation. Legitimation as in Williams's 'basic legitimation demand' is distinct from philosophical justification and relies on the historically contingent discourses and practices. The idea of rational justification, on the other hand, aspires to a standard that is not reducible to such historical contingency. Of course it might well be the case that there is no way to break out of this problem of the tyranny of historical contingency and no possibility of an ideal of reason which will vindicate rational social criticism: this pessimistic conclusion is boldly defended by John Gray and Raymond Geuss. Williams's view is rather more complex, as he remains a liberal realist who only asserts the priority of legitimation over justification rather than the impossibility of the latter. Yet Gray and Geuss's

---

[22] Something like this weak normative claim underlies James Tully's attempt to build an alternative approach to political theory from, amongst others, the work of Quentin Skinner. See Tully, *Public Philosophy in a New Key* (Cambridge: Cambridge University Press, 2008), vols. I and II.

sceptical reduction of justification to legitimation seems to be the question that needs to be addressed, and cannot simply be presupposed as the answer. The strong case in favour of the reduction of political philosophy to history or its abandonment in the face of brute power cannot withstand critical scrutiny; consequently bold claims for history in political philosophy are massively overstated. That at least is what I propose to argue.

The critique of historical reductionism in political theory – the solution

The Collingwoodian turn from philosophy to history has been used to show not merely that history is of value in the pursuit of a viable political theory, but rather the more controversial claim that the attempt to reach beyond mere contingency through abstract reason must fail, as it merely reproduces the local prejudices of a particular society or culture as the dictates of reason. In consequence we have no way out of the particularities of our own experience and therefore have to do our own political thinking and acting for ourselves, as Skinner and Geuss are happy to remind us. This fact is supposed to leave no space for the kind of political theory that moralists such as Rawls engage in. On this view there is only our contingent historical practice to rely on, so abstract political philosophy is only a reflection of our local practice and it is far too thin to carry any authority in confronting political practice.[23]

So the challenge from history is that philosophical reason is dependent upon the rich texture of political practices – so much so that, once it is distanced from them, its authority dissipates. This is certainly the realist challenge to political moralism advanced by Williams and Geuss. Philosophical political theory is historically contingent, and it is hopelessly weak as a source of authoritative practical guidance. If one can show that these criticisms are themselves controversial, weak and overstated, then the normativity of history in political theory is itself undermined. Let us start with the stronger claim that philosophical reason is always reducible to history. At first sight this is supported by the history of philosophy and the history of ideas. When we try and identify the deliverance of philosophical arguments we find ourselves locked into

---

[23] Williams, *Ethics and the Limits of Philosophy*, 93–119.

historically specific theories that are a reflection of the linguistic and political possibilities of the times in which they are constructed. The search for concrete universals or the embodiment of reason in history always seems to provide us with the concrete, but without the universal. As Skinner and his followers constantly remind us, there are no perennial questions nor are there perennial conclusions, there is just diversity and difference across time.[24] Any attempt to take the historically local and generalise it to others is to engage in a kind of cultural tyranny. Generalising across time, as in the case of criticising the Ancient Greeks for their support of slavery, it is claimed is at best redundant (hence Williams's argument about the relativism of distance), but when this approach is extended across space we have the more dubious problem of philosophical domination as a mask for political and cultural domination: this is precisely the claim made by James Tully, drawing on Skinner's historical methodology.

For this historicist argument to work as a restriction on the claims of political philosophy to transcend the tyranny of localism we need to be locked into local historical schemes and not be able to engage in transtemporal philosophical debates and conversations, for if these are possible they must use concepts that have meanings that are not confined to historically local practices and problems. Skinner's approach to the history of political thought has been to make precisely the claim that meanings are so confined, by rejecting the idea of perennial questions and instead locating particular locutions within specific linguistic contexts determined by the range of understandings of other participants. In this he takes himself to be following lines laid down by Collingwood, but with the additional support of speech-act theory.[25] Yet the updating of the argument for the particularity of historical meanings does not support the conclusions he wishes to draw. Skinner attaches almost exclusive priority to what an author intended by making a certain linguistic utterance so that all questions of textual meaning are reducible to the congeries of individual utterances that make up a complex philosophical text. Authors define the meaning of their texts. As a rule

---

[24] Skinner, *Visions of Politics*, vol. I, *passim*.
[25] See J. L. Austin, in J. O. Urmson and M. Sbisà (eds.), *How to do Things With Words*, 2nd edn (Oxford: Oxford University Press, 1980); H. P. Grice, 'Meaning', *Philosophical Review*, 66 (1957), 377–88; and J. Searle, *Speech Acts* (Cambridge: Cambridge University Press, 1969).

of thumb for the working historian this makes sense, as it encourages the reader to be attentive to the author and not simply impose a preconceived understanding on a text. Yet as an account of historical meaning it is by no means persuasive. Although the author's intention in making an utterance is important in understanding a text, so is our understanding of the context in which the utterance is made. Skinner's turn to speech-acts does much to illustrate the rhetorical strategies employed by thinkers in conceptual innovation and development, but whilst valuable, the focus on illocutionary and perlocutionary dimensions of speech-acts can divert our attention from the equally important locutionary meanings and deployment of canons of inference that are trans-temporal dimensions of the meaning of philosophical texts and arguments. At best we get a historical dimension to meaning, but not the reduction of meaning to historical context.

Such intentional or implicit semantic reductionism turns on the claim that linguistic contexts are composed of the range of possible understandings that contemporaries of an author could have had. But linguistic contextualism has been criticised on the grounds that it locks us into a vicious hermeneutic circle in which the parameters of the linguistic context are set by what contemporaries could have understood an author to mean. Yet we can only know that by locating contemporaries in further linguistic contexts, and so on and so on. The method becomes potentially incoherent unless it is possible to break into and out of the hermeneutic circle. Presumably a historian will claim to be doing this when she makes her interpretation, but that still leaves unaddressed the problem of how we assess her success in doing so. We are left with the problem of whether it is ever possible to get to an author's discrete linguistic intentions. The method proposed by Skinner is supposed to get us to the truth of the matter by closing in on the possible historical meanings of a text even if it cannot identify the final particular meaning, but even this qualified aim still locks us in a hermeneutic circle that we cannot break out of. To justify the priority of historical meaning or the absence of anything but historical meaning we need to be able to dispense with non-historicist semantics. If historical meaning can exist alongside non-historically particular meanings, then the turn to linguistic contextualism fails to support the critique of abstraction in political and philosophical arguments. At best it warrants interpretive caution and the need to carefully distinguish which level of claim one is addressing when discussing the arguments of past philosophers, yet if we turn

to ideas such as 'reception theory' and Ricoeur's claims about surplus
meaning, we can see that the situation is more complex still. For
Ricoeur, all texts and utterances contain, but are not exhausted by,
the author's particular intention in making the utterance. Meaning is
mediated by the author and the reader within traditions of understanding that give utterances meaning above and beyond the intentions of the
author. Indeed it is not possible to distinguish, in the case of classic texts,
where Plato's or Hobbes's intention ends and the historical meaning of
those texts, as they have come to us in the light of countless discussions
and interpretations, begins.[26] The important point here is not that we
now have two strands of meanings that are difficult to unravel, but that
the idea of meaning itself is complex and multi-stranded and that there
is no single pure or more authentic meaning. This point precludes the
familiar tactic of Skinner to retreat from the terrain of political theory
into the role of historian of rhetoric when faced with a philosophical
challenge, for at best this merely indicates the institutional interests of a
scholar, and nothing about the logic of interpretation. There is clearly
no reason why scholars cannot choose to ask narrowly historical questions of texts or more philosophical questions, but the point of linguistic
contextualism was to do more than signal different scholarly career
choices. It was supposed to show that the primacy of historical understanding was not an option but a necessity, and one which precludes a
purely philosophical approach to political ideas: for it is only in this way
that the turn to historical contextualism supports the critique of abstraction in political philosophy.

The acknowledgement of surplus meaning does not mean that anything goes, as the sophisticated hermeneutic theory developed by
Ricoeur shows, but equally it contradicts the idea that there is a pure
or authentic meaning that can be extracted from our complex hermeneutic practices that privileges the perspective of the author.

The critique of Skinner's historical method, and arguably that of
other historicists inspired by Collingwood, such as MacIntyre, has
much broader significance than that of making the history of ideas
difficult. Skinner's methodology presupposes a number of ontological
claims about the nature of historical meaning and the absence of trans-
temporal problems, which are used by his followers to limit the claims

---

[26] P. Ricoeur, in J. B. Thompson (ed. and trans.), *Hermeneutics and the Human
Sciences* (Cambridge: Cambridge University Press, 1981).

of political philosophy and to reduce political philosophy to history. His method cannot show that the claims of historical agents such as past political philosophers are indeed of merely local concern. Of course some past political thinkers will have had only temporally local concerns, and as such will remain of interest to specialists. Others will have had a broader range of concerns, and attempted to make general claims about political phenomena that are universal in scope. Among such figures we might include Plato, Aristotle, Hobbes and Hegel. It is simply implausible to claim that they are merely interested in temporally local questions. Furthermore, there are thinkers who are concerned with both the local and the universal; Aquinas, Locke and Marx are good examples. In each case the words and the natural languages used will be specific, but that does not entail that they are not employing concepts and ideas that are comprehensible across extended periods of time, or indeed which have universal scope and application. Whether they do so or not is a complex question, but it is not one that we can simply dismiss. Skinner's method cannot show that all utterances are temporally local; this is merely an assertion and not the conclusion of an argument or the lesson of historical experience.

Skinner and his defenders might reply that allowing for trans-temporal concepts that range beyond the words of discrete natural languages merely extends the scope of the discrete languages in which such concepts function[27] whilst still asserting that political concepts remain essentially contingent and local. In support of this claim one can argue that however successfully one might be able to translate different words using the concept of 'the state' or 'rights', there will come some point in the past, beyond which such translations become meaningless and without value. All we ultimately have is patterns of language use that are historically contingent and at some point temporally discrete.[28] This in essence is the historicist's basic claim and it underpins the Weberian idea that ideas are not fundamental in politics except in terms of our understanding of discrete political contexts. At some point our normative language and our language of politics run up against the contingency of history. Collingwood, MacIntyre or Skinner might be mistaken about the precise point where this occurs, but this is a

---

[27] See Q. Skinner, *Visions of Politics*, 103–27 and 175–87.
[28] Essentially the claim of J. G. A. Pocock in *Political Thought and History: Essays on Theory and Method* (Cambridge: Cambridge University Press, 2009), Part 1.

mere detail: essentially they are all making the same point and essentially they are correct, at least according to the historicist. Yet this assertion of historical contingency is neither as interesting nor as fatal as they contend.

The idea of contingency is a central concept of historical understanding, yet its relevance for the critique of philosophical political theory depends on what the assertion of contingency is supposed to show. The arguments of Skinner, MacIntyre, Geuss and on occasions Williams turn on the idea of non-objectivism, or the idea that philosophical arguments in political theory must fail because they appear to refer to a species of timeless objects which do not exist. The primacy of history is premised on the truth of non-objectivism which is bolstered by the evidence of historical and social diversity and the absence of non-contingent features of historical experience. The appraisal of so-called perennial ideas that forms part of Skinner's early critique of the 'political theory tradition' of the history of political thought is an example of non-objectivism.

The idea of non-objectivism is central to Collingwood's critique of the prevailing realism of Cook-Wilson, Pritchard and Joseph[29] that forms such an important part of his *Autobiography*. While the critique of non-objectivism may well be an appropriate challenge to a certain type of Oxford realist at the beginning of the twentieth century, it is not obvious that it has quite the force intended when recycled in the 'historicist turn' of Skinner, MacIntyre and Geuss.

In order for the objection to do any serious work, two things must hold. First, it must be the case that there are no objective real properties that persist beneath the normative concepts of political theory, and second, it must be the case that the moralist political philosophers are committed to asserting this version of objectivism. The first of these conditions cannot be defended from within the terms of historical experience, but secondly it does not matter because moralist political philosophers are not required to assert this form of objectivism. So even if we can resolve the matter of the status of the non-objectivist claim, nothing need follow from it.

If we turn to the first condition, namely the truth or warranted assertability of non-objectivism, it is clear that this is a metaphysical

---

[29] See J. Passmore, *A Hundred Years of Philosophy* (Harmondsworth: Penguin, 1957), 240–57.

claim that cannot be vindicated by historical experience. As we cannot merely dismiss the claim as self-contradictory or meaningless, we must interpret the claim as one about what is the case. Yet this creates a problem, because the denial of objectivism requires that we can break out of the constraints of historical experience and adopt a wholly external perspective in order to vindicate the non-objectivist's claim. The historicist claim is that we cannot break out of historical experience into an ultimate and timeless realm of objectivity, as all we have is historical experience which shows us contingency and difference. But in arguing that the objectivist needs to provide some access to a higher metaphysical realm to vindicate his appeal to objectivity, the historicist is caught up in the same claims. Just as the truth of objectivism needs us to transcend historical experience, so does the truth of non-objectivism seem to require the same capacity. The anti-Archimedean view of the historicists must itself rely on a form of Archimedeanism if it is to defend non-objectivism. Thus the historicist is caught trying to prove a negative thesis: namely that there is nothing on which the Archimedean view rests. What the historicist cannot do is change the terms of the argument to one of meaning, as logical positivists and ordinary language philosophers have tried to do, because the assertion of real political and moral entities is certainly not meaningless, albeit that we might have difficulty showing what they are. Non-objectivism, if it is to be effective, needs a stronger argument.

But why cannot the historicist simply assert the non-objectivist thesis on the grounds that there is no good evidence for believing in real moral and political properties of this kind? Why does the evidence of contingency and diversity not provide sufficient warrant for the non-objectivist thesis? This takes us back to the original claim of the historicist that the testimony of historical experience is merely difference and diversity, as opposed to uniformity, coherence and the emergence of universal truths.

There are three responses to this challenge to non-objectivism. In the first instance the argument that there are no real properties in the fabric of the universe that vindicate the normative claims of moral and political theory matters if one is to make the reverse claim that all moral and political arguments are merely ideological abstractions from present experience. This is precisely the claim that Geuss wishes to make in his critique of Rawls and post-Rawlsian political philosophy when he claims that 'a major danger in using highly abstractive methods in political philosophy is that one will succeed in merely generalising one's own local prejudices and repackaging them as demands of reason'.[30] This is a version of a familiar but invalid inference from the denial of moral objectivism to a version of relativism, precisely because it assumes that objectivism must be committed to making some claim about real properties in the world.[31] The denial of this spurious ontology does not necessarily undermine the possibility of objectivism, as we shall see shortly. However, the claim that all normative claims are merely ideological does rely on the assertion of an anti-realist metaphysic which itself entails the possibility of an external perspective beyond the first-order status of our ordinary normative claims. Yet it is precisely the impossibility of adopting such an external perspective to deny the existence of real moral properties that also undermines the possibility of asserting the truth of the negative claim of Geuss. One can only make the anti-realist claim that there are no such properties, or the historical realist claim that all normative claims are merely ideological and reducible to natural properties such as economic, racial, gender or biological interests from an external point of view, or a 'view from nowhere' as Thomas Nagel puts it.[32] If, however, we are locked into historical experience, we cannot make negative or critical claims that depend upon adopting an external perspective. We certainly cannot make the claim that all normative political philosophy is merely a species of ideology, as long as that claim is a metaphysical claim about the non-normative nature and epistemological status of those claims. As far as I can make sense of Geuss's argument, he is not simply making a claim about the causal origin of the claims of normative political theory, but is actually making a stronger claim that this causal story constrains or undermines the claims of such theory to have normative force or validity. The stronger claim is certainly the more interesting one, but it is also a claim that is impossible to make. The weaker causal claim is less interesting, because it is irrelevant to the normative status of the claims of political and moral philosophy, which is precisely the preoccupation of the moralist political theorists that Geuss and others wish to challenge.

---

[30] Geuss, *Outside Ethics*, 39.
[31] Berlin and Williams, on whom Geuss relies in many of his arguments, both deny this claim; see Berlin, *The Crooked Timber of Humanity*, 70–90, and Williams, *Ethics and the Limits of Philosophy*, 22–9.
[32] T. Nagel, *The View From Nowhere* (New York: Oxford University Press, 1986).

The second response to the non-objectivist challenge comes from within the realm of history itself, and touches on the reason why we cannot merely infer the truth of non-objectivism from historical experience of difference and diversity. The historicist theories of Skinner, MacIntyre, Geuss and Williams all presuppose an opposition between the perspective of history and the perspective of philosophy, and reject the latter in favour of the former. Yet it is precisely this dualism between history and philosophy that creates the problems that can be identified within their theories. This is because they wish to make sceptical philosophical claims about the status of philosophy based on the claims of historical experience. Yet this is precisely what they cannot do. If one is to take seriously the reality of historical experience, then one cannot assert this dualist opposition between the realm of philosophical understanding and the realm of historical understanding. Instead of two perspectives in opposition there is actually one, but this perspective of historical understanding does not justify the negative arguments that the historicist critics of political philosophy wish to make. This is precisely the historicist perspective on human understanding advocated by hermeneutic theorists such as Gadamer.[33]

Gadamer's hermeneutic theory is a complex philosophical vision of the historicisation of human understanding that has implications for the nature and status of philosophical and all other claims. The precise details of his position are beyond the scope of this argument, but they are relevant at least in respect to the supposed challenge of history to philosophy in contemporary political theory, not least because Gadamer is concerned to deny the opposition. This has two consequences: first, it rules out the possibility of a philosophical metaphysic or meta-ethic that attempts to reach beyond the boundaries of historical experience, and secondly, as we have seen, it also removes the possibility of a negative 'objectivism' which denies the existence of real normative facts as part of the fabric of the world. But thirdly and more importantly it also transforms our understanding of history itself from a more 'real' pre-philosophical mode of experience to one of seeing history and its objects as themselves part of the hermeneutic enterprise

---

[33] H-G. Gadamer, *Truth and Method* (London: Sheed and Ward, 1975). Gadamer's hermeneutic approach to philosophical understanding has had a significant impact on the legal philosophy of Ronald Dworkin; see especially *Law's Empire* (Cambridge, MA: Harvard University Press, 1986).

of coming to an understanding of human experience. This is precisely the reason why we cannot base the inference to non-objectivism on historical experience. This hermeneutic process has a considerable impact on how we understand the idea of historical experience and claims about historical difference which underpin the idea of the particularistic as opposed to universalistic dimensions of experience. This hermeneutic perspective emphasises an idea derived from Heidegger about the 'thrownness' of human experience, by which he means that human understanding is always locked within the traditions of interpretation of all others and their complex language games and discourses. In the hands of the careful historian, this fact should make us attentive to the differences of others, but at the same time this fact of 'thrownness' precludes the fact of radical otherness. To recognise and understand others is to assume overlaps of schemes of interpretation which make possible trans-generational communication. This precludes the possibility of identifying fixed and discrete contexts within which the meanings of others are locked. Contexts are fluid and overlapping, and meaning is mediated through all of these moves within complex traditions. Meaning is therefore not something that is the sole prerogative of the author, and to claim otherwise is to reintroduce some variant of the private language argument. Meaning is public and part of traditions and languages within which we are always situated and we cannot break out of these contexts to ask questions about the status of our traditions and practices, as such philosophical questions would also have to be asked from within the context of our traditions and practices. One consequence of this hermeneutic method is that historical questions become interpretative questions, and the practice of historical understanding and action in history is intricately connected with philosophical understanding. Rather than reasserting an opposition between historical experience and philosophical experience and expecting an adequate political theory to make a choice, a hermeneutic understanding of experience forces history to become philosophy, just as it forces philosophy to become history. The philosophical task, insofar as it makes sense, is part of the comprehension and understanding of human experience and is not something that can be dismissed as remote and unrealistic. The reality of historical experience is something that has to be recovered and made sense of by hermeneutic enquiry. Gadamer has his own views about how this is done and what its consequences are, which he develops at length. We need not follow Gadamer in all the

details; indeed I would not want to because he takes a much more
sceptical view about the prospects of normative social criticism of the
kind found on much contemporary political theory than is required by
his theory. Jürgen Habermas is only one of many who note Gadamer's
refusal to acknowledge the possibilities of his philosophical hermeneutics for underpinning a post-rationalist conception of social criticism of
the kind that Habermas develops in his later political works. But what is
clear from Gadamer's version of hermeneutic enquiry, or that practised
by Habermas, is that we cannot simply have recourse to a more 'real'
world of history. History is not a pre-given datum but the consequence
of interpretation that itself involves theoretical or philosophical techniques. The hermeneutic approach clearly allows for a more sophisticated
and broad conception of philosophical enquiry than the deployment of
abstraction and logical analysis. Yet as long as it is not thought that
these tools are the appropriate way to break out of historical experience
and into a realm of pure objects and, therefore, presuppose a 'realist'
ontology, there is no reason why these tools cannot be part of a
hermeneutic philosophical science. Indeed if they make any sense at
all that is what they must be, whatever some practitioners may claim
for them.

Once again, we can see that asserting the opposition of history and
philosophy and the primacy of the former over the latter only works
when we adopt a simplistic conception of historical experience as a pre-
interpreted mode of experience. Once we acknowledge that this is not so
the question turns to how we understand that mode of experience, and
that involves many things including the aspects of our current philosophical practice such as abstraction and analysis. Those who wish to
criticise the deployment of such methods need to offer stronger arguments than those which attribute to them a false metaphysics, or which
alternatively presuppose that historical experience is somehow a more
epistemologically certain basis for political or moral judgement.

Much of the apparent strength of the turn to history in moral and
political theory can be traced to those who use the lessons of historical
experience to vindicate claims about relativism, value pluralism and the
ineradicability of moral and cultural diversity. Philosophers of a realist
persuasion simply assert the truth of value pluralism as if it were some
kind of incontestable datum of moral experience. Political moralists
such as Rawls and his followers are accused of neglecting the fact of
value pluralism and merely assuming, against all the evidence, that

some kind of rational consensus amongst conflicting and diverse political values can be achieved. In defence of this realism we merely have
assertion or reference to authority.[34] What is lacking is a careful assessment of the way in which our moral practices, or those of others, are
characterised and interpreted by historians, anthropologists and social
scientists, and a similarly careful account of how these characterisations
are used to underpin a sceptical meta-ethical position such as non-
objectivism.[35] The inference to non-objectivism is based on a simplistic
account of historical experience and a claim that normative objectivism
must be based on a crude realist metaphysics. What none of the arguments so far considered show is the impossibility of a form of objectivism that does not depend on crude realism and its use in advancing
moral and political arguments that are more than a mere appeal to local
conventions and practices.

So far my argument has been an internal critique of the claims made
for history over philosophy as a prelude to defending the possibility of
normative political theory or political moralism. I have argued that the
inflated claims for history over philosophy depend on attributing to
political philosophy a false ontology and assuming in its place a naive
realist conception of history that fails to acknowledge the unavoidabil-
ity of interpretation. These arguments are enough to challenge the
necessity of the reduction of political theory to history or to support
the idea that political theory should acknowledge the priority of history.
In making this argument I have focused on the ways in which history is
supposed to constrain or challenge the possibility of philosophical
political theory; I have done this in particular because of the more
strident claims of critics such as Geuss who claim the turn to history
makes the whole activity of political philosophy redundant. He poses
the choice between philosophical political theory and a turn to history,
whereas I want to deny that we are faced with that choice. The

---

[34] John Gray is one of the most vocal defenders of value pluralism as an irreducible
fact of moral experience that undermines the Rawlsian liberalism and the search for
an overlapping consensus. Yet his argument for this complex meta-ethical claim
relies on reference to a series of assertions by Isaiah Berlin and a general allusion to
the historical record. See J. Gray, *Isaiah Berlin* (London: HarperCollins, 1995)
and *Two Faces of Liberalism* (Cambridge: Polity Press, 2000). For a critique of
Gray see P. Kelly, 'The social-theory of anti-liberalism', *Critical Review of
International Social and Political Philosophy*, 9 (2006), 137–54.

[35] See M. Moody-Adams, *Fieldwork in Familiar Places: Morality, Culture and
Philosophy* (Cambridge, MA: Harvard University Press, 1997).

opposition between history and political philosophy (including the claim that the history of ideas is categorically distinct from political theory) is a false one and one that has ill served political theory over the last forty years; but worse than that, it is also irrelevant to understanding the task of political theory, as we can see if we turn to the last of the challenges to non-objectivism.

In my first two responses I have focused on the coherence and implication of the non-objectivist challenge, and in so doing have been concerned with the nature of historical and philosophical experience and understanding. What I have not considered is the implication of the non-objectivism thesis for normative political and moral theory as such. One might concede that the non-objectivist response would have considerable purchase if political philosophers were committed to making claims that depended on that kind of realist objectivism, but fortunately few if any interesting political philosophers make this crude Platonist claim; indeed it is not even clear that Plato makes this kind of claim. For those who do not make objectivist claims of this sort, the challenge of non-objectivism is merely irrelevant. Thus a liberal political philosopher such as Thomas Nagel is able to dismiss the challenge in a couple of sentences:

I take it for granted that the objectivity of moral reasoning does not depend on its having an external reference. There is no moral analogue of the external world – a universe of moral facts that impinge on us causally.[36]

In a more extended response, Ronald Dworkin also rejects the idea of crude realism as the only basis for objectivism using a distinction between internal and external scepticism. Using the example of objective judgements about an interpretative object (in this case the meaning of Shakespeare's *Hamlet*) he writes:

Suppose someone says that *Hamlet* is best understood as a play exploring obliquity, doubling, and delay: he argues that the play has more artistic integrity, that it better unites lexical, rhetorical, and narrative themes, read with these ideas in mind. An 'internal' sceptic might say 'You are wrong. Hamlet is too confused and jumbled to be about anything at all: it is an incoherent hotch-potch of a play.' An 'external' sceptic might say, 'I agree with you; I too think this is the most illuminating reading of the play.' Of course, that is only an opinion we share; we cannot sensibly suppose that

---

[36] Nagel, *The Last Word*, 101.

Hamlet's being about delay is an objective fact we have discovered locked up in the nature of reality, 'out there' in some transcendental metaphysical world where the meanings of plays subsist.[37]

Dworkin's point can be extended to moral claims and normative claims in political theory, such as whether a given distribution is just or not, or whether there are rights of the kind that are claimed by certain groups against others. His point is that the claim to objectivity or rightness of such first-order claims about what we should do, what we should prevent and how we should live is not dependent upon some prior set of metaphysical or meta-ethical claims about what sorts of objects there are in the world and whether values or moral properties are amongst them. This is not to deny that there are ethical realists who make claims about moral objects as if they are part of the fabric of the universe, yet despite this there are very few notable realists in political philosophy and none of those considered political moralists are ontological realists when it comes to moral properties.[38] In short, Dworkin's claim, and that of Nagel,[39] is that the non-objectivist's claim is irrelevant. This is because the realists' critique of any claims made by a moralist political philosopher must take place within the first-order realm of moral and political argument if it is to succeed: an argument against equal rights for women that proceeded on the basis of there being no external moral properties, and therefore no right or wrong, would be irrelevant. Similarly an argument against a substantive moral position, such that discrimination against homosexuals is wrong, cannot be supported by appeal to any fact of history, if such things exist. To think that history settles any first-order moral or normative political issue is to commit a category mistake. At best the appeal to history can explain the causal origin of moral practices, but it cannot provide the right kind of justification for them. Consequently, modus vivendi arguments of the sort beloved of realist theorists such as Gray and Newey fail in their own terms because, whilst they can offer an account of what Dworkin calls

---

[37] Dworkin, *Law's Empire*, 78.

[38] Perhaps this is because in the case of political values this already implausible view becomes even more implausible.

[39] 'I take it for granted that the objectivity of moral reasoning does not depend upon its having an external reference. There is no moral analogue of the external world – a universe of moral facts that impinges on us causally. Even if such a supposition made sense, it would not support the objectivity of moral reasoning.' Nagel, *The Last Word*, 101.

consensual promise, they cannot provide the categorical force that we expect of a normative argument.[40] They give an account of how social conventions arise as a justification for why we should accept them as obligation-creating; hence they conflate *is* and *ought*.

The anti-anti-realism of Dworkin and Nagel does not settle the truth of any first-order claim about political morality, instead it merely sets out an agenda of enquiry and difficult arguments. On any particular issue it might well endorse a sceptical conclusion; for example the failure to find any normative defences of gender discrimination in terms of political rights does indeed support the view of gender equality against traditionalists. Nothing further is gained by searching for some external level of justification in a realm of moral objects, just as nothing is gained by appealing to history. Yet this sceptical conclusion also lends support to an alternative and contrary moral claim about gender equality, so it is not possible for the accumulation of refuted first-order claims to support the kind of global scepticism of the sort claimed by the external sceptic. Where does this leave the conflict between history and philosophy?

In short, the impossibility of global internal scepticism rules out the rejection of normativity or moralism as a potential part of an adequate political theory. If normative argument is part of political theory, then an appeal to history can only provide an assistance to but not replacement of political philosophy, as at best, the turn to history has nothing to say about questions of political rights. At best, history can contribute to an understanding of the causal contexts of political agency and the origins of political and ethical discourse, but it cannot provide the justification for normative judgements. The contribution of social, political and economic history or the history of ideas can provide contextual material for political judgements and allow us to assess causal claims. How it is supposed to replace political theory remains a mystery, unless it can show that political philosophy is either impossible or completely devoid of normative content. Only a sceptic would make such a thoroughgoing claim, and such a form of scepticism is untenable. If we return to Geuss's original challenge at the beginning of this

---

[40] R. Dworkin, 'Foundations of liberal equality', in G. B. Peterson (ed.), *The Tanner Lectures On Human Values XI* (Salt Lake City, UT: University of Utah Press, 1990), 3–119 and P. Kelly, 'Justifying justice: contractarianism, communitarianism and the foundations of contemporary liberalism', in D. Boucher and P. Kelly (eds.) *The Social Contract From Hobbes to Rawls* (London: Routledge, 1994), 226–44.

chapter, we can draw the following conclusions. A fully adequate political theory will require historical contextualisation and sociological nuance, but it will also require abstraction from pre-given social norms if it is to engage in normative social criticism. In this respect a political philosophy that is narrowly abstract, such as Nozick's, needs to be corrected, but a more nuanced theory such as that of constructivists such as Rawls and Habermas is free from the challenge of false abstraction. Within this conception of political theory there will be many overlapping tasks; some will be more abstract and constructive, and others will have a more historical or sociological dimension. Within the academic division of labour there will be a variety of ways of contributing to an adequate political theory. What I have described is not a new approach to political theory, but one which seems to capture the current practice of political theory without forcing false choices between history and philosophy or between methodologically respectable and unrespectable ways of doing political theory. In so doing I suggest that the kind of arguments offered by constructivists such as Rawls can be brought together with historically informed social criticism and textual reconstruction. Instead of claiming a series of discrete categories of thought or modes of enquiry that vie for authority, I would suggest that these activities are perspectival points on a continuum of enquiry. My point is not even to deny the value of the sort of contextual history of political thought practised by Skinner and his disciples. On the contrary, my only intention is to dispel the second-order claims made about these activities, namely that they are all that is left to political theory, or that they are the only intellectually respectable ways of studying ideas, because philosophical reconstruction and critique are impossible. Following Dworkin, my point, in short, is that the interesting questions in political philosophy and the history of political thought are first-order ones, and these are unaffected by claims about the reduction of philosophy to history or the discovery of the appropriate methodology of historical enquiry.

If Geuss is offering this kind of advice, then it can indeed be gratefully accepted, and is accepted even by followers of Rawls, whom Geuss regards as a dangerous apologist for the prejudices of contemporary liberal politics. But if his claim is the stronger one, namely that philosophical contructivism is impossible, then his argument and that of those like him must fail. In short, the claims for history over philosophy in the practice of political theory are massively overstated.

2 | From historical contextualism, to mentalism, to behaviourism

JONATHAN FLOYD

What is the significance of history for political philosophy? Or, what do political philosophers need to know of history, if they are to do their work as it ought to be done? Or, as a third formulation, what do we need to know of how societies have thought and lived in the past, in order to decide how they ought to be governed in the future? Whichever way one puts it, it is an unusually tricky question to answer, and not just because it admits of numerous plausible answers, most of which are perfectly compatible with at least one of the others, but also because it requires an unusual degree of clarity regarding the answer we give to a still further question, namely, what *is* political philosophy? What I should like to do here, therefore, is to begin by saying something about both what I take political philosophy to *be* and what I take political philosophers to *do* (and just why I treat these as two distinct questions will be clear from the answers I give to them). Following that, I shall then examine just one particularly plausible account of the significance of history for this subject – an account which I am going to call 'historical contextualism' – and then, following *that*, examine two alternative suggestions regarding just what we might learn when we consider not just the significance of history in general to political philosophy, but also the significance of 'historical context' in particular. My conclusion, ultimately, will be that whilst historical contextualism as a *form* of political philosophy fails to deliver the goods, adopting a historical perspective on the *method* our subject employs may well prove invaluable.

Political philosophy as a question; political philosophy as a project

What political philosophy *is*, I would suggest, is a subject organised around the following four-part question: How – should – we – live? This is a question we can distinguish both from the moral philosopher's question, 'how should *I* live?' and the political scientist's question 'how *do* we live?' It is also a question which, in everyday conversation, we tend to reformulate as something like 'what sort of government ought we to have?', although, as that reformulation invites the anarchist's retort 'why have any government at all?', it is important to remember that it is the former, more open and abstract problem that we have always to try and solve. I shall call this problem, from now on, political philosophy's 'organising question'.

Understanding that this is what political philosophy is, I think, now helps us to get a better handle on just what it is that contemporary political philosophers *do*, which is this: they attempt to answer their organising question by trying to work out just what it is that we 'really think', beneath all of our conflicting opinions, and after sufficient quantities of reflection, about each of the many answers given to it by various political philosophers. Such 'working out' takes the form of an argument between different philosophers regarding just which of the many judgements and principles they propose stands up to critical scrutiny. Every test of consistency, coherence, example and counter-example is applied in order to work out whether our 'truest thoughts' are libertarian, egalitarian, or communitarian in nature; whether they follow utilitarian or contractarian patterns of evaluation; whether they point towards more democratic or perhaps more constitutional forms of ideal government – and so on and so forth. This way of attempting to answer its organising question I call contemporary political philosophy's 'project'.

Yet even this very broad characterisation of our subject (I am tempted to say banal, although I trust it will seem less so when I return to the matter later) cannot quite capture all of the ways in which it might be practised – although it will help to clarify just what it is that makes those other ways distinctive – for there exists still at least one further interpretation of the described project which puts the emphasis in 'what we really think' not just on the 'really', but also on the 'we'. That is, in addition to producing a precise account of what gets to count *as* real thoughts, together with a precise account of just what those thoughts *are*, there exists a cluster of political philosophers who seek further to narrow down just *who* we take to be the relevant 'we' – which in this context means the 'we' both from whom these thoughts are drawn and, in turn, for whom the products of those thoughts (i.e. answers to the question 'how should we live?') are intended. Communitarians such as

Michael Walzer belong to this cluster, together with those relativists we find both in civil society and in the imaginations of practising political philosophers (though rarely actually *in* political philosophy itself), but still, they are not the only ones, for there exists at least one other group which both belongs to this cluster and interests me a great deal more than either of these two. This group I am going to call, from here on in, 'historical contextualists'.

Historical contextualism as a form of political philosophy

I define historical contextualism in terms of the following two beliefs: first, the belief that when we reason about normative political questions, we always reason from within a contingent context of certain shared and relatively fixed moral convictions; second, the belief that in order (a) to recognise that we do inhabit such a context and (b) to understand its nature, we require *history*.[1] We cannot understand ourselves as moral beings, say the historical contextualists, unless we know first just what set of core beliefs we have been left with by our past. Or, to put the same point another way, the significance of history for political philosophy here is that we will not learn *how to live* until we learn just *who we are*, and will not learn *that* until we learn first just *who we have become*. Or, in a third formulation, this time from Charles Taylor, 'In order to understand properly what we are about, we have to understand how we got where we are.'[2] It is not, however, on Taylor's work that I want to focus here, but rather on the more recent writings of Charles Larmore and Bernard Williams. They are easily the most persuasive proponents of the position I want to examine, and, in what follows, I shall consider each of their arguments in turn, beginning with Larmore's.[3]

---

[1] I am grateful to the editors of *Critical Review of International Social and Political Philosophy* for permission to draw in this section on an earlier discussion of historical contextualism. See J. Floyd, 'Is political philosophy too ahistorical?', *Critical Review of International Social and Political Philosophy*, 12: 4 (2009), 513–34.

[2] C. Taylor, 'Philosophy and its history', in R. Rorty, J. B. Schneewind and Q. Skinner (eds.), *Philosophy in History* (Cambridge: Cambridge University Press, 1984), 28.

[3] Given more space, I might also have considered Taylor here, together with the more recent work of a further contextualist, Alan Thomas. Yet it is not vital, in this

Larmore's first and most fundamental claim is that 'modernity has shaped our moral thinking in fundamental ways [which means that] we will not see our way through these problems as clearly as we must unless we take stock of what has made us what we are'.[4] And, although there are presumably many formative experiences and resultant norms which, when taken together, make up what he would consider to be the modern moral consciousness, there is one feature of it in particular which he thinks fundamental. This feature is the phenomenon of 'reasonable disagreement',[5] by which he means the fact that, in this modern world of ours, there will always be perfectly reasonable people who disagree with each other about the fundamental ends of life. What is therefore needed by political philosophers, he argues, is some locally available minimal moral conception upon which even those individuals locked in permanent reasonable disagreement will be able to converge.[6]

All of which then begs the question: is such a conception available? Well, Larmore certainly thinks so, and also that it is defined by two contextually present norms: 'rational dialogue' and 'equal respect'.[7] The first of these, 'rational dialogue', holds that if we are to settle our conflicts and dilemmas through discussion rather than force, we shall have to fall back upon common or neutral ground, which means in practice finding some other stock of commonly available reasons, whilst the second, 'equal respect', which Larmore intends as an interpretation of the Kantian injunction to treat others as ends and not means, is presented by him as an answer to the inevitable question: 'why should we insist upon settling our problems through discussion?' Its content, in

---

context, for me to do so, because whilst Taylor provides a rightly famous application of historical contextualism to moral philosophy in general, rather than political philosophy in particular, Thomas presents only a non-historical form of the same general approach, even though that form is then briefly applied to specifically political problems. So, neither scholar, in short, provides a full test case for historical contextualism as political philosophy in the way that both Larmore and Williams do. For their respective contextualist statements, see: C. Taylor, *Sources of the Self: The Making of the Modern Identity* (Cambridge: Cambridge University Press, 1989); and A. Thomas, *Value and Context: The Nature of Moral and Political Knowledge* (Oxford: Oxford University Press, 2006).

[4] C. Larmore, *The Morals of Modernity* (Cambridge: Cambridge University Press, 1996), 16.

[5] *Ibid*. 12–14, 63.

[6] C. Larmore, *The Autonomy of Morality* (Cambridge: Cambridge University Press, 2008), 1–15.

[7] Larmore, *The Morals of Modernity*, 134–6.

brief, is that our political order, if it is to be legitimate, must be justifiable to all who are made subject to it.

So, Larmore is claiming that even in the modern, pluralistic West, where we should always expect to encounter reasonable disagreement at all sorts of levels of moral and political discourse, there does exist real agreement on these two basic moral norms. Yet to this we might respond: even if that is so, which is doubtful, is it not also likely, especially in this context, where critical reason is at least as established a norm of moral and political practice as anything else, that some people are going to ask the question: 'even supposing that we have been living by these norms unreflectively, why should we now affirm them in the cold light of day?' Larmore anticipates this objection, and answers it as follows. For him, what grounds the norms is simply the fact that they are *ours*. According to the historical narrative he presents, they were forged for our culture in the fires of past violent conflicts – and in particular religious conflicts – over the nature of the good life, and have become a cornerstone of our modern, Western way of life.[8] As he himself puts the point on one occasion: 'the source of their authority is our form of life insofar as it embodies these two norms [and, in turn] this form of life is authoritative for our conduct if, however historically contingent it may be, it has made us what we are'.[9]

This then leaves us with one final question: if these norms are authoritative for our conduct, what exactly is it that, politically speaking, they authorise? Well, according to Larmore, what they authorise or, more precisely, *obligate*, is our support for a neutralist liberal constitution, by which he means a constitution that is neutral between all those different conceptions of the good life about which reasonable individuals will always disagree.[10] This is an answer to the question 'how should we live?' which Larmore, following Rawls, calls 'political liberalism', and it is called that, for his purposes, just insofar as it is a political conception which itself supposedly has no foundations in any one conception of an ideal existence, individual or collective. Larmore's finished argument can thus be summarised as follows: a historical process has occurred; it has bequeathed to us a particular set of norms; and these norms imply, politically, a certain form of liberal politics. That is one historical-contextualist form of political philosophy, or, alternatively put, this is

---

[8] *Ibid*. 40.   [9] *Ibid*. 57.
[10] *Ibid*. 121–51. See also Larmore, *The Autonomy of Morality*, 139–49.

what Larmore thinks 'we', by which he means the modern West, 'really believe' about the matters which concern political philosophers, which is to say, those matters of right and wrong and better or worse which bear upon the answer we should affirm to the question 'how should we live?'

We can now compare these arguments with those provided by Williams who, like Larmore, also wants to justify a liberal answer to political philosophy's organising question, although his reasoning to this effect is both simpler in structure and more modest in ambition. At the heart of this answer is the following non-historical claim: that in all political societies there exists a 'basic legitimation demand', the essence of which is that there must be a justification of the present order which 'makes sense' to at least a majority of those who are subject to it.[11] That is, if there is to be any politics at all, and not just brutal rule by force, then some justification has to be given for the present structure of authority that is accepted as at least minimally reasonable by those who are subject to it.

It is this claim that allows his historical argument to kick in because, according to Williams, the forms such justifications take are always going to be affected by historical circumstances.[12] And, just like Larmore, those circumstances in which he is most interested are those which prevail in the modern West. *And again*, just like Larmore, getting to grips with these circumstances means, for Williams, getting to grips with modernity in general and the 'fact' of serious moral and political disagreement in particular. For societies living under these conditions, Williams explains, the only justification of political order which 'makes sense' is a liberal one, with other answers being simply 'unacceptable'.[13] We can therefore summarise Williams as follows: given both our historically produced cultural circumstances *and* our historically inherited attitudes regarding what is 'unacceptable' in political life, the only possible form of political legitimation for modern, Western societies is a liberal one. Or, as Williams put it on one occasion, 'modernity + the basic legitimation demand = liberalism'.[14]

So, whilst Larmore claims that modern life is expressive of a certain set of norms, the upshot of which is some form of political liberalism,

---

[11] B. Williams, *In the Beginning was the Deed: Realism and Moralism in Political Argument* (Princeton, NJ: Princeton University Press, 2005), 4.
[12] *Ibid.* 3.   [13] *Ibid.* 8.   [14] *Ibid.* 9.

Williams claims that the only acceptable answer to political philosophy's organising question for modern individuals is, again, a liberal one. Or, alternatively put, whilst it is simply the case for Larmore that we live a certain way of life in the modern world which embodies and holds to a certain set of norms, it is simply the case for Williams that we find non-liberal political principles unacceptable. In what follows, I should like first to explain what I take to be the basic problem shared by these arguments, second to explain what I think this problem means for historical contextualism in general, and third to consider just what further suggestions we might yet entertain regarding the importance of historical context to political philosophy.

The problem with historical contextualism

The basic problem shared by these two arguments is that they appeal to non-existent consensuses. That is, although they both claim that at some level there is widespread agreement to be found on something which, in turn, generates a determinate (and, in both cases, liberal) answer to political philosophy's organising question, their failing is that there is no such pre-existing agreement to be found, and not just at the level of thought in which they are interested, but also at any other.

The simplest way of demonstrating this failure involves dividing up 'our' moral context into three levels of at least minimally informed and reflective thought. These are (1) the level of elite political argument, (2) the level of the educated public and (3) the level of our most reasonable individuals. What we can now ask is: How much agreement do we find in each of these three domains? Well, certainly there is scant consensus regarding even values or principles found at (1) – where different political parties oppose each other on the basis of very different notions of equality, liberty, justice, etc. – just as there is scant consensus at (2) – where the educated public at large disagrees about, again, such things as the proper senses and relative priorities of equality, liberty, justice and community, etc. – which then only leaves us with (3), the level of fully reasonable individuals. But the problem here, surely, is that we can find no more reflective, rational and theoretically coherent group of individuals than political philosophers themselves, a group that is no more known for agreeing about the proper way to resolve these fundamental oppositions than the politicians or public they are supposed to be guiding. All of which then means that the claim that fully reasonable individuals agree on, perhaps norms such as equal respect, or perhaps values such as republican liberty, is really no more plausible than the suggestion that Robert Nozick agrees with Ronald Dworkin, or that luck-egalitarians agree with communitarians, and so on and so forth.

This basic problem, however, plays out slightly differently in each case. For Larmore, it certainly seems as though moral contextualism in general – understood as a broad approach to ethical enquiry, the key feature of which is that it does not require foundational justification for already locally accepted judgements – is on considerably safer ground when dealing with such imperatives as 'don't torture babies for fun' than when considering such norms as 'rational dialogue' and 'equal respect'. So, whilst modern individuals may well have little trouble either agreeing upon or doing without a further justification for the former imperative – and I do not dispute the occasional philosophical significance of this point – they also cannot help but disagree with each other regarding both the relative worth and grounds of the latter norms. And this difficulty – that in our actually existing present context, many if not most individuals fail to prize these two norms above all other values – then brings with it a further implication, namely, that if individuals would rather promote their own way of life and its ideals than prioritise these two suggested norms and, with them, a putatively neutral liberal political order, it follows that a liberal order of the proposed sort cannot be justified to them in the intended fashion and, as a result, that the norm of equal respect is unrealisable. Or, to put this same point another way, because not all individuals can be brought to accept that they *already* subscribe to the described norms, they also cannot have the proposed political constitution justified to them in the way Larmore claims 'equal respect' requires.

Williams's arguments, on the other hand, suffer for a slightly different reason. Whereas the problem with Larmore is that he fails both to establish his putative contextual norms and, in turn, to justify his very precise political prescriptions, Williams's difficulty is that his line about 'only liberal answers being acceptable' only stands *itself* as justifiable just so long as we take his understanding of 'liberal' to be so broad as to radically under-determine 'our' political options. That is, even if we grant (1) that no illiberal, democratic majority is likely to politically develop anytime soon in any known modern state, and (2) that there is very little support to be found in any of them for some kind of a conversion to, say, monarchy or theocracy or aristocracy, there is still no obvious consensus to be found as regards all of those various particular answers which *are* currently being given to the question 'how should we live' by both elected politicians and academic political philosophers. Accepting, for instance, that modern populations *do* find the notion of the divine right of kings unacceptable does nothing to guide our choices between, say, social democracy or neo-liberalism, let alone luck-egalitarianism or libertarianism, or communitarianism or deliberative democracy, or a rights-based constitution versus a sovereign parliament, and so on and so forth.

The fundamental problem, then, is that *our* context under-determines *our* political options: we have not been historically shaped into political liberals any more than we have been shaped into market socialists or left-libertarians. Or, alternatively put, because the moral context of the modern West is one characterised by, not some minimal agreement upon moral norms or political principles, but rather a plurality of norms, principles, values and conceptions of the good, it radically under-determines those answers we might seek to give to the question 'how should we live?' There is good reason, it seems, why arguments which begin with an acknowledgement of diversity and an ambition to find deep-lying common ground soon start to distinguish between relevant and irrelevant forms of disagreement and diversity. It soon becomes necessary, clearly, to talk of 'reasonable disagreement' rather than disagreement as such, just as it soon becomes necessary to talk of 'reasonable pluralism' rather than pluralism as such.[15] For consider: just as an attention to context functions as a means of narrowing down the 'we' in 'what we really think', so does an attention to 'reasonable' function as a means of narrowing down the 'really', which means that if one has failed to extract sufficient mileage from the first, one will soon have to try and finish the job by returning, however reluctantly, to the second.

Some clarification regarding targets

Let me be very clear though about what I am *not* saying here. I am certainly not claiming, at least on the basis of the argument presented so far, that the kind of agreement on either norms or principles described by these two scholars could not *ever* be achieved, but rather only that

---

[15] See J. Rawls, *Political Liberalism* (New York: Columbia University Press, 2008).

the emphasis needs to be on 'creating' rather than 'discovering' it, whatever form of argument such creation might require – and nothing about
that task, I would suggest, will be unfamiliar to political philosophers of
any kind. Yet this caveat by no means changes the essence of my point,
which is that the attempt to simply identify and then reconcile us to some
putatively latent set of ideals in our local way of life is on a hiding to
nothing on account of that very plurality of ideals which surrounds us.
Beliefs regarding both the content and priority of justice, for example,
differ both amongst political philosophers and even those most reasonable members of the educated public, so any simple attempt by the former
to work up directly from what the latter 'already believe', rather than
trying to correct those beliefs themselves, is surely doomed to fail.

A further qualification is that this rejection of historical contextualism
as a *form* of political philosophy does not by any means entail ruling out
those very different utilisations of historical context *for* political philosophy undertaken by, for instance, Raymond Geuss and James Tully (even if
we might have independent reasons to question both).[16] Consider here
that whereas Geuss invokes our historical context solely in order to
identify whatever constraints on political action and legitimation currently exist in a given political environment, and thus in turn to make
whatever prescriptions are formulated by political philosophers for that
environment considerably more realistic, Tully uses history simply in
order to draw out the surprising contingency of present institutions and
assumptions.[17] Now, as far as I can see, there is nothing that needs to be
particularly objected to here in either project, just as there is nothing to be
objected to in the historical-cum-politico-philosophical labours of
Quentin Skinner, who retrieves and then dusts off certain concepts and
arguments from the past, such as neo-Roman liberty, in order that we can
then properly compare those items in the light of day to later, more
hegemonic ideals.[18] And again, if there is no objection to be drawn

---

[16] For extended discussion of Geuss's argument, see the chapters by Kelly and by
Honig and Stears in this volume. For discussion of Tully's argument, see again the
chapter by Honig and Stears.
[17] R. Geuss, *Philosophy and Real Politics* (Princeton, NJ: Princeton University
Press, 2008); J. Tully, *Public Philosophy in a New Key, Vol. I: Democracy and
Civic Freedom* (Cambridge: Cambridge University Press, 2008).
[18] Q. Skinner, *Liberty before Liberalism* (Cambridge: Cambridge University Press,
1998). And if this exercise undertaken by Skinner is acceptable – and I can see no
reason why it would not be – then it is perhaps also worth noting that this is in fact

from my arguments above against the kind of work undertaken by these thinkers, then there is also no objection to be drawn against Alasdair MacIntyre who, like Charles Taylor and Larmore, does want to draw an illuminating picture of our existing moral context, and yet, unlike them, considers that picture to be one of discord and dissonance, rather than concord and consensus.[19]

So, all I have argued so far is that historical contextualists, understood here as a class of thinkers who attempt to work up from (1) a putative description of contextual moral consensus to (2) a determinate answer to political philosophy's organising question, are on an impossible mission – not that those thinkers who want to invoke historical context either for other reasons (e.g. Geuss, Tully, Skinner), or with both other reasons and more plausible contextual descriptions (e.g. MacIntyre), need to rethink what they are already doing.

Two alternative suggestions

I do wonder, however, whether there is still more that might be gained for political philosophy from the general kind of endeavour described above, and in particular whether two suggestions to this effect might hold considerably greater potential than the argument I have so far considered. Both of these suggestions, as we will see, instruct us to think of historical contextualism not as a *form* of political philosophy, and thus an attempt to answer that subject's organising question, but rather as something we can apply to political philosophy *itself*.

The first of these holds that rather than focusing on norms, values, or principles (etc.), political philosophers would do well to look for patterns or commonalities in the kinds of question they tend to ask of themselves and each other. That is, even though they might fail to find agreement on either contextual norms or universal principles, perhaps they do agree more than is usually noticed regarding the kinds of

---

the very same task which Bernard Williams undertook in that earlier work of his, *Shame and Necessity*, wherein he draws out an alternative, pre-Socratic vision of human motivation and responsibility in order that we might better assess, and then either affirm or reject, our own, perhaps confused, and perhaps even partially Greek themselves, modern assumptions regarding these things. See B. Williams, *Shame and Necessity* (Berkeley, CA: University of California Press, 1993).

[19] A. MacIntyre, *After Virtue: A Study in Moral Theory* (London: Duckworth, 1981).

problems they seem always to be trying to solve. Candidates for such questions might include: how can liberal-democratic forms of government be justified under modern, pluralist conditions? Or, perhaps better, is there some form of political system to which no reasonable person, given a genuine commitment to working out mutually acceptable terms of association, could reasonably object? The problem with such enquiries, however, is that although such questions can be quite widely shared, they are also contestable moral aspirations themselves – just think of the second of the two, for instance, when reformulated as Rawls's 'principle of liberal legitimacy', or when expressed in pretty much the same terms in Alasdair MacIntyre's description of the 'Enlightenment Project'.[20] All of which means that if political philosophers are to learn something useful by studying their own context of enquiry, they shall certainly have to learn something less obvious and more significant than the fact that, at present, there is relatively little work being done outside of the well-worn libertarian-egalitarian (and always democratic, one way or another) axis of concern.

This then leaves us with my second suggestion, which is that rather than looking at either answers or questions, we should instead consider methods. That is, rather than looking to see (1) whether modern, Western individuals agree on some unexamined set of moral or political norms, or (2) whether modern, Western political philosophers agree on the kinds of question they tend to ask themselves, perhaps we should attempt to find out (3) whether there is something useful to be discovered about the way in which they argue with one other about the rival answers they provide to those questions. We can ask: how do political philosophers argue what they argue? Or, how do they try to prove what they want to prove? And then, in turn, if it just so happens that they always apply the same method in their attempts to prove those arguments, we can subsequently enquire: does adherence to that method, particularly when viewed from a long-term historical perspective, seem like a promising or futile endeavour?

I propose that when we do try to gain a historical perspective on this question, which is to say a perspective which enables us both (1) to identify that element of contingency in things which would otherwise appear natural – as Tully's recent work has illustrated – and (2) to compare our currently hegemonic viewpoint with rival alternatives to

---

[20] *Ibid.* 36–78.

it – as MacIntyre has always done – we shall learn something very interesting about the character and value of the method currently employed in (the context of) contemporary political philosophy. And not just something *about* its character, because bringing into historical focus the question of method in contemporary political philosophy will not simply help us to assess the worth of that method, but also to work out just exactly what that method *is*. This is so because unless we manage to individuate our subject by distinguishing exactly what makes it distinctive from other methods, we shall not properly be able to grasp its particular nature, let alone its value relative to other ways of doing things. So: we shall compare in order to distinguish, and distinguish in order to evaluate.

Mentalism in focus

What then do we see when we zoom out to a historical distance, and consider contemporary political philosophy's method from afar? Well, what I would suggest we see – particularly when one considers what I described as this subject's 'project' earlier on – is this: contemporary political philosophers proceed in their work by attempting (1) to discover and then (2) to apply whatever set of normative political principles is already implicitly expressed within the existing moral thought patterns of human beings. This model of enquiry I call 'mentalism', because what I take to be its defining feature (particularly when contrasted with an alternative method I shall mention in a moment) is its basic *introspective* quest to find foundational regularities in the evaluative *thoughts* of human beings, just as a natural scientist would look for patterns in, say, the movements of planets or the formation of clouds. This is the 'scientific' way of approaching moral and political philosophy which Hume canonically expressed in his *An Enquiry Concerning the Principles of Morals*, and which Rawls refined and formulated in a number of his early articles including 'Outline of a Decision Procedure for Ethics', 'The Sense of Justice', and also the slightly later work, 'The Independence of Moral Theory'.[21] Consider here, for example, Hume's statement that:

---

[21] D. Hume, *An Enquiry Concerning the Principles of Morals* (Oxford: Oxford University Press, 1998). All of the listed pieces by Rawls can be found in J. Rawls, *Collected Papers* (Cambridge, MA: Harvard University Press, 1999).

a philosopher ... needs only enter into his own breast for a moment, and consider whether or not he should desire to have this or that quality ascribed to him, and whether such or such an imputation would proceed from a friend or an enemy ... to observe that particular in which the estimable qualities agree on the one hand, and the blameable on the other; and thence to reach the foundations of ethics, and find those universal principles from which all censure or approbation is ultimately derived ... we can only expect success, by ... deducing general maxims from a comparison of particular instances.[22]

Or Rawls's statement that:

one tries to find a scheme of principles that match people's considered judgments and general convictions in reflective equilibrium. This scheme of principles represents their moral conception and characterises their moral sensibility. One thinks of the moral theorist as an observer, so to speak, who seeks to set out the structure of other people's moral conceptions and attitudes.[23]

So, to adopt this historical viewpoint is, in the first instance, to see the line of methodological continuity which runs through both Hume's and Rawls's endeavours. But not just this line – because what I should further like to claim is that it also brings into focus its flaws. To understand mentalism, I would suggest, is also to begin to see that it cannot deliver the goods, because when political philosophers move to inspect any one of what I believe to be the three levels of moral thought from which they could potentially extract determinate political principles (and note the parallel here with my earlier discussion of Historical Contextualism), they do not find consensus – which is to say universal and principle-determining thoughts *shared* by all those human beings in whom they are interested – but rather dissonance. Or, to put the same point another way, what I am suggesting is both (1) that it is impossible for contemporary political philosophy's model of enquiry to deliver what it is intended to deliver, and (2) that this impossibility can be demonstrated by (a) distinguishing and (b) dismissing each of the three levels of moral thought out of which mentalism might hope to extract the sort of determinate foundational thoughts it requires.

   I shall now provide a brief sketch of how this demonstration works by moving as concisely as possible through each of what I take to be these

---

[22] Hume, *An Enquiry Concerning the Principles of Morals*, 7.
[23] Rawls, 'The independence of moral theory', in *Collected Papers*, 288.

three levels. They are, in order: (1) those decisions we are all supposed to make in hypothetical choice situations; (2) those beliefs which Rawls, and others, refer to as considered moral judgements; and (3) our intuitive responses to abstract moral dilemmas. Following this, I shall present what I take to be two plausible alternatives to this method, and then, following *that*, defend the second of these against those objections most likely to be raised against it.

So, consider first hypothetical choice situations, such as Rawls's well-known 'original position'. The problem with them begins with the simple fact that in order for it to be the case that anyone occupying a given situation *really would* make exactly the same choice as anybody else, controversial conditions have to be placed on either – and often both – (1) the criteria by which the chooser chooses or (2) the kinds of knowledge to which they have access. But then, such conditions, as is well known, inevitably trigger the question 'what justifies them?', and in turn an attempt to find such justification either at the level of considered judgements or at the level of intuitive responses to abstract dilemmas. So, wherever the requisite justification for such conditions is to be found, it cannot be found at the level of hypothetical choice situations themselves, which means that hypothetical choice situations are incapable of operating as foundations for the kinds of normative political principles in which political philosophers are necessarily interested (even if they can play some kind of a role further up the justificatory line).

This then takes us to considered moral judgements. Can they provide any better grounds for our arguments than hypothetical choice? I think not. The problem with them is that they are either (a) universal and indeterminate or (b) contested and determinate. Judgements such as 'slavery is wrong' or 'don't torture babies for fun', for example, are universal just insofar as everybody shares them, yet also indeterminate just insofar as they fail to help us select between any of the major systems of government proposed by modern political philosophy. Judgements such as 'every child deserves an equal opportunity in life', on the other hand, are, again, either plausibly universal and indeterminate, if what is meant by them is that no child should be discriminated against on the basis of race or sex, *or* contestable and determinate if what is meant is that all children should be raised by the state in order to compensate for the problems caused by unequal parents. So: Even if there do exist fixed points in our moral convictions of the sort described by the concept of considered moral judgements, such points are just as incapable as hypothetical choice situations of playing the required foundational role.[24]

All of which then leaves us with intuitive responses to abstract moral dilemmas. Can they salvage our project? Unfortunately not, because the problem with them is that different intuitions can be produced in one and the same person – not to mention different intuitions in different people – simply by framing any given dilemma in multiple ways. This problem can be illustrated by way of a well-worn thought experiment. Imagine a runaway railway carriage which, if it carries on as it is going to at present, will kill five people strapped down to the tracks up ahead, but, if a lever is pulled in the carriage, will switch to a different track, on which one railway worker is working. When asked what they would do if placed in such a carriage, most people would say 'pull the lever'. But now imagine a second dilemma. This time there is no fork in the tracks and, rather than finding yourself in the carriage, you are instead placed to the side of the tracks where, in front of you, stands a very large man. Now, you know that if you push this man onto the tracks, he will die whilst the five people will be saved, whereas if you do not he will live and they will die. So, again, what do you do? This time most people would say 'don't push the man'. But here's the rub: the problem with these two very natural, perfectly intuitive responses from the point of view of moral and political philosophy is that they are *different* responses to *one and the same* dilemma. That is, in both cases one is faced with a choice between killing one in order to save five, or allowing one to live and five to die.[25] How, therefore, could moral intuitions be any more fit for purpose than hypothetical choice situations or considered moral judgements?

These problems can be summarised as follows.

---

[24] For two excellent discussions of both considered judgements in general and Rawls's use of them in particular, see P. Singer, 'Sidgwick and reflective equilibrium', *Monist*, 55 (15974), and T. M. Scanlon, 'Rawls on justification', in S. Freeman, *The Cambridge Companion to Rawls* (Cambridge: Cambridge University Press, 2003), 139–67.

[25] These findings are summarised in K. A. Appiah, *Experiments in Ethics* (Cambridge, MA: Harvard University Press, 2008), esp. 89–120. See also J. M. Doris and A. Plakias, 'How to argue about disagreement: evaluative diversity and moral realism', in W. Sinnott-Armstrong, *Moral Psychology, Vol. II: The Cognitive Science of Morality: Intuition and Diversity* (Cambridge, MA: MIT Press).

Table 1 *Mentalism – three strikes and you're out.*

Level of moral thought	Problem encountered
(1) Hypothetical choice situations	Either different people make different decisions, or those people are restrained in ways which, although they generate uniform answers, also require justification elsewhere.
(2) Considered judgements	These are either (a) universal and indeterminate, or (b) contentious and determinate.
(3) Intuitive responses to dilemmas	By framing a single moral dilemma in different ways, we can elicit different decisions from one and the same person.

There is unfortunately too little space here to either elaborate upon or defend this argument to the extent that its potential implications demand, so what I should like to do instead is simply make as clear as possible just what I take these implications to be. The most important one is this: the upshot of the failure to find consensus at each of the three levels described is that human moral thought as a whole is unfit for the role intended for it by mentalist political philosophy, which means in turn that this subject, as currently practised, is doomed to failure. Our thoughts are simply too dissonant and multi-vocal to admit of the kind of patterns-into-principles theoretical move that modern political philosophers have always tried to make, which means that political philosophy as it is currently undertaken would never be able to achieve consensus of the sort to which it aspires. Mentalism, I would therefore suggest, is not just what puts the armchair in armchair philosophy (by virtue of its fundamentally introspective character), but also what grants political philosophy a considerable part of its reputation for being utopian in the wrong way – that is, for never producing arguments capable of truly convincing other political philosophers, let alone wider publics, of the superiority of one single, determinate answer to the question 'how should we live?'

It is perhaps useful here to note the apparent parallel to MacIntyre's verdict that what he deems the 'Enlightenment Project' should be deemed a failure. Certainly there is a parallel, but still, what divides my case and his is that whilst he claims this project must be deemed a futile endeavour simply because it has not succeeded after 300 years of effort, I have tried to prove that it did necessarily *have* to fail on account of the method it has always employed (or, at least, I have tried to present a sketch of how that proof would run).[26]

Revisionism and behaviourism considered

What I should like to do now is compare this method with two alternatives, the first of which shares with mentalism its taste for human thoughts as the basic data of politico-philosophical enquiry, and the second of which holds that our subject should not be so confined.

The first of these is a minority position in contemporary scholarship I call *revisionist mentalism*, because in addition to wanting to revise our political opinions by recourse to our deeper moral thoughts, it also wants to revise the kind of confusion we find even at that level (as I have tried to show above) by recourse to what its practitioners take to be the most important of those.[27]

This is a method we find classically exemplified by Plato, in whose dialogues we find Socrates engaged in argument with various interlocutors, the point of which is to reveal that deep down, those interlocutors are confused about what they 'really think' about matters of right and wrong, justice and injustice, etc. And in turn, the point *then* is to replace those now openly confused thoughts with an entirely new and systematic way of thinking about the matter in question. Plato's hope was that the confused yet open mind that is produced by means of such argument is now ready to have its bundle of conflicting opinions replaced with genuine wisdom. And this hope is not, at least when broadly understood, unique to Plato's oeuvre, because the same basic idea can also be found at play in the work of contemporary thinkers

---

[26] MacIntyre, *After Virtue*. For my own rejection of MacIntyre's case, see J. Floyd, 'Is Political Philosophy too ahistorical?' *Critical Review of International Social and Political Philosophy*, 12 (2009), 4.

[27] In calling this model 'revisionism', I am deliberately echoing Parfit, who in turn follows Strawson when he writes: 'Descriptive philosophy gives reasons for what we instinctively assume, and explains and justifies the unchanging central core in our beliefs about ourselves, and the world we inhabit. I have great respect for descriptive philosophy. But, by temperament, I am a revisionist ... I try to challenge what we assume. Philosophers should not only interpret our beliefs; when they are false, they should *change* them.' D. Parfit, *Reasons and Persons* (Oxford: Oxford University Press, 1984), x.

such as Peter Singer and Derek Parfit, for whom the basic philosophical quest is to revise our weaker intuitions and beliefs by reference to what they deem to be our stronger and more rational ones, not so much in the manner of Rawls's reflective equilibrium, whereby mildly unsystematic thought is trimmed and cleaned up at the edges, but rather by taking just one or two apparently golden intuitions and beliefs and then using *them* to remake our further thoughts in accordance with *their* character.[28]

This approach, however, is ultimately no more compelling than mentalism proper, on account of its fatal and unavoidable tendency to prioritise both (1) theoretical coherence, and (2) whatever golden intuitions or beliefs particular philosophers feel particularly attracted to, over (3) everything else any given individual might believe. Examples of priority (1) are easy to find in all kinds of political philosophy. Both MacIntyre's work on moral dilemmas and Rawls's final chapter of a *Theory of Justice*, for instance, make perfectly clear their conviction that achieving full systematisation of one's moral and political beliefs is ultimately more important than having an inconsistent (or at least frequently indeterminate) framework with which, potentially, one is considerably more comfortable.[29] Priority (2), however, is confined to revisionists proper, although it is easy to find expressions of it in members of this group such as, again, Singer and Parfit, each of whom uses certain compelling moral intuitions in order to then override whatever else we might already believe about matters of right and wrong, simply because doing so would result in a less ad hoc, and thus more coherent, normative viewpoint. And yet, however neat and theoretically satisfying we might find this work to be, we will still ultimately have to ask: what possible normative force could such obsession with system hold for the vast majority of perfectly reasonable individuals? To this, I think, we will ultimately have to answer 'not much', because what really needs to be understood here is that revisionism, to its great detriment, combines the philosopher's professional predilection for system with the proselytiser's predilection for replacing whatever cocktail of values others might hold with whichever handful of values he or she

---

[28] See, for instance, P. Singer, 'Ethics and intuitions', *The Journal of Ethics*, 9 (2005), 331–52; and Parfit, *Reasons and Persons*.

[29] A. MacIntyre, *Ethics and Politics: Selected Essays, Vol. II* (Cambridge: Cambridge University Press), 85–100; J. Rawls, *A Theory of Justice* (Cambridge, MA: Harvard University Press, 1971), 577–87.

already holds most dear, all of which tends to render its arguments as persuasively blunt as they are theoretically elegant.

A second alternative to standard mentalism, however, seems considerably more promising. This suggestion, which is of my own design, holds that rather than looking solely at human moral thoughts and then attempting either (1) to find their inner system, or (2) to radically revise them in a systematic direction, political philosophers might do well (3) to look at certain kinds of *behaviour*. That is, rather than only studying how humans think, perhaps they would do well, sometimes, to consider how they act. We find elements of this way of thinking, I think, in a number of famous treatises, such as Machiavelli's *Discourses*, Montesquieu's *Spirit of the Laws* and, most clearly, book V of Aristotle's *Politics*.[30] And indeed, there is even a small move in this direction in a handful of contemporary thinkers. These include Jon Elster, whose work connects theoretical discussions regarding what a just distribution would be with empirical studies into how we try to make just decisions in particular allocation situations;[31] David Miller, whose work connects survey data on popular attitudes towards particular concrete practices and distributions with normative theories of the same;[32] and Amartya Sen, who insists that arguments regarding exactly which conception of justice we ought to adopt need to be informed by enquiries into the kinds of behaviour patterns they can realistically be expected to both encounter and encourage.[33]

I do think though that political philosophy could go considerably further in this direction than even any of these scholars have indicated, because surely if political science tells us *anything at all* about the tendencies of different structures of human organisation, it also tells us something of fundamental importance about both 'human nature' in general and what I would call 'expressed political preferences' regarding those structures in particular. And in turn, if it genuinely does tell us

---

[30] N. Machiavelli, *The Discourses* (London: Penguin, 2000); C. Montesquieu, *The Spirit of the Laws* (Cambridge: Cambridge University Press, 1989); Aristotle, *The Politics and the Constitution of Athens* (Cambridge: Cambridge University Press, 1996), esp. 119–52.

[31] J. Elster, 'The empirical study of justice', in D. Miller (ed.), *Pluralism, Justice, and Equality* (Oxford: Oxford University Press, 1995), 81–98.

[32] D. Miller, *Principles of Social Justice* (Cambridge, MA: Harvard University Press, 1999).

[33] A. Sen, *The Idea of Justice* (London: Allen Lane, 2009), esp. 68–9.

something at least a little reliable about those preferences, then surely it also tells us something very important about the relative value of those institutions – which, when all is said and done, is normally what political philosophers do ultimately spend their time trying to establish (by which I mean it is the relative worth of such institutions that the principles to which philosophers devote themselves are supposed to establish). The thought, therefore, that we should completely isolate facts about how humans *do* behave from considerations of how they *should* behave may well be a very deep mistake in modern political philosophy, and perhaps even one which accounts for much of its contemporary failings; all of which then raises the question: why is this suggestion never considered?

The answer to that is that there exists an incredibly deep-set philosophical resistance to connecting facts about any kind of behaviour to justifications of any kind of principle. You cannot, say contemporary philosophers, connect an 'is' to an 'ought', or a 'fact' to a 'value', or, I think most persuasively of all, a 'fact' to a 'principle'. Consider here, for example, the reasoning which supports the third of these three separations, as deployed by the late G. A. Cohen. He argues as follows: for any fact, such as 'all human beings share moral intuition X', to be relevant to political philosophy, there has to be some principle which makes that fact relevant, which means that there can be no facts at the foundations of normative arguments, but rather only principles.[34] I would suggest, however, not just that Cohen's reasoning is flawed, but also that it can be flipped. It is flawed, first of all, for the same reason that it would be incorrect to say of the following statement to a bumblebee that it lacks any real normative force: 'Because building your hive at the top of the tree will make your home less vulnerable to bears, you ought to build your hive at the top of tree.' Why, in short, would this statement have no normative force if we can observe both that the bumblebee wants to keep his hive away from bears, and that building at the top of the tree would do so? Exactly the same kind of reasoning applies to human beings, to whom we might say: 'If you want to avoid famine, crime, war and political instability, you would do well to try and construct a reasonably prosperous liberal democracy, because we know, from observation, that this type of system is much more likely to avoid

---

[34] G. A. Cohen, 'Facts and principles', *Philosophy and Public Affairs* 31: 3 (2003), 211–45.

those things, just as we know, from observation, that the vast majority of you want to avoid them.'

Yet to this the mentalist will reply, 'ah, but human beings are not like bees: they can reflect upon both what they do and why they do it, and, as a result, require *reasons* for their actions.' This instinctive objection rests, I think, upon an important mistaken assumption, which is that reason can in some way produce preferences, whereas *by reason* it cannot. Consider here that it is not reason that instructs me to prefer food to starvation, or one partner to another, or one career to another, or one political state of affairs to another, but rather the intuitions or preferences about those things I already have. All reason can do, when properly understood, is help me work out both what are, *to me*, the most relevant or important intuitions or preferences and, in turn, just which partners or careers or governments would best serve them. Or, alternatively put, because at least one pre-existing conviction (preference, desire, intuition, etc.) has to have the first say in any operation of practical reasoning, Humeans ineluctably get to have the final say in the theory thereof.[35]

All of which then means that Cohen's argument can be flipped, because if it *is* the case that facts about existing intuitions or considered moral judgements can be used as foundations for entailed answers to political philosophy's organising question, then why not, to give just

---

[35] I realise that this passage is much more of a subscription to Humean practical reasoning than it is an argument for it, as well as a rather glib way of siding with Bernard Williams regarding the priority of 'internal' over 'external' reasons. That much, I think, is unavoidable in this context, although it is perhaps worth briefly noting here that even in the works of Joseph Raz, that anti-Humean scholar who has done more than any other to give reason its due in the theory of practical reasoning, it can still play only a limiting role. Reason, in Raz, *under-determines* those valuable options with which it would be reasonable for us to engage, a fact which in turn supports both pluralism as a theory of value and autonomy as a political ideal. So: how are we then to decide amongst those options left standing by reason? For Raz, the answer to that is either going to be that we are *already socialised* to have a taste for some values or – and he says considerably less about this – simply the fact that we do *already have a desire* for them. As he says on one occasion, 'our chemistry rather than our rationality explains why some like it hot'. And consider: 'values guide action . . . but there are many of them, and one's taste may favour some rather than others'. See B. Williams, *Moral Luck: Philosophical Papers 1973–1980* (Cambridge: Cambridge University Press, 1981), 101–13; J. Raz, *Engaging Reason: On the Theory of Value and Action* (Oxford: Oxford University Press, 2002), 66; J. Raz, *The Practice of Value* (Oxford: Oxford University Press, 2003), 55.

one example, facts about what those considered judgements are in local contexts, as has been suggested by the historical contextualists – even if I think they are wrong to do so, for reasons given above. But more importantly still, if facts about the decisions we allegedly *would* make in hypothetical political choice situations can be used as foundations, then why not facts about those decisions we actually *do* make in concrete political circumstances? Might it not be the case, in short, that regardless of whether or not in general actions speak more loudly than words, certain political actions do sometimes speak more clearly than certain moral thoughts?

Let me provide a brief illustration of how this utilisation might work in practice. For example, I would suggest that rather than trying to gauge the worth of liberal democracy solely by reference to, say, our negative considered judgements about either such institutions as slavery or such processes as selection on the basis of birthright, we might try to measure it by reference to the comparative performance it exhibits in producing (1) political collapse, (2) political resistance (protest marches, riots, terrorism, etc.) and (3) violent crime. Why, though, should we be especially interested in these three forms of behaviour? My answer to that question is as follows: what unites these three measures is the thought that engaging in the activities they describe generally requires one to put one's life and person at serious risk, which means that doing so requires a degree of commitment that would not normally be required for, say, a vote, or a consumer purchase, or a choice of holiday destination. It is this common element, I think, that both grants these actions a significant kind of normative status and enables us to focus on three things which, when monitored, produce discernible patterns of a sort that is distinctly lacking in human moral thought.

If one needs a term for such actions, we might call them 'strong expressed preferences', but that is by the by; what really matters here is that patterns of the kind described can be found in all sorts of works of social and political science, from Adam Przeworski's work on the comparative performance of democracies and non-democracies,[36] through

---

[36] A. Przeworski, M. E. Alvarez, J. E. Cheibub and F. Limongi, *Democracy and Development: Political Institutions in the World, 1950–1990* (Cambridge: Cambridge University Press, 2000), 273. See also A. Przeworski, 'Democracy as an equilibrium', *Public Choice*, 123 (2005), 253–73.

Ted Gurr's work on the causes of revolutions and state collapse,[37] to Arend Lipjhart's work on the comparative performance of different types of democracy.[38] Each of these studies, we might say, reveals a variety of interesting 'behavioural facts'. For example, we know from Przeworski that no democracy with a GDP/capita of $6,055 or more has ever collapsed, just as we know from two further scholars, Richard Wilkinson and Kate Pickett, that more equal democracies generally experience fewer crimes than less equal ones.[39] And what *that* then enables us to begin to argue, I would suggest, is that there is a case to be made for egalitarian-liberal democracy – that kind of answer to political philosophy's organising question to which more political philosophers are attracted than any other – which depends not on, say, those intuitions we are said to hold about abstract conceptions of 'fairness', but rather on those 'expressed political preferences' which political scientists have managed to observe by studying (what else?) human political history.

But still, we have to be careful here, because although I think it rather odd that contemporary political philosophers do commonly spend their time asking such questions as 'what do our intuitions about fairness tell us of the constitution of an ideal state?', without ever considering the fact that, in practice, illiberal, non-democratic states exhibit a strong tendency over time towards transformation or collapse, a mentalist will still inevitably reply: even if your 'facts' are accurate, let alone 'relevant' in even some minimal sense, there still remains the fundamental question of what precisely it is that makes these indicators of behaviour normatively significant in the way that you suggest, and surely that significance, if nothing else, has to come from a more traditional, mentalist endeavour? Well, perhaps, but perhaps not. Consider here a parallel with the ordinary practice of mentalism. If a mentalist claims that all of our considered judgements conform to the principle

---

[37] T. R. Gurr, *Why Men Rebel* (Princeton, NJ: Princeton University Press, 1970). See also J. A. Goldstone, R. H. Bates, T. R. Gurr, M. Lustik, M. G. Marshall, J. Ulfelder and M. Woodward, 'A global forecasting model of political instability', paper presented at the Annual Meeting of the American Political Science Association, Washington, DC, September 1–4, 2005.

[38] A. Lijphart, *Patterns of Democracy: Government Forms and Performance in Thirty-Six Countries* (New Haven, CT: Yale University Press, 1999).

[39] R. Wilkinson and K. Pickett, *The Spirit Level: Why More Equal Societies Almost Always Do Better* (London: Allen Lane, 2009).

'maximise social utility', then whichever set of practical rules and whichever set of political institutions best fit with that rule will be, *ex vi termini*, the right ones. But note: they do not then ask 'what justifies *that* baseline principle?' If we think it *then we think it*, and there is nothing more to say, which then raises the question: if such reasoning is good enough for mentalism, why not also for behaviourist political philosophy? That is, if we can call a halt to our regressive search for justification in a *thought*, then why not also in an *action*, particularly when that action might ultimately prove more indicative of our political preferences than our own armchair inclinations about the same?

And indeed, there is still at least one further point here, which is that when a behaviourist political philosopher declares 'I advise you to pursue x as a means to y, not just because, in practice, y tends to be the best means to x, but also because, in practice, x tends to be what you prioritise', he or she is actually saying more than can be claimed by a mentalist, because often all they can really say is 'I advise you to do a because it would serve b, *even though in practice* b is not what you prioritise, and *even though in practice* b may bring with it consequences c which, again *in practice*, you tend to abhor'. Of course, the mentalist might still want to claim that there could still be reason to choose what we prefer in the course of abstract moral reflection over what we prefer in the course of real-life endeavour, but then, even if one were to grant that priority as a rule, as I would not, that ultimately only returns us to the problem, as explained above, that even in their most abstract and reflective domains of moral thought, human beings tend to disagree with each other. And not just with each other, for as we have already seen in the case of intuitive responses to abstract moral dilemmas, they also disagree even within their own individual minds. So, not only is there no obvious reason to prioritise hypothetical decisions over real ones, or armchair judgements over expressed preferences, there is also good and independent reason, as noted above, to abandon both of these options, given that both of them may well turn out to be less stable – despite what we might intuitively assume! – than the described empirical alternatives.

Some tentative conclusions

Let me now try and tie these various threads together. I have argued – or at least begun to argue – many things in the above. First, I argued that although history does help to reveal both the nature and sources of our present moral context, that context is not one defined by a single, minimal moral conception, or even a single, determinate and acceptable answer to political philosophy's organising question, but rather *plural* conceptions and *plural* answers. So, contra historical contextualism in general, and Larmore and Williams in particular, history cannot be used as the magic key to a context which, in turn, provides us with those determinate normative principles which political philosophers so desire.

Second, I argued that although history might not be particularly useful in identifying and then reconciling us to some or other set of normative political principles, we may still want to gain a historical perspective on the context of our own philosophical endeavours, and in particular on the methods we employ in the very same. Doing this, I think, allows us to bring into view a method which I call mentalism, and also to both reject that method and compare it with at least two alternatives – revisionist mentalism and behaviourism.

These two alternatives then took me to my third argument, which was that behaviourism – a politico-philosophical method which, like historical contextualism, attempts to harness historical facts in the generation of normative political principles – could perhaps aid political philosophers in breaking that stalemate of conflicting principles which so marks their work in modern times, and which has led many thinkers, such as Alasdair MacIntyre, to think that the subject must fail as it is currently practised, simply because it has already failed so much. All of which then means that if we now ask again 'what is the significance of history for political philosophy?', what I would answer is this: history is significant for at least *all* of these reasons. And indeed, even if it is only significant for just one – which is to say, even if only one of these arguments really stands up to scrutiny – that would still be more than enough to be going on with.

This concession is, though, a very important one here, and not just for the usual reason of acknowledgement of fallibility, both personal and epistemological, but also because I have barely had space here to make the second and third of these arguments to what would really be the required extent. I have not, for instance, provided as many examples as would be ideal to either illustrate what mentalism *is* or demonstrate *why* it has to fail. Nor have I considered as many objections to behaviourism as it is inevitably going to encounter. For instance, when I say that observable patterns of political behaviour seem to provide just that kind of support for liberal-egalitarian-democratic forms of political organisation for which many political philosophers have long been searching, it will be wondered by some whether I might actually be intending to defend some kind of absurd 'end of history' thesis to the effect that past behaviour displays the absolute limits of human progress. Well, to that I can only reply that, *perhaps*, behaviour simply shows just what the best form of political organisation that has been experimented with *so far* is, and that it would be good if, in the future, not just newer forms of organisation were to be tried out (rather than the same old recycled failures), but also if political philosophers were to think of those forms not as things which could be justified in the course of abstract reflection, but rather, to paraphrase Mill, as 'experiments in political living' which could be 'tested' in practice. But still, the real point remains that there are still many more such objections to be answered, even if there has been insufficient space on this occasion to answer them.

Certainly then, although I do believe that we can think of history, not just as a series of dates, but also as a series of *data*, I am aware that there is still much work that needs to be done in the future to prove it. And so, as regards behaviourism, if I have merely managed to make readers consider that patterns in human behaviour *might* be more relevant to political philosophy than has generally been assumed, and in turn that the question of whether there *do* exist such clear trends is not something that has already been proven one way or another, but rather something which might still be up for grabs, then that would clearly be more than enough for here and now. Or, if one prefers, it would clearly be enough, given both the nature of modern political philosophy and the state of my arguments about it – which is to say, given one very important aspect of the historical context of this chapter.

3 | Contingency and judgement in history of political philosophy: a phenomenological approach

BRUCE HADDOCK

The issues raised in this book go to the heart of an endeavour to do the best we can for ourselves in the light of past experience. In our reasonable moments, none of us would embark on a hazardous course of action without thinking long and hard about problems other individuals had confronted in comparable circumstances. And though our interest in studying history of political philosophy is unlikely to be motivated by quite the same practical urgency, it nevertheless constitutes a repository of the very best thinking that has been recorded, often advanced in exceptionally challenging circumstances. How we should live, what we owe to each other, what are the limits of our tolerance, are questions that can crop up in any conceivable society, understood as a scheme of social co-operation. Not to ask ourselves how such questions were addressed in the past would be the height of practical folly, though we perfectly understand that no two situations are exactly alike. What we have to focus on is the nature of a normative engagement in a variety of circumstances. We need to be clear about what it is to think hard in any conceivable circumstance. Our awareness that circumstances change is a subordinate element in a larger concern to think clearly.

Yet the past is not incidental to history of political philosophy. Methodological debates in the 1960s and 1970s highlighted in a variety of ways that normative engagement in texts is an actual engagement with identifiable interlocutors.[1] Quite how a context of debate should

---

[1] See Q. Skinner, 'Meaning and understanding in the history of ideas', *History and Theory*, 8 (1969); Q. Skinner, 'Some problems in the analysis of political thought and action', *Political Theory*, 2 (1974); Q. Skinner, 'Motives, intentions and the interpretation of texts', *New Literary History*, 3 (1971–2); J. Dunn, 'The identity of the history of ideas', in P. Laslett, W. G. Runciman and Quentin Skinner (eds.), *Philosophy, Politics and Society*, fourth series (Oxford: Blackwell, 1972); J. G. A. Pocock, 'The history of political thought: a methodological enquiry', in P. Laslett and W. G. Runciman (eds.), *Philosophy, Politics and Society*, second series (Oxford: Blackwell, 1962); B. Parekh and R. N. Berki, 'The history of political

be construed was much disputed. Quentin Skinner's view of a 'linguistic context' gained considerable currency, focusing specifically on a logic of conversation as a limit to the range of meanings that could (in principle) be attributed to a statement.[2] Skinner's concern was narrowly methodological. He was effectively asking how we (as historians) might best understand a conversation we had not been involved in. *Ex post facto* reconstruction, however, is notoriously neat and tidy. Hard thinking does not work like that. Thinkers push the boundaries of meaning in order to make the best sense of experience. They cannot be sure where their ideas will take them. They are pursuing implications, and implications are necessarily open-ended. This is not a pretext for playing fast and loose with texts, conjuring up whatever meaning might best suit our analytical purposes, but a recognition that thinking is agonising and tentative. Tidying up too much of the messiness at the edges can be deeply misleading.

The Limits of Revisionism

The (so-called) revisionist debate plainly heightened the level of methodological awareness across the sub-discipline of history of political thought. No one could now read texts innocently, as if Plato simply had something deeply interesting to say. The stress on context obliged even the most analytical readers to pay scrupulous attention to detail. Anachronism became a cardinal sin.[3] Yet worry about imputing meanings to texts also led to exaggerated interpretative caution. Even historically sensitive thinkers like Isaiah Berlin were chided for casually opening themselves up to startlingly original thinkers simply as readers. Discipline was the watchword, but it tended to come in narrowly historical form. Philosophers had to make sure that the Hobbesian argument they devised as a possible critical position could actually be

---

ideas', *Journal of the History of Ideas*, 34 (1973); C. D. Tarlton, 'Historicity, meaning, and revisionism in the study of political thought', *History and Theory*, 12 (1973); and D. Boucher, *Texts in Context: Revisionist Methods for Studying the History of Ideas* (Dordrecht: Martinus Nijhof, 1985).

[2] Skinner, 'Meaning and understanding in the history of ideas', 49.

[3] I became obsessed with the issue in the early part of my career: see B. Haddock, 'Vico and anachronism', *Political Studies*, 24 (1976), 483–7; B. Haddock, 'Vico: the problem of interpretation', *Social Research*, 43 (1976), 535–52; and B. Haddock, 'The history of ideas and the study of politics', *Political Theory*, 2 (1974), 420–31.

attributed to Hobbes. Some lost heart, and ran the argument without the attribution. Initial excitement about context has over the last forty years or so given place to a discernible parting of the ways, with historians and philosophers going about their business much as they had before, but with history of political thought seen as very much the domain of historians.

In methodological terms, of course, we are all pluralists now, though there remains something deeply unsatisfactory in the thought that we should slip back into old habits, as if the philosophical grounds for reading texts in specific ways should be quietly set aside. One of the prime reasons for thinking about approaches to texts was precisely that normative argument had been misconceived. Nobody could be taken at his word if he claimed to be addressing posterity. An argument is addressed to positions that do not hold true. They may resonate in the future, but they are devised to remedy problems in argument here and now. Note that the focus is not on what is going on in this or that argument; it is a limiting feature of engaging in argument at all. If this is true, and it is hard to see how it could not be in some sense, we can hardly invoke an idealised conversation of great minds as a substitute for the actual arguments thinkers were immersed in.

What we see in the literature, in fact, is a strange convergence on the question of contingency, though the issue is seldom addressed directly. The fact that ideas are (in some sense) contributions to contingent debates in specific cultural circumstances is assumed to be sufficient justification for a clear distinction between political philosophy and history of political philosophy as conceptual engagements. Beyond (rather narrowly conceived) methodological debates in history of political thought, this is part of a reaction against foundational argument in moral and political philosophy. Searching criticism over the last thirty years, culminating in postmodern celebration of moral and political construction rooted in sociological (rather than principled) consensus, has undermined the critical ground that innocent readers of political texts presupposed as they tried to sort out their own thinking. The impact in the English-speaking world has been especially acute, where the canon has generally been read from the perspective of a developing liberal tradition. Classic liberal foundational arguments, typically dependent upon conceptions of rationality and progress, have seemed to be especially vulnerable. Some liberal and post-liberal theory has simply accepted that the liberal position is one among many, dominant especially in cultures that benefited most from nineteenth-century industrialism, but with little or no trans-historical or cultural appeal.[4] In a world of agonistic politics, everything is up for grabs. In democratic contexts, in particular, the status of public argument has shifted significantly, with stress on rhetorical rather than theoretical persuasion. What counts is what is accepted, with fingers crossed that the consequences of being on the wrong side of a consensus may not be too costly. Readers of texts are not quite so exposed. For the most part they can continue with their musings relatively undisturbed. Their critical antennae, however, are accorded barely any critical status. In the circumstances, they can be forgiven if they turn to sad and sentimental stories.

Plainly it is a feature of most philosophical texts in the canon that they do address foundational questions, though a significant range of texts, from the sophists down to our own day, have always challenged the credentials of foundational theory. To approach these texts as if the foundational game is up is really very odd indeed. If your interests are philosophical, and the philosophy is wrong, why read them at all? Historians can carry on satisfying their curiosity, but that will not change the way we think. And that is a body-blow to any philosophical interest in the canon. We used to read these texts to clarify our own thinking in very basic ways. They served as building blocks in an edifice that no one could have dreamed of building. If conceptual clarification at the most abstract level is a forlorn hope based on misleading assumptions, we really do have to ask what we think we are doing.

The logic of normative argument

When we look closely at the pattern of normative argument, however, retreat from foundationalism is more apparent than real. Typically discussion will focus on the secondary ground that liberals largely share, such as different conceptions of distribution or rights. But the question of why these issues should be regarded as pressing is left to one side. This is theory addressed to the normal concerns of liberal democratic politics, where the status of that politics is taken for granted. When challenged about basic priorities, however, liberals can find

---

[4] See R. Rorty, *Contingency, Irony and Solidarity* (Cambridge: Cambridge University Press, 1989); and J. Gray, *Endgames: Questions in Late Modern Political Thought* (Cambridge: Polity, 1997).

themselves embarrassed, as is evident in the complex liberal response to multiculturalism.[5] Ordinary dilemmas about the limits of liberal toleration are especially difficult to handle if the formal liberal consensus is excessively narrow. In these circumstances, whether we like it or not, we are led to address foundational issues.

The problem is nicely illustrated in Rawls's *Political Liberalism*.[6] A book that purports to describe the possibility of principled consensus in liberal democratic states depends upon a deeper commitment to the free and equal status of persons (and not simply citizens). Rawls may feel able to take free and equal status for granted, but defence of that commitment was a principal achievement of seventeenth-century political philosophy, especially as it has come down to us in Hobbes, Locke and the great natural-law theorists. History of political philosophy serves effectively to temper the parochialism of analytical theory, where complacency can so easily blind us to the controversial nature of our presuppositions. The fact of pluralism, as Rawls in other moods reminds us, limits what we can legitimately hope to achieve through an interventionist state.[7] Deep pluralism obliges us to exercise restraint in our use of politically sanctioned violence. Recollection that what we take for granted might be anathema to some societies, groups, or individuals commits us to think long and hard about when we might legitimately invoke the coercive apparatus of the state. We are led back to foundational argument, despite our (perfectly understandable) worries about the range and relevance of our commitments.

Everything hinges in these discussions on the moral standing of persons, and, more specifically, whether that standing can be philosophically defended. The argument plainly has implications beyond the family of liberal democratic states. In this view, the question of what can be tolerated must be addressed to the plight of human beings universally, though the political response to that normative awareness will clearly be dependent upon circumstances. The fact that our thinking must be both universal and sensitive to context is deeply revealing. It reminds us precisely how tough questions arise. In a fix, we simply have

---

[5] See P. Kelly (ed.), *Multiculturalism Reconsidered* (Cambridge: Polity, 2002); and B. Haddock and P. Sutch (eds.), *Multiculturalism, Identity and Rights* (London: Routledge, 2003).

[6] See J. Rawls, *Political Liberalism* (New York: Columbia University Press, 1993).

[7] See *ibid*. 3–4.

to think hard, summoning up all the resources at our disposal. Imagination, as well as analytical flair, counts here. What we can possibly conceive is a function of the range of our intellectual experience. Exposure to
the best thinking that has survived is one way of keeping our minds open.
This, surely, is the kernel of truth in the (much derided) humanist claim
that history is moral philosophy teaching by examples.

The significance of context for argument thus takes us in a variety of
directions. Skinner's stress on 'linguistic context' makes eminent sense
when we are dealing with what we might style middle-range theory,
where discussion is concerned with policy and prescription, rather than
the most abstract questions about the status of persons. But, especially
in times of crisis, we can be led to more basic thinking that focuses more
specifically on what it may mean to be a human being.[8] Indeed Michael
Oakeshott, whose *Lectures in the History of Political Thought* are
deeply sceptical about the status of normative argument, nevertheless
acknowledged in his celebrated introduction to Hobbes's *Leviathan*
that in some cases the relevant context of argument is nothing less
than the history of philosophy as a whole.[9] How we are to interpret
that wider context is, of course, deeply problematic. One way to make
sense of the point is to assume that nothing should be ruled out. We
draw on whatever may be available, the more sophisticated the better.
This matches our intuitive understanding of hard thinking, though
doubtless a great deal of philosophical work needs to be done before
we can model more precisely what might be going on. The point to
stress here is simply that our thinking resonates at a variety of levels,
some of which will be latent when we are operating within comfortable
assumptions. When we push ourselves to the limits of our understanding, deeper resources come into play. Thinking hard is never comfortable. Circumstances force us to try to do things that may very well be

---

[8] Skinner, of course, is well aware that 'linguistic contexts' change; and, indeed, he
has shown how in a number of important writings. See his methodological essays
collected in *Visions of Politics, Vol. I* (Cambridge: Cambridge University Press,
2002). My point is that a historian's description of change is significantly different
from an agent confronting the demands of an urgent and unpredictable situation.
The agent's dilemma has to be modelled in quite different ways.

[9] See M. Oakeshott in T. Nardin and L. O'Sullivan (eds.), *Lectures in the History of
Political Thought* (Exeter: Imprint Academic, 2006). Oakeshott's introduction to
Leviathan is reprinted in his *Hobbes on Civil Association* (Oxford: Blackwell,
1975).

beyond us.[10] Every so often, however, someone pulls off something remarkable (like *Leviathan*). And the conceptual world never looks the same again.

Thinking at this level of abstraction can crop up in the most unlikely philosophical contexts. Anglo-American jurisprudence in the 1950s and 1960s was dominated by scrupulous attention to the way the legal world worked. But questions of legality and legal redress could not be effectively considered without wider discussion of political stability and moral redress. In the revealing controversy between Hart and Fuller the debate involved direct discussion of the status of natural law, though in a philosophical style very different from the great seventeenth-century archetypes.[11] Discussions of international law have continued in the same vein, extending our understanding of legal and civil order to embrace the complex interdependence of the modern world.

Challenges to traditional foundational theory must, of course, be taken seriously. The critique of liberal foundationalism, in particular, has a distinguished pedigree, drawing on Hegelian and Marxist ideas developed throughout the nineteenth century. The assault on unhistorical conceptions of rationality and individuality, combined with sociological critique of the idea of an individual outside a historically specific web of culture, had already exposed 'timeless' liberal theory to serious objections by the end of the nineteenth century. The addition of the Freudian critique of rationality left liberalism without its traditional grounding assumptions. In modern discussions the larger claim has

---

[10] This is not to suggest that 'thinking hard' guarantees good outcomes. Nor that we have the resources to work our way through any conceivable difficulties. Some things are simply too much for us. And in some contexts, we simply have to react instinctively. Bernard Williams has always worried that the seminar model of hard thinking is quite unlike our actual response to personal crises. See his *Ethics and the Limits of Philosophy* (London: Routledge, 2006). The crucial point to focus on here, however, is that political thought addresses co-ordination problems. We confront issues that need to be addressed collaboratively. In these contexts, instinct and intuition only take us so far. We have our hunches, and we cannot do without them. But, in the last resort, the form of political thought is very much dictated by the demands of public justification, no matter how limited the relevant public might be.

[11] See H. L. A. Hart, *The Concept of Law* (Oxford: Clarendon Press, 1961); and L. L. Fuller, *The Morality of Law* (New Haven, CT: Yale University Press, 1969). For discussion see N. Simmonds, *Law as a Moral Idea* (Oxford: Oxford University Press, 2007).

been advanced that all theory is context-dependent, rendering any talk of foundations absurd.[12]

Sceptical positions such as these have made much more headway in political and social theory than in philosophy of mind. We should remind ourselves that the 'revisionist turn' in the 1960s was very much fuelled by a reading of the implications of key philosophical positions. Austin, Wittgenstein and Collingwood were much cited, and their positions adopted, sometimes in bowdlerised form. There was much less sustained discussion of the cogency of their basic arguments. Yet when we look at serious philosophical scholarship on Austin, Wittgenstein and Collingwood, in particular, and beyond to the complex world of post-structuralism, it is clear that these are not simply positions that can be taken up and used for methodological purposes. They are too contentious, indeed too interesting, for that. This is not the place to engage in close philosophical discussion of specific arguments, simply a reminder that we run the risk of making ourselves look rather foolish if we pick too casually from the philosophical goods on display.

Thinking, writing, acting

The methodological debate focused very much on the retrospective understanding of historians, as it should. What was rather left out of the account was the writers of texts themselves, agonising about the inadequacies of received understandings and trying to galvanise support for positions and projects. The relevant philosophical material here concerns the status of normative judgements. We actually have a burgeoning literature to work with, but very little has surfaced in methodological discussions of history of political thought.[13] Looking back on

[12] See R. Rorty, *Philosophy and the Mirror of Nature* (Oxford: Blackwell, 1980); and J. Lyotard, *The Postmodern Condition: A Report on Knowledge* (Manchester: Manchester University Press, 1984).
[13] See C. M. Korsgaard, *The Sources of Normativity* (Cambridge: Cambridge University Press, 1996); C. M. Korsgaard, *Self-Constitution: Agency, Identity, and Integrity* (Oxford: Oxford University Press, 2009); A. Gibbard, *Wise Choices, Apt Feelings: A Theory of Normative Judgment* (Oxford: Clarendon Press, 1990); A. Gibbard, *Thinking How to Live* (Cambridge, MA: Harvard University Press, 2008); A. Gibbard, *Reconciling Our Aims: In Search of Bases for Ethics* (Oxford: Oxford University Press, 2008); and S. Darwall, *The Second-Person Standpoint: Morality, Respect, and Accountability* (Cambridge, MA: Harvard University Press, 2006).

the earlier debate, it is surprising that more productive use was not made of Searle's thought after his seminal work on the notion of a 'speech act'.[14] Skinner, in particular, but others following him, was quite right to treat writing as an act, but writers of texts in political thought are engaged in an act of a very specific kind. The image of conversation is helpful here, but not in the (oddly detached) Oakeshottean form.[15] Conversations among texts are about persuasion, in contexts where good argument counts quite as much as rhetorical force. Outcomes are crucial, lives and interests are at stake, in ways that they are manifestly not for the historian of political ideas.

Conventional methodology takes the drama out of theorising. Typically political action, including theoretical statement, involves risk, in the sense that we necessarily have imperfect understanding of the reverberations of our actions. Participants in a scheme of social co-operation will have their own views and priorities, and may not even have a strong commitment to continued co-operation. They are very unlikely to accept the thought that co-operation at any price is in their interest. Uncertainty and vulnerability are thus key to an understanding of political statement and response. If co-operation is conditional, reasonable terms must somehow be fashioned. What might constitute reasonable terms will doubtless vary in substantive terms in relation to shifting circumstances. A formal conception of reasonableness, however, even if only tacitly grasped, will remain a factor in the evaluation of social practices.

Public justification, even if the relevant public is exceedingly narrow, thus provides an appropriate context for reading a text that can plausibly be described as political. Viewed in this light, the theoretical context for reading texts shares basic features with the context of agents seeking reasonable terms of co-operation. We are faced with individuals thrown into situations where they have to respond to challenging issues as best they can. No matter what reservations we might have about conceptions of individual rationality, we cannot avoid thinking in terms of more or less adequate schemes of co-operation. The commonplace observation that values shift with contexts has very little bearing on

[14] See J. R. Searle, *Speech Acts: An Essay in the Philosophy of Language* (Cambridge: Cambridge University Press, 1969); J. R. Searle, *Rationality in Action* (Cambridge, MA: MIT Press, 2001); and J. R. Searle, *Mind, Language and Society: Philosophy in the Real World* (New York: Basic Books, 1998).
[15] See M. Oakeshott, 'The voice of poetry in the conversation of mankind', in his *Rationalism in Politics and Other Essays* (London: Methuen, 1962).

arguments pitched at this level of abstraction. If, as historians of political thought, we are alert to the implications of philosophical argument for our conceptions of appropriate method, we really have to tackle the vexed question of what it means to be an agent in any circumstances. It is immediately apparent that anti-foundational argument has often been misleadingly construed in moral and political philosophy. Wittgenstein, in particular, is routinely invoked as a social reductionist, yet a close reading of *Philosophical Investigations* and *On Certainty* yields a much more nuanced view.[16] This is not the place to pursue a detailed reading of Wittgenstein. It is worth noticing in passing, however, that his distinction between 'depth' and 'surface' grammar in *Philosophical Investigations* has barely been acknowledged in conventional 'sociological' readings of his work.[17] It remains unclear precisely where the distinction might take us, but it clearly offers scope to defend the status of critical thinking. The point, of course, is not that we can read off a method from an appropriate philosophical position, rather that we should take care not to restrict the scope of our thinking unduly.

What makes history of political thought so vital to normative theory is precisely that critical thinking is unavoidable in the contingent circumstances in which we find ourselves. This is true of all periods, though the slow pace of change in some contexts will often give agents an impression of permanence and solidity. Far from being an argument against the universality of normative thinking, however, the fact of change and diversity obliges us to think in terms of shifting possibilities. It is the universality of thinking (rather than values) that makes the historical record of hard thinking so important to us.[18] Our daily experience of deep pluralism actually heightens the salience of the historical record. The business of maintaining a normative consensus is never complete. In a world where a precarious status quo can never be taken for granted, the reality of the human response to changing circumstances is indispensable to our political education.

When we try to defend a particular conception of agency, it is intriguing to see where we turn. The simple thought that you cannot be an agent

---

[16] See L. Wittgenstein, *Philosophical Investigations*, trans. G. E. M. Anscombe (Oxford: Blackwell, 1968); and *On Certainty*, ed. G. E. M. Anscombe and G. H. von Wright (Oxford: Blackwell, 1969).

[17] See Wittgenstein, *Philosophical Investigations*, para. 664.

[18] This is the connecting theme of my *A History of Political Thought: From Antiquity to the Present* (Cambridge: Polity, 2008).

on your own was forcefully defended in Hegel's *Phenomenology of Spirit*, while in the *Philosophy of Right* he focused in revealing detail on the relationship between individual and community.[19] Hegel throws down a challenge that we recognise in our (significantly different) situation. Not to take Hegel seriously, in analytical as well as historical terms, is to miss something crucial for our understanding of thinking in practice. Hegel's account is, of course, one contribution among many, significant for us now precisely because we appreciate the force of a conception of individual identity that takes social context seriously. We do not follow Hegel, but explore his insight in addressing an issue that still taxes us. We approach Hegel's problem with a mass of empirical material to hand that was not available to him. But Hegel adds something that is not readily available in empirical studies – the thought that a struggle for recognition is essentially a normative exercise. Hegel helps us to frame that question. Not to take him seriously for our purposes is to impoverish our thinking.

Serious metatheoretical work is thus essential if we are to regain our bearings in both history of political thought and political theory. The 'linguistic turn' of the 1960s looks in retrospect like a promising detour that was taken on trust. It still seems to me that we can learn a great deal from reflection on language as a phenomenon. Philosophers over the last couple of decades have done important work on the 'sources of normativity', and speaking a language remains the most universal model we have of a normative engagement in a necessarily social setting.[20] Wittgenstein and his followers are still crucial to our efforts to understand the nature of argument, though we may well have to be more patient in our exploration of the implications of their thinking.[21] Here I can do no more than hint at promising directions we might do well to pursue. Part of the problem is that political theory as a sub-discipline is to some extent a victim of its own success, acquiring something of a life of

---

[19] See G. W. F. Hegel, *Phenomenology of Spirit*, trans. A. V. Miller (Oxford: Clarendon Press, 1977); and *Philosophy of Right*, ed. and trans. T. M. Knox (Oxford: Clarendon Press, 1952). The contemporary relevance of Hegel's position is discussed in M. Quante, *Hegel's Concept of Action* (Cambridge: Cambridge University Press, 2004).

[20] The phrase is borrowed from Korsgaard, *The Sources of Normativity*.

[21] Peter Winch's *The Idea of a Social Science* (London: Routledge and Kegan Paul, 1958) now reads like a programmatic manifesto, though it retains its value as an introduction to Wittgensteinian thinking for social and political theorists.

its own, unhealthily separated from mainstream work in philosophy. Hyper-specialisation is a problem for us all in an age of information overload. Every so often, however, we have to take stock, and that might involve looking again at resources we may well have started taking for granted.

Second thoughts

We have grown accustomed to asking ourselves what we are doing when we read texts. Oddly, however, at least in our glib moments, we tend to treat the texts themselves as raw data. We thought we were addressing the activity of writing when we sought to recover original linguistic contexts, but the way that enterprise was portrayed was dominated by the concerns of readers. What are we to make of Hobbes, writing in another context, almost in another world? But note, the question 'what was he thinking?' presupposes that we have a sufficiently clear view of thinking itself, and that may well not be the case. If we try to focus, instead, on the peculiar demands of thinking and writing as primary activities, we are led to a subtly different literature that raises new questions for us.

Thinking about thinking is hardly a novelty in philosophy. Indeed if we want a one-sentence definition of philosophy, that may very well be it. My point, however, is that our (second-order) preoccupations with explanation and understanding have led to neglect of first-order thinking. It is a daunting undertaking, from where we stand as historians of political thought and political theorists, to commit ourselves to systematic study of first-order philosophical questions. I have nothing quite so foolhardy in mind. What concerns me is not that we should set philosophy right, rather that we should not be too reckless in our borrowing.

Consider, for example, Donald Davidson's discussions of agency and first-person awareness.[22] In a series of seminal essays, Davidson focuses on what we might be said to be doing when we are thinking and speaking. Revealingly Davidson's is an approach that develops from Wittgenstein, but is leavened with insights from the logic of Quine and

---

[22] See, especially, D. Davidson, *Inquiries into Truth and Interpretation* (Oxford: Clarendon Press, 2001); *Essays on Actions and Events* (Oxford: Clarendon Press, 2001); and *Subjective, Intersubjective, Objective* (Oxford: Clarendon Press, 2001).

Tarski. Steps in the argument are very cautious indeed, reminding us that the most basic human activities may be philosophically problematic. Note that the problem is not what people do or say, but what philosophers say about them. Ordinary folk manage their world remarkably effectively; philosophers introduce complexity and confusion. This is very much (in true Wittgensteinian mode) philosophy as therapy.

Detail here is for illustrative purposes only. What I commend is not Davidson's conclusions, so much as his attention to basic questions. This is an invitation to simplify the way we go about our work, in a sense, to trust our understanding. In this view, ordinary understanding is actually quite remarkable. In order to make sense of ourselves, we have to assume that most people are right about most (very basic) things most of the time. Our capacity for individual thought and action actually presupposes a shared picture of a mundane world. Descriptions may change, but our initial point of reference does not. Here Davidson stresses the simple thought that anything said in one language can (in principle) be translated into any other, at least for practical purposes.[23] What we work on, as our thinking develops, is more or less adequate ways of putting things, in relation to a world that all possible speakers share.

In light of this insight, what sense can we make of celebrated discussions of incommensurability in political theory or strong relativist conceptions in history of political thought? Very little, if Davidson is right. In a much-cited essay, Davidson criticises Kuhn's use of the language of paradigms as a deeply misleading account of any possible thinking.[24] The fact that we each look at issues from a particular perspective has no bearing whatever on the truth claims we might advance. We check truth claims by trying to put things in different ways. Doubtless we frame truth claims with (more or less plausible) metaphors. But, crucially, we do not make truth claims for the metaphors.[25]

Language remains crucial for Davidson, but retains an open texture, enabling us to respond in infinite ways in any given situation. This is a logical point about what we can possibly say. The fact that, as historians

---

[23] See Davidson, 'Radical interpretation', in *Inquiries into Truth and Interpretation*, 125–39.

[24] See D. Davidson, 'On the very idea of a conceptual scheme', in *ibid*. 183–98.

[25] The thought is taken from W. V. Quine, 'Two dogmas of empiricism', in his *From a Logical Point of View* (Cambridge, MA: Harvard University Press, 1961).

confronting a particular set of evidence, we are concerned to attribute meanings in relation to contextual understandings, leaves open the possibility that an agent could have said anything at all. We are fortunately no longer quite so obsessed with an author's intentions as we once were, which leaves us to construe meanings as best we can in relation to an array of ideas held in relation to one another. This is critical reading as it was always done, opening a book and thinking hard about it, looking beyond the text when specific arguments seem odd. It also explains why we see more in a text when we reread it. Ideas can hang together in all manner of ways. We fix on meanings that are most fruitful in relation to our particular concerns. And in the nature of the exercise, as with the resources of a finite language, the possibilities are literally endless.

In retrospect, the 'linguistic turn' of the 1960s seems to have been inspired by a very narrow reading of philosophy of language. Certainly the social constructivist reading, popular in social psychology, sociology and anthropology, in addition to history of political thought, looks untenable. For my purposes here, it is enough simply to acknowledge that it is problematic. Controversial conceptions of language will have different methodological implications. We have wonderful resources to work with here, but they cannot be regarded as definitive. If we open ourselves to different possibilities in philosophy of language, we may well find new themes in our substantive material. Yet the measure of our work must always be substantive interest, not methodological correctness.

The most intriguing possibility in Davidson's work is that the conception of language use as a primitive model of thinking shifts our focus of attention in both history of political thought and political theory towards a common source in normative engagement. Stress on the form of language highlights structured relations in our dealings with one another, even in the basic distinction between speakers and listeners. Indeed the stable expectations embedded in language use are a necessary condition for our making any sense of ourselves at all. Modelling complex situations in political philosophy often involves stripping engagements down to bare essentials. The fact that language use is necessarily rooted in social relations enables us to distinguish minimal conditions for regulation and self-correction. It is worth noting that we draw this insight from Wittgenstein's rejection of the idea of a private language (is this philosophy or history of philosophy?), though we really cannot say how far he would have been prepared to follow us. Happily that worry can be quietly set aside.

History and theory

What links history of political thought and political theory together finally is a shared concern with public justification. In any specific context, of course, a range of different background assumptions will be invoked, whether knowingly or not. The fact that values may differ markedly, however, disguises remarkable continuity in the forms of argument advanced over recorded political history. Recognition that, as various groups of strangers, we may have an interest in pursuing at least some projects together, commits us to acknowledging the status of partners in a scheme of co-operation. Precisely how benefits and burdens are distributed may always be contentious. Equal partnership will only ever be one position among many, depending upon the variety of bargaining positions that come into play. Knowledge may now be more valuable than land as a resource. How things are weighted will depend upon circumstances. Yet there will always be priorities, defended more or less effectively from different perspectives. Some commitments will be treated as basic; others may be traded off for the sake of continuing co-operation. Outcomes in practice will depend on much more than argument, but public persuasion commits us to a measure of reciprocity.

Relevant examples can be drawn from a range of situations. Once it is acknowledged that justification is necessary, elaborate procedures come into play that constitute normative commitments. In the extreme case, war marks the end of dialogue. Yet it is instructive to note the formal affinity in justifications of war over time. Thucydides's discussion of the Peloponnesian War strikes us as remarkably modern, despite its cultural distance.[26] Grotius's special pleading in his *Commentary on the Law of Prize and Booty* invokes natural law in order to justify a form of piracy.[27] And (something like) natural law arguments continue to be used in defence of the most dubious causes in modern diplomacy. The fact that argument is used and abused is a secondary consideration.

---

[26] See Thucydides, *History of the Peloponnesian War*, trans. R. Warner (London: Penguin Books, 1972).

[27] See H. Grotius, *Commentary on the Law of Prize and Booty*, ed. M. J. van Ittersum (Indianapolis: Liberty Fund, 2006).

What must be noted is the logic of argument itself, which has normative force.

The features of social co-operation stressed here are highly abstract. They constitute basic building blocks for practical life in any conceivable context. But they have been taken up in contemporary theory, along with much else, in compelling accounts of practical engagement. This is political theory in skeletal form, without the social and cultural detail that gives daily life a shape for us. Yet when we turn to classic statements of political philosophy, this is precisely the level of abstraction we seek. We are drawn back time and again to Hobbes's account in chapter 13 of *Leviathan*, despite the fact that his view of human nature fails to convince us. We are perfectly able to distinguish Hobbes's philosophy from his personal opinions and preferences. That is why we continue to read him as political philosophers.

A primary motive for reading history of political thought had, of course, always been philosophical. That has not changed, despite our vastly increased awareness of middle-range texts that offer philosophical insight while addressing more narrowly political issues. Other interests in past texts in political thought are entirely proper. Indeed there is no theoretical justification for restricting the scope of the interests that take us back to past texts. Understanding ourselves can never be effectively attained if we merely reiterate the conventional concerns that shape a given period or context. Thinking in unfamiliar ways can alert us to dimensions of our own experience that might previously have been ignored. The discovery of an exquisite psychological world of childhood experience, for example, has had a major impact on the way we see ourselves and organise our social life. To make any sense to us at all, these insights have to be seen as more than accounts of conventional understandings.

What this shows is that substantive interests drive our historical enquiries. The discussions of human nature in Hobbes, Locke, Spinoza and other seventeenth-century philosophers now strike us as dated, ignoring as they do the deep impact of social, economic and political change on conceptions of the person. The fact that we can no longer treat foundational concerns within these terms of reference, however, should not deter us from addressing foundational questions at all. Thinking about our deep historicity, for example, goes beyond the historical awareness that is now a dominant feature in our experience. The fact that we once saw ourselves very differently remains an incentive to grasp what it is to be human (and not simply a person who happens to be historically aware).

Philosophical texts may be viewed as building blocks in an exercise in self-understanding, extending throughout recorded history. Middle-range political theory, focused on legal, distributional or constitutional problems, can take all manner of foundational assumptions for granted. If, as a matter of fact, we largely share assumptions about the free and equal status of individuals, we are absolved from the task of establishing foundational premises for resolving practical arguments. And because practical concerns are pressing, it is right that we should devote our efforts to matters that are unresolved. A foundational consensus, however, is a privilege of settled political cultures. A Chinese proverb has it that to live in interesting times is a curse. At the very least, interesting times oblige us to think through issues that challenge our self-understandings. Assumptions about progress that our liberal pre-decessors took for granted look sadly out of place in a troubled world. What we can safely take for granted then becomes a philosophical problem. It matters hugely in times of crisis, when the basic standing of persons might be challenged, that foundational questions can be addressed in an appropriate idiom. Texts in the history of political philosophy do not provide direct answers to our questions, but they enable us to frame discussions in which basic building blocks have become problematic. It is in the nature of our historicity that contexts are unique. But without a repository of hard thinking, our best endeav-ours are likely to be disappointing.

In the view I defend here, substantive debates in political philosophy/theory have a direct impact on the way we read past texts. This is not to say that the methodological debate has been a distraction. One of the most important philosophical problems that currently confront us is the moral, political and cultural significance of the fact that we are histor-ical creatures, formed in relation to contingent circumstances that shape the way we see ourselves. Doubtless this is dangerous ground, littered with failed projects in speculative philosophy of history that worry us. The sharp distinction between analytical and speculative philosophy of history in Anglo-American philosophy mirrors the distinction between substantive and methodological issues that has been such a pervasive feature of discussions of approaches to history of political thought. What we seem to be facing in both cases is an analytical point pushed too far. Grandiose political projects were very much discredited by the baleful history of the first half of the twentieth century. Recoiling from the impact of extravagant utopian theory, however, can easily disable us in more mundane normative arenas. Whatever reservations we might have about the abuse of normative theory, we cannot avoid tackling normative issues as we try to fashion effective schemes of social co-operation in shifting circumstances. This is demanding work, made no easier by our loss of nerve. Recurrent themes in history of philosophy provide deep consolation here, offering models of hard thinking in deeply challenging contexts.

We go back to the best arguments precisely because normative theory is unavoidable. Textual scholarship is, of course, different from practical argument in obvious ways. Yet recovering a context of argument takes us back to very familiar normative conditions – reflective individuals wondering what to do for the best in situations involving complex co-operation. Modelling a context of argument is contentious in itself. We cannot deploy approved methods and models in order to get at the 'truth'. Understanding past texts is always tentative and conditional, much like understanding conversation. It is very easy to pick up the wrong end of any number of sticks. The only corrective to hard thinking that goes wrong is more hard thinking. That takes us back to substantive philosophy, whether we like it or not.

Our awareness of contingency has been heightened by experience of deep pluralism and interdependence, quite as much as theory.[28] One response has been to focus on the specific questions that thinkers were seeking to answer. Collingwood's celebrated account of the logic of 'question and answer' in his *Autobiography* has become an article of faith for many of us.[29] Collingwood's worry was that disregard of historically specific thinking would obscure the fact that we are historical creatures, whatever that might mean. Philosophers preoccupied with perennial truth claims would not have an appropriate language to portray the business of generating truth claims in the first place.

Answers might not be perennial, but thinking most certainly is. Collingwood always insisted, even at his most historicist, that thought, as 'an eternal object . . . can be apprehended by historical thought at any time'.[30] Hence we can reconstruct the questions we did not actually ask.

---

[28] See B. Haddock, 'Liberalism and contingency', in M. Evans (ed.), *The Edinburgh Companion to Contemporary Liberalism* (Edinburgh: Edinburgh University Press, 2001), 162–71.

[29] See R. G. Collingwood, *An Autobiography* (London: Oxford University Press, 1939), 29–43.

[30] R. G. Collingwood, *The Idea of History* (Oxford: Clarendon Press, 1946), 218.

And there is no theoretical limit to the range of questions that can (in principle) be reconstructed, though each of us will have finite competence. Collingwood's use of the term 'logic' to describe a process of question and answer is revealing, suggesting an objective criterion of intelligibility, rather than empathetic identification. We can show how thinking goes wrong. False moves are part of the tentative business of thinking, at any time, in any place.

The specific thinking that we call political is designed to establish terms of social co-operation that are fit for purpose. Co-operation can, of course, be coercively induced, though it is unlikely to be effective over time unless key players agree to work together. Where goals are shared, we can assume that co-operation may be sustained relatively easily. It is precisely because circumstances change that we have to adapt our practices to meet the demands of new situations. Often discussion will be merely strategic. In difficult situations, however, terms of co-operation themselves may be in question. It may not be clear who should count in a scheme of co-operation, or how far their voices should be heard. We then find ourselves wondering what 'we owe to each other', rather than pondering the best means to attain given goals.[31] A stipulative definition of political philosophy is unhelpful, but we can recognise a change of idiom when terms of reference are under scrutiny.

On this view, the history of political philosophy can be seen as an exercise in grasping what goes on when we explore a context of hard choices. Contingency leaves the question of normative relevance entirely open. We have to do our thinking for ourselves, but we simply cannot begin unless we take the historical record seriously. Starting points are given. We have to use whatever conceptual resources may be to hand, in political thought as in any other sphere. The fact that our arguments are addressed to a public, however, imposes a discipline of its own wherever schemes of social co-operation are in place. Thinking about a text is critical in precisely the same way as any other exercise in practical reason, whenever and wherever conducted. Where history of philosophy differs from hard practical thinking is in a lack of urgency. What we might choose to do with our (provisional) conclusions is quite another matter.

---

[31] The phrase is borrowed from Scanlon. See his *What We Owe to each Other* (Cambridge, MA: Harvard University Press, 1998).

4 | *Political philosophy and the dead hand of its history*

GORDON GRAHAM

This chapter explores the relation between political philosophy and the history of political thought. It focuses on this question: are they allies or rivals? The question arises in part because the two disciplines so evidently share a very large number of figures and texts. That the list stretches from Plato and Aristotle through Hobbes and Locke to Marx and Mill is probably non-contentious. Whether it extends to (say) Rawls and Habermas is more problematic. Certainly, these authors are very likely to be studied in courses on 'contemporary political philosophy' and much less likely to appear in reading lists for 'history of political thought'. For the purposes of studying their philosophical ideas they are *not* historical figures – at least not yet.

I

Why might we separate Rawls and Habermas from other major political philosophers in this way? One plausible suggestion is that we, their current readers, are also their contemporaries, and this means that we share an implicit context of thought and understanding with them that we do not share with Hobbes or Locke. It is this that enables us to read their philosophy straight off the page, so to speak, whereas by contrast, the context of important thinkers from the past needs to be made explicit, if we are to understand them. That is why we need to engage in historical inquiry – the history of thought.

On the surface, this plausible suggestion allows us to construe the relationship between 'political philosophy' and 'history of political thought' as a natural and helpful alliance in which the latter simply supplies a necessary condition for the former. Closer examination, however, uncovers a deeper tension. Consider the appeal to implicit context as a way of identifying what is 'contemporary'. Implied in such a view is the supposition that the meaning of *all* political texts is contextual. The difference between implicit and explicit contexts on

84

this account is a purely contingent one, and in fact need not have any necessary connection with historical period; a context that can be taken for granted by one reader may be opaque to another. Thus the distinction between 'implicit' and 'explicit' leaves 'context' central to the understanding of texts, and this raises a question about the possibility of strictly philosophical engagement, even with contemporary texts. At most, the distinction supports the idea that the understanding of contemporary texts does not generally require historical investigation of any kind. There are many who would contend that this is only very rarely the case, of course, but in any event it is not an issue of any great significance. Just as the texts that Hobbes and Locke have left us were once contemporary, so the context that gives modern texts their meaning will recede into the past. Sooner or later the context in and for which Rawls and Habermas wrote will require historical recovery and excavation. What this shows (if true) is that their philosophical reflections are as historically localised as any other. Whereas political philosophers typically believe that they are engaged in a relatively 'context-free' inquiry, this is something of an illusion, generated by the fact that in the case of contemporary texts, historical context need not be made explicit. But if this is true, it means that political philosophy, as many people have understood it, is impossible.

Why should it mean this? The answer is that historical understanding has a powerful tendency to encroachment on the human sciences. Consider a parallel with the natural sciences of physics or chemistry. The history of these sciences is possible, important, interesting and valuable. But it can be separated sharply from the study of the sciences themselves. Neither owes anything to the other. Historians of chemistry are not expected to contribute, even indirectly, to contemporary issues, and even expert chemists need know little or nothing of the history of their subject. It is true, obviously, that scientific investigation does not take place out of time and that natural science is itself a historical accomplishment. Yet this does not alter the fact that the theoretical significance of contemporary experiments is not context-dependent. In no sense is it determined by time and place. Indeed, the evidential value of an experiment relies upon its being repeatable in indefinitely many other times and places. That is why successful natural scientists can be ignorant of their history. By contrast, to claim that philosophical ideas are context-dependent in the way just outlined is to say that their meaning is a function of historical time and place. Such meaning, of course, is precisely what historical inquiry aims to uncover and to offer us. The problem is that it uncovers it at the expense of every other kind of meaning.

The problem I am alluding to here is a familiar one. It lies at the heart of what I shall call the 'analytic *versus* contextualist' debate about political thought. 'Contextualism' in political theory is identified especially with the intellectual historians John Dunn,[1] J. G. A. Pocock[2] and Quentin Skinner. In a celebrated essay first published in 1969, Skinner writes:

The whole point, it is characteristically said, of studying past works of philosophy (or literature) must be that they contain (in a favoured phrase) 'timeless elements' in the form of 'universal ideas', even 'a dateless wisdom' with universal application. ... [T]o suggest instead that a knowledge of the social context is a necessary condition for an understanding of the classic texts is equivalent to denying that they do contain any elements of timeless and perennial interest, and is thus equivalent to removing the whole point of studying what they said.[3]

Skinner, of course, does not think that the contextualised study of texts is pointless; he only thinks it cannot have the point that others have thought. His contention (as he acknowledges) was anticipated thirty years earlier by the Oxford philosopher R. G. Collingwood. In his *Autobiography*, Collingwood recalls his growing doubts about the 'realism' that prevailed in the Oxford of his student days.

Was it really true, I asked myself, that the problems of philosophy were, even in the loosest sense of that word, eternal? Was it really true that different philosophies were different attempts to answer the same questions? I soon discovered that it was not true; it was merely a vulgar error, consequent on a kind of historical myopia which, deceived by superficial resemblances, failed to detect profound differences.[4]

---

[1] See for example J. Dunn, *Political Obligation in its Historical Context* (Cambridge: Cambridge University Press, 2002).
[2] See 'The history of political thought: a methodological enquiry', in Laslett and Runciman (eds.), *Philosophy, Politics and Society* (Oxford: Blackwell, 1962).
[3] Q. Skinner, 'Meaning and understanding in the history of ideas', *History and Theory*, 8: 1 (1969), 200.
[4] R. G. Collingwood, *An Autobiography* (Oxford: Oxford University Press, 1939), 60–1.

These 'profound differences' of course can only emerge through historical sensitivity to time and place. That is why history of philosophy is central rather than peripheral. The problem is that the very profundity of the differences it reveals threatens the idea that in 'even the loosest sense' philosophical problems transcend time and place (we can perhaps leave aside the somewhat rhetorical term 'eternal'). Thus the historical transcendence to which 'realist' political philosophy aspires turns out to be an illusion, and the philosopher who treats what Plato has to say about 'the polis' as though it were a theory of 'the State' comparable to Hobbes's say, is like the evidently foolish person who translates 'trireme' as 'steamship'.[5] When it comes to the study of politics, '*historia vincit omnia*', we might say. The consequence is that far from being political philosophy's helpful handmaid, the history of political thought becomes its assassin.

When 'realists' strike back (as it were), the effect works in the other direction; the history of political thought becomes the casualty. What is important, on this conception of the subject, is the kernel of ideas to which contemporary philosophical debate can relate. Uncovering this kernel can require the assistance of the linguist and/or the historian, but only in the sense that their skills may be needed to translate philosophical texts from the past into the language of the modern reader. Philosophy really only begins once such a translation is completed, and any historical work involved in completing it is not more significant for philosophical engagement than is the technology of print and paper that puts it in our hands. Whereas Locke could describe philosophy as an under-labourer to empirical science, on this 'realist' conception it is philosophy that is master, and history little more than the hired help.

In what follows I shall argue that any antipathy between political philosophy and the history of political thought can be overcome if we abandon the inclination to think of them as *either* rivals *or* allies. This solution, it seems to me, has much to offer our understanding of moral and political philosophy, where the debate has perhaps attracted most attention. But it is not restricted to this arena. The 'ally *versus* rival' dichotomy beckons in all areas of philosophy and its history, and in most other humane disciplines as well. For this reason, I shall begin the next step in the argument by considering an interesting parallel – the relation between music and musicology.

[5] *Ibid.* 64.

II

In the nineteenth century, musical taste formed by the high Romantic style of Tchaikovsky, Mahler and others led performers to adapt and alter both the music and the instruments characteristic of the Baroque and Classical eras. Massed choirs, pipe organs with hundreds of stops, and a large orchestra were used to perform works that were originally written with small vocal groups, chamber organs and a few stringed instruments in mind. Handel's *Messiah* is a notable instance of this general trend. Originally composed in 1742 for a small choir, by the late nineteenth century it was invariably performed by a huge number of voices as, famously, in the Huddersfield Choral Society. By the mid-twentieth century reaction had set in. Prompted by the rediscovery of 'Early Music' – which is to say, music composed before the invention of modern instruments – the 'authenticity' movement eventually created a quite different climate of opinion. 'If you want the best that any music has to offer', Robert Donington, an authority on early music declared, 'you do well to go at it in the authentic way'.[6] This new climate was one in which Victorian practices were frowned upon, and even came to be viewed as a sort of shameful travesty – the musical equivalent, in a way, of Dr Bowdler's notorious amendments to original texts in *The Family Shakespeare*, a ten-volume edition of the plays that eliminated all words and expressions 'which cannot with propriety be read aloud in a family'.

The remedy was to engage in 'authentic' performance, i.e. to perform the music as near as possible to the way in which it would have been played in the period it was composed, to restore it, we might say, to its historical context. Obviously, this required musicians to turn to musicologists, since only with the help of musicology could contemporary scores be stripped of their Romantic accretions, and only historians could give the necessary advice for reconstructing the sort of instruments with which Bach or Handel would have been familiar. With a 'clean' score and 'authentic' instruments, it was supposed, a modern audience might come to hear the music as an audience would have heard it at the time of its composition, and thus the way the composer intended it to be heard.

---

[6] R. Donington, *Early Music* (Oxford: Oxford University Press, 1983), 45.

The parallel with history and normative political theory is evident. The musician asks a normative question – how should this music be played? The musicologist provides the answer, thanks to careful historical inquiry that makes us sensitive to the context of its composition. So, too, the political philosopher asks: how should this text be understood? – and the historian of political thought provides the answer, once again on the basis of historical sensitivity to the context of its composition. The 'contemporary' political philosopher assumes an implicit context and thus, like the Victorian musician, distorts the object of study by inadvertently locating it in the wrong one. The intellectual historian, like the musicologist, corrects this distortion, by making its historical context explicit, thereby allowing the text to speak out of its own times.

The parallel between the two cases seems to me a striking one, and this raises the possibility that the music/musicology debate might throw valuable light on what I have called the analytic-contextualist debate. It can do so partly because enthusiasm for 'authenticity' in music has waned in recent decades, thanks to a growing consensus both that the movement invoked an impossible standard and that the dispute ultimately turned on false dichotomies.[7]

Consider the first point in relation to the ideal of 'recreating' the original musical experience of the Dublin audience that heard the premiere of Handel's *Messiah*. For a start, there is a certain measure of simple impossibility confronting such a goal. We can certainly strip the score of later accretions, but in most cases interpretative gaps will remain. We can also reconstruct instruments more like those that Handel used, but these will be made out of modern materials. Moreover, they will be played by people who have learned on modern instruments, and who have acquired a second mastery of old instruments, rather than mastering them *de novo* as did musicians who only knew the old ones. Even more obviously, it is impossible to reconstruct

---

[7] For a useful summary of the philosophical problems confronting authenticity in music, see J. O. Young, 'The concept of authentic performance', *British Journal of Aesthetics*, 28: 3 (1998). It has also met with practical objections. The entry on 'authenticity' in the *Oxford Companion to Music*, A. Latham (ed.) (Oxford: Oxford University Press, 2002) concludes that 'the inconsistency with which ideas of historical performance are applied, combined with the gaps in our knowledge of historical practice, make a literal interpretation of the term "authenticity" impracticable' (74).

the acoustic in which the performance was heard. Different buildings have different acoustics, and the acoustic also varies in accordance with the number of people present, the weather, competing noise, etc., etc. All this detail is irretrievably lost, so that trying to reconstruct the acoustic is a fruitless endeavour. If this is what authenticity requires, then authentic performance is impossible.

But it is impossible in another way too. Musical experience is neither passive nor episodic. The sound of music is not something that we merely *hear* on some occasion, such as a clap of thunder or a fire siren. We *listen* to it, and this intentional aspect makes a crucial differ-ence to the experience. For one thing, the practice of listening changes from period to period. Mozart complained to his father about the noisy chatter that people engaged in when he played the piano at aristocratic social gatherings. We listen to that same music with careful attention in specially constructed concert halls. Ought we to inculcate in ourselves a more careless way of listening in the interests of 'authenticity'? Could we do so? In any case, our musical history is *necessarily* different from theirs. This is a logical point, not merely a practical one. For those eighteenth-century Dubliners, Handel's great oratorio was something quite new; for us it is very familiar, and we hear it as the forebear of music that did not exist in 1742. For us, Baroque music is part of a sequential development that includes the Classical and the Romantic. For Handel's audience this was logically impossible, since no such music had as yet been composed.

In defending the claims of 'authentic' performance in the light of these observations, Stephen Davies has argued that 'authenticity' should be regarded not as a determinate goal to be accomplished, but a regulative ideal by which to be guided.[8] Let us leave aside the question as to whether this distinction will solve much. Instead we should ask what it is about authenticity that would make it an ideal that we might endorse. Davies's answer is that the ultimate test of an 'ideal' musical performance is faithfulness to the composer's intentions as specified in the score. That is to say, an 'ideal' performance creates for its audience the musical experience the composer intended, and a performance may be judged more authentic to the extent that it approaches this ideal. In the philosophy of literature, this invocation of the author's intention as

[8] S. Davies, 'Authenticity in musical performance', *British Journal of Aesthetics*, 27: 1 (1987).

a critical standard was labelled a 'fallacy', in a famous article by
W. K. Wimsatt and Monroe C. Beardsley.[9] It is not necessary to explore
all the complex philosophical issues surrounding this contention to see
that the relevance of intention depends crucially on a further assumption, namely that the only legitimate use to which something may be put
is that for which it was intended. It is only if there is something wrong
about deviating from the intended purpose (or interpretation), that
alternative purposes are to be regarded as defective.

This is a highly implausible assumption. Its implausibility derives from
the ease with which we can cite instances and circumstances in which it
would constitute an absurd restriction. For example, Ming vases and
wine cups were made for domestic use. Does this suggest to anyone that
displaying them is a gross error? Does anyone think that the posters
Toulouse-Lautrec painted for the opening of the Moulin Rouge in 1891
can have no proper use so long after the event which they were intended
to promote? Is there something wrong about using old beer barrels as
patio flower pots? No one does think these things, and by implication no
one thinks that in these cases authorial intention is decisive when it comes
to the use, value, understanding or treatment of the objects in question.
Why should it be any different with pieces of music?

It is worth noting that the dispute about authenticity is essentially
normative. It is about the right and wrong way to do things. The language
of 'distortion' and 'correction' shows this. Dr Bowdler's emendations of
Shakespeare were made in a moralising spirit. His aim was an educational
one – rendering the works of the great playwright fit for the classroom.
The twentieth-century repudiation of 'Bowdlerisation' is no less moralising, however – an affirmation of historical faithfulness against the incur-
sions of nineteenth-century prudery. This normative character is of great
importance. If the issue is about the right and wrong ways to do things,
then there is only a genuine dispute if music and musicology are aiming
to do the same things. And this is what I think most worth questioning.

It is true that music-making and musicology are both activities essentially related to music, but they are not the same activity. I shall mark the

---

[9] 'The intentional fallacy' by W. K. Wimsatt and M. C. Beardsley was first published
in the *Sewanee Review*, 1946. A revised version was included in *The Verbal Icon:
Studies in the Meaning of Poetry* (Lexington, KY: University Press of Kentucky).
I discuss the general point in G. Graham, *Philosophy of the Arts* (London:
Routledge, 2005), esp. 207–13.

difference by saying that music-making is concerned with *appropriation*, while musicology aims at *reconstruction*. Arguments about authenticity arise from the confused supposition that all appropriation is misappropriation. The confusion arises because appropriating something for present purposes invariably leads us to alter or deviate from the standards that faithful reconstruction requires. But there are plenty of contexts in which such deviation and alteration is quite unobjectionable. Consider historic properties. The historic conservation of buildings is neither better nor worse than their modernisation. It is simply a different purpose, and can itself be done well or badly. If a house built long ago is to be a home rather than a historic relic suitable only as a 'heritage site', I must appropriate it as such. This usually means installing modern plumbing, heating and so on. Such work can be done unsympathetically or sympathetically to the original design. The difference is not a matter of change *versus* no change. It is a matter of retaining (or renovating) those features that both at the time of its construction and now make it recognisably a place in which human beings can live satisfactorily.

A similar point can be made about musical compositions. Suppose that someone rearranges a violin concerto by J. S. Bach for a saxophone quartet. It is incontestable that this could not have been the way in which Bach intended it to be heard, since the saxophone was not invented until almost 300 years after his death. It follows, truistically, that anyone who wants to know how Bach would have expected the piece to sound will not use saxophones. What does *not* follow is that the saxophone version has no musical properties that Bach would have recognised. Nor does it follow that every good musical purpose will be better served by a performance on original instruments; such a performance will be of no value at all to those who want to explore the potentialities of the saxophone. It does not even follow that there is something false or misleading about describing the resulting arrangement as a piece by Bach. The criteria of identity for pieces of music are not so rigid. In fact, once we have said that it is an *arrangement* of Bach for saxophones, we have said everything that needs to be said. The further question: but is this *really* Bach? – is both unanswerable and pointless.

III

The relevance of this extended discussion of musical authenticity lies in its parallel with the tension that has widely been thought to arise between the contextualism to which the history of political thought seems firmly wedded, and the non- (or even anti-) contextualism to which political philosophers often subscribe. If the parallel holds, then we are able to say that the purpose of political philosophy is to *appropriate* the texts of past philosophers, while the purpose of intellectual history is to *reconstruct* them. Both activities are essentially connected to thinking about politics, of course. That is why they are so easily viewed as occupying the same territory, and why the question 'Are they rivals or allies?' so readily arises. But once we take seriously the thought that, despite this commonality, they are nonetheless distinct activities, we open up the possibility that they are markedly different, in the way that (for instance) house building and home making are importantly different. Both are concerned with aspects of human habitation, certainly, but the house builder needs to know things about walls and windows which the home maker can safely ignore, and vice versa.

Does the parallel hold, though? I have chosen the term 'appropriating texts' quite deliberately since, as it seems to me, contextualists might well use the term 'appropriation' in criticism of 'analytical' political philosophy. Used in this way, 'appropriation' often has the connotation of a cavalier treatment of the text, one that licenses a disregard for its integrity, and at the same time encourages its egregious manipulation for the sake of contemporary relevance. With such treatment, it is implied, philosophical texts come to say whatever contemporary philosophers want them to say, and this may bear little resemblance to original authorial intent. This is, more or less, the accusation that Collingwood brings against his Oxford colleagues, and in doing so he articulates a point of view that can be encountered quite widely amongst intellectual historians. The description is at best an exaggeration, however, and at worst a caricature. Even the most 'analytic' of political philosophers insist upon good editions and accurate translations of the texts that their students are to read and about which they debate with other philosophers. Perhaps there is some respect in which 'appropriation' of a text is academically suspect – though I shall argue to the contrary – but however that may be, appropriation is still importantly different from fabrication and falsification. Modernising the plumbing in a medieval castle (to invoke an earlier parallel) requires us both to know and to respect important features of its original construction; its ramparts are not merely a façade for the 'modern' building within.

How then might a more judicious reservation about appropriation be expressed? As every teacher knows, it is possible for competent speakers of a language to misunderstand a philosophical text drastically, even when it is written in their native tongue. There is thus always a potential gap between what a text says and what someone thinks it says. It seems eminently reasonable to infer from this that bringing our beliefs about what a text says into line with what it *actually* says is a necessary pre-condition of assessing its philosophical merits. And clearly, a pre-condition of ensuring this correspondence is establishing what the text does say. Now an important theme of the contextual school is that linguistic entities, whether spoken or written, are *actions*, acts of communication between human beings. Accordingly, if they are to be understood, we have to understand the audience to which the communication is addressed as well as the mind that means to communicate with it. Both are necessary to a proper grasp of meaning. Plato (or Hobbes or Locke, etc.) did not write in a communicative vacuum. Nor did they write for an atemporal 'ideal' audience. They wrote for an actual one. That actual audience (for obvious reasons) was not the modern reader, but the contemporaneous reader. Taken together, these considerations make knowledge of the historical context indispensable. Without it, the text ceases to be an act of communication at all. It follows that while we may (to use a phrase of Derrida's) 'play' upon the text, its character as a historically specific *action* prevents it from providing us with 'answers' to 'timeless' questions. Very much in the spirit of Collingwood, Skinner writes:

All I wish to insist is that, whenever it is claimed that the point of historical study of such questions is that we may learn directly from the *answers*, it will be found that what *counts* as an answer will usually look, in a different culture or period, so different in itself that it can hardly be in the least useful even to go on thinking of the relevant questions as being 'the same' in the required sense at all.[10]

Viewed from this perspective, the parallel with musical works breaks down. A musical work is not a linguistic communication. It is an object of appreciation, not of understanding. We cannot be mistaken about its meaning, because strictly speaking it has none (in the normal sense of that word). There is no gap between how we hear music, and how it

[10] Skinner, *Meaning and Understanding*, 230.

really sounds. How it sounds, just *is* how we hear it. It is not something we can be mistaken about.[11] This is not to deny that there is often (perhaps always) a 'personal' element in the experience of music as we listen to it. Previous experiences, both musical and non-musical, past associations and present circumstances may give the music a different emotional 'feel' to the feel it has for others, or even for ourselves on another occasion. Strictly speaking, however, this is a not matter of the sound itself, but of our affective response. The simplest way of making the point is to say that we respond differently to the same piece of music; it just confuses matters to suggest that, in some way, a different response makes it a different piece of music. If this were so, then we could not say what seems to be obviously true – that the music affects us differently – since each of us would be confined to a personal musical world with boundaries determined by affective response.

By contrast, philosophical texts do have meaning, precisely because they are linguistic entities. I can grasp the meaning of a sentence whether I hear it in French or English, or read it in Roman or Cyrillic script. Its meaning thus transcends the media of sound and sight. A transcription of Bach for saxophones may be questionable on some level, but it is not a counterpart to (say) a badly edited text or poor translation of Plato into English.

This defence of contextualism undoubtedly has considerable plausibility, and the rejection of the parallel with music does rest on a real difference between the two cases. Yet further reflection will reveal, I think, that neither the point about communicative action nor the difference with music implies quite as much about the use of philosophical texts as might be supposed. The first pertinent observation is this. Not all political texts are philosophical texts. Only a very few are, in fact. Most are speeches, pamphlets, manifestos, propaganda and so on. All of these, of course, are also communicative acts, so we need to mark some of the features that differentiate them from philosophical texts if we are to account adequately for the difference. Two such features come immediately to mind. First, there is a plain sense in which these other

---

[11] Jerrold Levinson has argued for a version of 'authenticity' in music that rests on the distinctive sonic properties of the instruments available in the period of a piece's composition. J. Levinson, *Music, Art, and Metaphysics* (Ithaca, NY: Cornell University Press, 1990). Whatever merits his case may have, it is clearly compatible with the point being made here, since it rests on a claim about sonic properties, not historical contingencies.

political texts are addressed to specific audiences to which we do not, and could not, belong. For example, Adam Ferguson's *Reflections Previous to the Establishment of a Militia* (1756) is a political text by a philosopher of some significance and repute. This 53-page pamphlet was written in a highly specific political context – England after the defeat of the Jacobites – concerned with a specific issue – the creation of an English militia – and addressed (anonymously) to a specific political audience – those who had voted against the Townsend militia bill. Since the context, the issue and the audience are long since gone, it is incontestable that, though Ferguson's pamphlet is of continuing interest to the intellectual historian, it is without philosophical interest or practical connection to contemporary politics. (Ferguson himself later described it as 'a tedious performance'.) By contrast, Ferguson's *Essay on the History of Civil Society* (1767) cannot be declared philosophically inconsequential or politically irrelevant with equal assurance.

The difference lies in this. Ferguson wrote both the pamphlet and the *Essay* with historically specific audiences in mind, and, let us agree, in neither case was he invoking any conception of an 'ideal' (still less an 'eternal') audience. Nevertheless, he wrote the *Essay* for posterity as well as for the social theorists of his own time. In other words, he wanted and expected it to retain its relevance beyond the historical period of its composition. How far beyond? I choose the example of Ferguson with care, because the *Essay* ran through a great many editions and translations, before falling into general neglect something less than a hundred years after its first publication. Though there is a Cambridge Text edition of the *Essay* available once more,[12] its editor, Fania Oz-Salzberger, says quite openly that 'Readers of the *Essay* today would hardly consider its author as "our contemporary"'.[13] This is not just a matter of age, however. Students of political philosophy are more likely to find it 'dated' than (for instance) Locke's *Second Treatise of Civil Government*, published seventy years earlier. Ferguson, we might say, has yet to find his Nozick. In *Anarchy, State and Utopia*, Nozick appropriated elements of Locke's *Second Treatise* for the purposes of debating a dominant view in contemporary political philosophy, namely Rawls's *Theory of Justice*. The question of whether the posterity

---

[12] A. Ferguson, *An Essay on the History of Civil Society* (Cambridge: Cambridge University Press, 1996).
[13] *Ibid.* xxv.

for which both Ferguson and Locke wrote extends to the twentieth century is to this extent an empirical question. Did readers in the twentieth century find themselves engaged by it in a non-historical mode? The answer appears to be 'Yes' in the case of Locke, and 'No' in the case of Ferguson. But this might change. In the same place, Oz-Salzberger also notes that its central thesis 'has re-surfaced with new relevance in the last few decades'.

'Writing for posterity' is an intelligible intellectual ambition, yet it is not something that is within our power to secure. Whether I succeed or not is a matter for posterity, not for me. To that extent, a text takes on a life (or fails to) beyond the intentions of its author. In this respect, it seems to me, the parallel with music is restored. Whether transcriptions of Bach for the saxophone are a valuable musical innovation or not is a matter for the judgement of contemporary saxophonists and their audiences. Personally, I am inclined to think that they are, while the reverse transcription of saxophone music for Baroque organ is unlikely to be. But the point is that these are matters of experiment and judgement. The obvious truth that Bach could not have anticipated this does nothing to settle the matter.

In the case of philosophical texts written for posterity there is an equivalent phenomenon to the freedom that allows Bach to be transcribed for saxophone. This is what I shall call 'interpretative gap'. 'What did Hume mean when he wrote ...?' This kind of question in the mouth of an intelligent reader calls for something other than simple reiteration of the text. It signals a request for interpretation. Sometimes, this means *translation*, as in the question: 'What does the Greek word "trireme" mean?' The translator may need to look beyond the text to the community of speakers from which the text came, gathering evidence from historically contemporaneous sources. It is a matter of finding out what 'trireme' meant to the ancient Greeks. Both how it is to be translated into modern English (and whether it can be) are matters that only sensitive historical inquiry will determine.

For many purposes the words 'translation' and 'interpretation' can be used interchangeably. But when it comes to the study of philosophical texts, it is important to distinguish them. Some interpretative questions are indeed effectively matters of translation, matters that is to say of mastering the connotations that words had for those who wrote them and originally read them. But many are not of this kind. In response to the question 'What did Hume mean when he wrote ...?', it is often appropriate to turn to the text itself, not beyond it, and to seek to find a coherence within it that will dispel the perplexity this question expresses. This, I take it, is what philosophers often do – to excess, some would say. However, even when our best efforts in this regard have been exhausted – when, that is to say, the translation is as good as we can get it and the complete text as coherent as we can make it – there may remain interpretative questions. These are what I am calling interpretative gaps.

How are they to be filled (if they are)? It is tempting to suppose that other writings of the same author are especially valuable in this context. Wouldn't it fill the gap conclusively if we were able to call up the shade of Hume and ask him: 'What did you mean when you said . . .?', or less fancifully, if we were to find a letter to Adam Smith or Adam Ferguson (say) in which he amplified his remarks? But tempting though this thought is, it is importantly mistaken. In either circumstance, all we would have is more text, and in making this larger entity (text plus extras) cohere, further interpretative gaps may arise. Odd though it may sound, authors are not authoritative interpreters of their texts. Between writing the *Treatise* and the *Inquiries*, to continue the example, Hume may have changed his mind, or misremembered, or mistakenly thought that a different formulation meant just the same as a former one, or inadvertently contradicted himself. All the same possibilities arise for any letter we might find. Whether errors and confusions such as these have entered into the supplementary material is not a question exclusively for Hume or for his contemporaries, but for everyone who thinks it worth reading his text.

It is of great moment in this context to observe that the possibilities just sketched raise normative questions – is this a mistake? Is Hume misremembering here, etc.? – but these questions are not confined to what is normally thought of as textual criticism. They require us to have some independent grasp of what counts as a mistake in the context of doing philosophy. That is why a reader whose understanding of a language is excellent may nevertheless be perplexed by a philosophical text written in that language. Moreover, such questions lead on seamlessly to more wide-ranging normative questions: is this true? Does this make sense? Does A contradict B? It is at this point, I am inclined to say, that the text becomes a philosophical text. Such questions are at best mere curiosity when applied to Ferguson's pamphlet about the militia. The only questions that can matter to us now are all historical – in the past tense. What *were* the issues he thought important? How *was* his pamphlet received? *Did* it make any difference? And so on. By contrast significant questions relating to his *Essay* can be expressed in the present tense. 'Is there anything to be said for his "stadial" view of history?' for instance, and some questions of this kind will intelligibly raise issues about historical location and continuing intellectual value: 'Are Ferguson's arguments about the dangers of prosperity anything more than the expression of concerns typical of his times?'

Philosophical appropriation of the text shows itself when attempts are made to bridge interpretative gaps by innovative means. 'Would Hobbes's account of human nature be more cogent if we abandoned his pseudo-geometrical method?' This is the point at which historians of philosophy begin to get nervous. Once moves of this kind are made, they think, we have abandoned the text and its author. 'Improved' Hobbes is not Hobbes. It might be what we think Hobbes *ought* to have said, but it isn't what he *actually* said. Their objection, however, requires us to make a very sharp distinction between fact – what Hobbes said – and value – whether it is true and important. What the various examples I have used are intended to show, on the contrary, is that the trajectory from editing to translation to interpretation to extrapolation to innovation is a seamless one. The first stage is undoubtedly different from the last, but contrary to Hume's famous contention about 'is and ought', nothing has gone wrong in between.

Editing and translation can often require a significant effort at historical reconstruction, and people who are good at this may find that the activity of reconstruction stimulates them to reconstruct the wider intellectual world of the period, and even its broader cultural character. Trying to understand a text in terms of content may reveal interpretative gaps that it is intellectually challenging to try to fill. Such challenges may eventually involve us in appropriating the text as a vehicle by means of which we can think through some of the issues for ourselves. Similarly (to pursue my parallel one last time), the student of Bach may be led to reconstruct the wider musical world of the early eighteenth century, and from there to explore its religious and ecclesiastical context. Alternatively, students of Bach, captivated by his harpsichord music for example, may come to wonder whether some of its properties would be more evident, or even enhanced, when played on a modern piano. They are appropriating Bach for purposes he could probably not have imagined. Have they abandoned Bach? Yes and no. Have they turned

him into a creature of their imagination? Certainly not. It is the genius of
Bach that still shines through the piano music he could never have heard
or even dreamt of.

IV

Collingwood's example of the person who translates 'trireme' as
'steamship' and counters text-based objections to this translation by
declaring that this simply shows how wrong the Greeks were about
steamships, is clever and amusing. But it is largely rhetorical. In the
real world of philosophy, no one makes errors of this magnitude.
Collingwood, of course, thought that the example was merely an
extreme case of something quite common, namely the consequences of
thinking that philosophy is a matter of assessing the truth of competing
theories, regardless of their origins in time and place. He goes on to
expound an alternative conception of philosophy as uncovering the
presuppositions of historically located thinking, understanding the
views philosophers have elaborated, not in terms of their adequacy for
our purposes, but in terms of the questions to which their authors
offered them as answers. It is not hard to show, in my opinion, that
this drastically fragments the subject and requires us to deny that there is
such a thing as a tradition of inquiry at all. It does not follow, however,
that the palm must then go to the 'Oxford realists' whom he was
attacking. On the contrary, their conception construes philosophy as
(potentially at least) a progressive science. This too is false to its history.
In philosophy, I shall say, there are no demonstrably right answers. This
does not mean that there are no perennial questions, and it does not
mean that possible answers to these questions are in some important
way time-bound. The 'analytic-contextualist' debate arises because of a
mistaken conception of the relation of the activity of philosophising to
its history. Here too, the analogy with music might serve as a corrective.
To compose today in the manner of Vivaldi would be pastiche, but
Vivaldi's music can still figure in the modern concert hall, and indeed in
the artistic successes of recording companies.

    Skinner concludes the passage about questions and answers quoted
earlier with this striking remark: 'we must learn to do our own thinking
for ourselves'.[14] His thought appears to be that since the passage of time

---

[14] *Ibid.* 230.

renders the questions and answers of earlier thinkers different from those of today, they cannot help us with finding answers to the questions of our own time. There is something obviously correct about this – when applied to the 'political questions of the day'. *Pace* Machiavelli and Bolingbroke (amongst others), history cannot be regarded as a repository of practical lessons that subsequent generations can usefully follow.[15] Applied to political philosophy, however, there is something radically wrong about this view, since it implies that the activity of philosophising itself has no history, and that each generation (each individual?) must begin to philosophise afresh. This can hardly be correct.

What is true, I think, is that we are mistaken if we think that the great philosophical texts are repositories of cumulative 'results' (negative as well as positive) upon which any new philosophical 'theory' must build. This broadly 'scientistic' conception applies only in part to the experimental sciences themselves, but not at all to philosophy. There are no 'results' in philosophy, if by this is meant propositions established beyond any rational question. There is no position in philosophy that cannot be revitalised. Sometimes certain doctrines are out of fashion for a relatively long time, and this gives rise to an impression that they have been refuted. Cartesian dualism is a good example. Sometimes too, it seems that some specific idea has been conclusively refuted – Hume's attack on miracles is a case in point. But it is never very long before a philosopher will make a compelling argument on the other side – David Chalmers in the case of dualism,[16] for instance, and John Earman in the case of Hume.[17]

Examples like these are rare, and especially hard to find in political philosophy.[18] For the most part, every recognisably philosophical position is potentially a 'live option'. In this way, I want to say, philosophical texts are like great novels. Though the works of Jane Austen, for

[15] I discuss some of the relevant issues here in ch. 8 of G. Graham, *The Shape of the Past* (Oxford: Oxford University Press, 1997).

[16] In D. J. Chalmers, *The Conscious Mind* (Oxford: Oxford University Press, 1998).

[17] In J. Earman, *Humes' Abject Failure: The Argument against Miracles* (Oxford: Oxford University Press, 2000).

[18] Locke's refutation of Filmer in the *First Treatise* [1689] is a plausible example, but a position not unlike Filmer's was defended 300 years later in S. R. L. Clark, *Civil Peace and Sacred Order* (Oxford: Oxford University Press, 1989). See J. Locke, *Two Treatises of Government* (Cambridge: Cambridge University Press, 1988).

example, are unmistakably products of their day and have value as historical documents of the period, they can still be read as fiction, with profit and enjoyment, 200 years later. Works of fiction can meaningfully be regarded as 'truthful', and they can continue to influence the activity of writing fiction. Their truthfulness is a merit in itself and part of the explanation for their continuing influence. Yet no one would ever infer from this that the 'truthfulness' of later novels might render earlier ones redundant, or that subsequent novelists would have to acknowledge and incorporate their 'truth'. The relevant contrast in fiction is not with falsehood, but with shallowness, sentimentality or romanticism. Similarly, the explanatory power that a philosophical theory offers us is not the same as the explanatory power that commends a scientific theory, and the empirical adequacy which is crucial to the latter is hardly a matter of great moment to the former. The aim of philosophy, I shall say, is to gain clarity and insight about some fundamental aspects of human existence. Politics is one of those aspects, and wrestling with the great texts of political philosophy is for most of us an indispensable condition of learning how 'to do our own thinking for ourselves'.

PART II

The challenge of realism

5 | *Politics, political theory and its history*

IAIN HAMPSHER-MONK

This chapter seeks to reflect on the differences and relationships between political philosophy, the history of political thought, and the conduct of politics itself. It seeks to sketch out political discourse as a kind of force field constituted by three nodes, identified by three idealised intellectual practices: History, Philosophy and Rhetoric. The kinds of intellectual enterprises that we conduct in the field of politics are characterised by blends of these, inasmuch as perhaps no one ever entirely succeeds in emancipation from the other of these categories. Yet each enterprise has its own distinctive properties, an understanding of which is important to understand their proper and effective conduct.

If we take the study, or writing, of the history of political thought (hereafter HPT) to be a historical exercise, and theorising about politics (hereafter PP) to be a philosophical one, then the relationship between the two becomes an instance or exemplification of the distinction between history and philosophy. Sharpening and idealising for a moment that distinction, the subject matter of history, we might say, comprises unique particulars, individuals, and individual sequences of actions (which might be utterances), and possibly, on the largest scale, the story of whole peoples and societies.[1] The history of political thought (HPT) is the history of particular utterances (ultimately written or recovered from other sign-bearing artefacts). The subject matter of philosophy, by contrast, is constituted by universals, or by whatever can be said to be universally true, or, at a meta-level, the necessary and universal conditions under which propositions can be advanced about, or within, a particular subject area.

These are idealised types. I realise it is more contentious to map these onto historical figures, but let me try. To start at the beginning, history

---

[1] It is of course true that, as practised, history involves all sorts of activities imported from other hermeneutic and the social sciences.

and philosophy were both 'istorie' – enquiry.[2] Herodotus's claim is to
reveal the truth about what has been done, to 'Set down and preserve
the memory of the past by putting on record the astonishing achievements both of our own and of other peoples'. And for Herodotus, part
of the past is what is, or has been, *believed*.[3] It is part of his genius to
stand apart from his sources ('The Egyptians say . . .', 'The Phoenicians
say . . .') and leave his listeners to judge, or on occasion to offer his own
assessment. But this distantiation is not only critical scepticism. His
authorial voice paradoxically both creates his presence in the narrative
and depicts the rules of a genre (that he himself is inventing) as imposing
duties on him as to how he conducts his enquiry: 'My business is to
record what people say, but I am by no means bound to believe it – and
that may be taken to apply to this book as a whole.'[4] In this sense
Herodotus is already a historian of thought, and the history of thought,
if not what all history is, is at least the *prima materia* of it.[5]

But this claim (the claim to discern what lies at the basis of reality) is
also a claim made by philosophy – at least what we now construe as
philosophy. Pre-socratic philosophers were preoccupied with identifying the enduring reality (if indeed there was one) beneath or inherent in
the surface features of experience. Philosophy's claims – ever since

---

[2] Herodotus's background is Ionian, and his immediate predecessors and
contemporaries include Thales and Hippocrates. But the Ionian philosophers
focused their thought on the physical world and it is only in Herodotus that these
intellectual qualities become focused on humankind in an ethnographical and
historical way. P. Cartledge, *Ancient Greek Political Thought in Practice*
(Cambridge: Cambridge University Press, 2009), 69–70.

[3] Herodotus, *The Histories* (London: Penguin Classics, 1996), Bk. I.1.1ff. Cf. 'so
much for what the Persians and the Phoenicians say; and I have no intention of
passing judgement on its truth or falsity . . .', *ibid.* 1.7. The distinction I make here
is not that discussed by Bernard Williams, *Truth and Truthfulness* (Princeton, NJ:
Princeton University Press, 2002), 155ff., which relates to whether or not
Herodotus distinguished between events in historical time and mythical
happenings. My point is Herodotus's claim that the historian can (indeed must)
record the fact of humans' claims and beliefs without necessarily having to
ascertain their truth or falsity.

[4] Herodotus, *Histories* 7.152.3. Also 2.123.1 [let he who will believe the Egyptians]
'As for myself, my task in the whole work is to write down what everybody says, as
I hear it.' On Herodotus's construction of the constraints inherent in his self-
created genre, see N. Laraghi, 'Meta-*historiē*: method and genre', in C. Dewald
and J. Marincola (eds.), *The Cambridge Companion to Herodotus* (Cambridge:
Cambridge University Press, 2006).

[5] The claim that all history is the history of thought is famously made in R. G.
Collingwood, *Autobiography* (Oxford: Oxford University Press, 1970), 110.

Plato – have involved, at least in part, claims about the necessary and enduring (timeless?) character of philosophical truths. It is not, of course, that philosophers wish to say that history's claims are untrue, rather that they are formulated to refer to, and to hold true only of, particulars in time. That Plato taught a theory of the forms in Athens around 375 BC, although an enduring truth, is a historical truth *about* philosophy, not a philosophical truth. It is an enduring truth precisely because it is formulated as a historical claim about the propositions advanced by a particular individual at a particular time in a particular place. The historical truth is that the theory as a set of propositions was taught, not the truth or falsity of the propositions themselves which is the province of philosophy. The philosophical claims advanced in the theory of forms by contrast lay claim to universal and timeless validity. For Herodotus the historian, the question is: '*what* was said written or believed?' For Plato the philosopher, the question is: 'were the beliefs true?'

Nevertheless it is not so easy to separate history and philosophy. I want to go on to explore as it were disciplinary claims each might make on the other, but before I do so it's worthwhile at least gesturing to the peculiar status of political thought or philosophy. (False) beliefs about natural phenomena do not belong at all to the (true) content of, say, physics (but only to its history[6]). Philosophical beliefs in the field of politics (even when 'false') can be constitutive of political reality for those communities, and constitute a part of political reality (in terms of the political culture, or the *long durée*) for their successors. If we think political communities are essentially hermeneutical and historical products (as opposed to, say, rational-choice products), the history-philosophy (as belief) distinction is much more tricky to negotiate than in the natural sciences, where the contemporary properties of copper, say, are quite unaffected by previous beliefs about it.

As disciplines, there is a tension between history and philosophy for two reasons, one contingent and the other not so. It seems to be a contingent feature of histories that alongside the particular story that any history tells, the aspiration to discern persisting features of human action and circumstance has emerged, either as a historical aim, or

---

[6] And the history of sciences, unlike the history of political thought, does not form part of their pedagogy. Part of the process of economics becoming a 'science' has been its (attempted) emancipation from its history.

as a condition of historical explanation.[7] Thus Herodotus's terribly politically incorrect explanatory aside on the origin of the Trojan Wars involves a generalisation that purports to be a universal truth about young females: 'Abducting young women ... is not a lawful act; but it is stupid after the event to make a fuss about it ... for it is obvious that no young woman allows herself to be abducted if she does not wish to be.'[8] Conversely, claims advanced as philosophical truth can come to look extraordinarily parochial in the light of later assumptions and beliefs. Indeed whole areas of investigation, such as the identity of natural slaves, or the vexed question of how many angels could occupy the head of a pin, can simply drop out of philosophical repertoires.

These observations about contingent reasons for the failure of historical and philosophical claims to vindicate their own characteristic qualities, as, respectively, particular and universal, suggest two more generic demands that each discipline can make, from within itself, on the other. Thus the historian can always claim that the status of any philosophical proposition is historically situated, and so liable to revision. And it is a claim that philosophy can always make about any historical explanation or indeed claim that it rests on certain (unexamined) philosophical presuppositions. So, whilst we may have here two modes of enquiry aspiring to truth, each mode is dependent on and vulnerable to propositions formulated in its alternative.[9] The philosopher on the one hand can always ask the historian for a philosophical account of her enterprise – what is the status of this claim, what is the principle of inclusion, what is the nature of the subject, how and under what conditions does her explanation explain? The historian, on the other hand, can always point out that the philosopher's questions are a product of a discipline at a particular point in time, of a particular historical set of preoccupations, beliefs about the nature of reality, causation, significance, etc.

Now it is sometimes claimed, by those who wish to preserve the independence of philosophy from history, that whilst *political* philosophy (or at least those examples of it that are interventions in a historically

---

[7] Indeed on one model of explanation the historical enterprise is impossible without adverting to some universally true features of humans' being as does any understanding of explanation that invokes a covering law conception of causality.

[8] Herodotus, *Histories*, 1.3.42ff.

[9] As sketched for example by Michael Oakeshott, in *Experience and its Modes* (Cambridge: Cambridge University Press, 1933). See further the chapter in this volume by Paul Kelly.

constituted problem or context) is indeed bound to be particular and historically situated, philosophy itself (and maybe those examples of political philosophy, if there are any, that aren't constituted as responses to immediate contexts) *is* immune to the counter-claims of history; since philosophers commonly do discuss (or at least take themselves to be discussing) – across time – problems formulated by their predecessors. This could then be held to constitute a trans-historical debate, or repertoire of positions that anyone, at any time, might participate in or utilise. Yet I take it that if we treat the historian's objections really seriously, this will not do. For the historian's point is not that political (and indeed other) philosophers don't sometimes *claim* to be evading the hermeneutic horizons of time and place. It is rather that even where they *aspire* to this, they don't – and can't in principle – succeed. It is not just that political philosophy (as opposed to, say, metaphysics), by being an intervention in a political situation, is historically anchored, as it were; it is that because meaning is intrinsically historically constituted, *any* philosophy draws on, and presupposes, a particular historical configuration of meaningfulness.[10] The historian's claim is that all attempts to transcend the limitations of one's own hermeneutic environment are bound to fail, simply because they must necessarily be formulated from within that hermeneutic, and even the most abstractly formulated philosophical claims cannot escape their historical origins. That the historian's claim is effectively a philosophical one (i.e. a claim about the universally parochial conditions of philosophical speech) is, of course, ironic, and is surely damagingly so when formulated in a language particular enough to be identified as itself a claim within a parochial philosophical position.[11] And of course the philosopher can counter at a similarly abstract and general level about the dependence of any historical story on philosophical presuppositions. In the absence of some kind of Hegelian account of the ultimate culmination of historical process and philosophical development in an absolute knowledge, these two competing claims do not look to be

---

[10] 'Understanding is, essentially, a historically effected event.' H. G. Gadamer, trans. W.Glen-Doepel, *Truth and Method* (London: Sheed & Ward, 1989), 300.

[11] Thus Quentin Skinner's formulation of this claim in the idiom of mid-twentieth century speech-act theory might be thought to hoist the historian's claim with its own petard. But the fact that similar claims to historical hegemony have been made in a variety of other philosophical idioms (e.g. by Collingwood, Oakeshott, Gadamer) suggests the claim itself might still be true.

resolvable, although of course one could always *simply* claim hegemonic authority for one or the other.[12]

The range of propositions for which philosophy's timeless truth-status could be claimed has waxed and waned over time. Plato seems to have held out the hope that all propositions, at least about the ideal-type of things in the world, could achieve this status – including propositions in ethics and politics. Augustinian-influenced Christian thinkers, on the other hand, seemed to think that there were vanishingly few such propositions, or at least few available to human intellects. In the high Middle Ages a view emerged that whilst certain, philosophical knowledge of the primary items of creation was in principle available, only prudential knowledge of human creations was possible, and prudential knowledge was as corrigible as were its objects – institutions, practices, moral rules of thumb, etc.[13] (a kind of division of the world, interestingly, that was largely replicated by some logical positivists[14]). On this view, any reflections on political institutions or conduct would be bound to fall short of philosophy, since there could simply be no enduring truth about such contingent phenomena. Thinking about politics was therefore necessarily prudential, casuistic and subject to *raison d'état*. There might be political *theory*, but there could be no political *philosophy*, although there were those who sought (thus far unsuccessfully) to construct enduring political maxims (the characteristic genre in this circumstance) derived from such reflections. These may be prudential: that it is better to be feared than loved, for example, or hover between the definitional and the empirical: that sovereignty is the power to decide the exception, for example.[15]

---

12 Thus Gordon Schochet characterises Quentin Skinner's work as 'an attempt to resolve a conflict between history and philosophy that by its nature cannot be settled'. G. Schochet, 'Quentin Skinner's method', *Political Theory*, 2 (1974), 269.

13 'Time, history, and eschatology in the thought of Thomas Hobbes', in J. G. A. Pocock, *Politics, Language and Time* (London: Methuen, 1972).

14 A. J. Ayer once said: 'Philosophical propositions, if they are true, are usually analytic.' But he adds in a curiously concessionary footnote: 'some empirical propositions, such as those that occur in histories of philosophy, may be counted as philosophical ... But in so far as they are not merely[!] historical I think that the truths discoverable by philosophical methods are analytic.' A. J. Ayer, *Language Truth and Logic*, 2nd edn (London: Dover, 1946), 26.

15 Machiavelli, *The Prince* (London: Penguin Books, 1999), ch. xvii; C. Schmitt, *Political Theology* (Chicago: Chicago University Press, 2005), 5.

This looks as though it might set the bar too high to admit any political theory as philosophy at all. Although Rawls's second thoughts about the reach of his theory of justice were more modest than his first, many modern practitioners – including the late lamented Jerry Cohen – have not so moderated their claims. For Ronald Dworkin the task of political philosophy was 'to find some inclusive formula that can be used to measure social justice in *any* society'.[16] It may, however, be that the range of statements that can be counted as philosophical in this sense are very small and have the character of Locke's ground-clearing activities or other such epistemological preliminaries. Nevertheless, even such preliminaries have led thinkers to adopt particular political positions. The political implications of cognitive indeterminacy for Hobbes formed an important part of his argument for the extensive reach of the sovereign's powers, and led Burke's thought in an ineluctably historical and conservative direction.

But no matter how much or how little material a political philosophy adhering to this position would generate, and no matter how confident it would find itself, there remain epistemically foundational claims to be made differentiating propositions in PP from claims in HPT. This is because, as I have been insisting, even in non-normative political philosophy predications in PP would be universal, not unique and particular, or culture-bound, whereas in HPT we report claims made by others in particular contexts without (necessarily) endorsing or even appraising their truth status. And once we take into consideration normative political philosophy there is at least one further difference. HPT *describes* normative beliefs, whereas normative PP seeks to *evoke* them. There is a dramaturgical quality to normative theory (not that its more austere practitioners would want to see it that way) which is, at least on first blush, lacking in HPT.[17] I say on first blush because history can instruct, even when not overtly didactic, and we may want to bracket – for later consideration – how some appreciation of HPT may indirectly affect our political practice. And it is to the conduct of politics itself, as opposed to the philosophy or history of it, that I now turn.

[16] *New York Review of Books*, 17 April 1983, my emphasis.
[17] The reluctance is revealing of the Kantian background to most contemporary political philosophising. The moral will is to be moved by recognition of the moral law, not (if moral) by naturalistic (enthusiastic or empirical) motivations. There is more to say about this in the last section.

Political practice and rhetoric

Up to now we have been considering the relationship between HPT and
PP largely in terms of the way they function as exemplars of history and
philosophy. But as we have begun to focus on their specifically *political*
character, we are led to consider the relationship between each of these
activities and the world of political practice.

Until the rise of a mass and politically mobilised electorate, examples
of both of what we now see as the history of political thought and
political theory, where they were intended to relate to politics, were
contributions to a controversialist or polemical debate conducted
amongst the relatively small and educated elites whose opinions counted
in political decision-making. Commonly these elites were relatively culturally self-contained to the extent that a particular mode of argumentation predominated, privileging claims formulated in legal, philosophical
or religious discourse, or specific variants of these, in legitimising
claims.[18] Periodically though – in classical Athens, in the self-governing
communes and cities of the Renaissance – and in the emergence of a
modernity in which epistemic elites could no longer enjoy an unreflective
isolation – such elite linguistic hegemony broke down altogether.
Emancipated from these insulated discourses, political argument takes
place within an unspecialised, demotic linguistic field.

Under these conditions we can identify a third force tugging at
political expression in addition to the rival claims of philosophy and
history – that of rhetoric. Rhetoric is the activity of persuading audiences to adopt or reject action or policies, or of the guilt or innocence,

---

[18] Pocock's concept of a political language and his deployment of it in constructing
histories of political thought is paradigmatic here. His *Ancient Constitution and
the Feudal Law*, exploring the dominance and breakdown of the language of the
common law, relies in part on the isolation of a particular elite – the common
lawyers – from alternative accounts of English pasts. The *Machiavellian Moment*
pursues a specific language – that of republicanism – as a 'tunnel history' through
the matrix of past political discourse, and its response both to changes in political
and social practice and exposure to alternative accounts of political reality. See
J. G. A. Pocock, *The Ancient Constitution and the Feudal Law: A Study of English
Historical Thought in the Seventeenth Century* (Cambridge: Cambridge University
Press, 1987); *The Machiavellian Moment: Florentine Political Thought and the
Atlantic Republican Tradition* (Princeton, NJ: Princeton University Press, 2003).
For further discussion, see also A. Pagden, *Languages of Politics in Early Modern
Europe* (Cambridge: Cambridge University Press, 1987).

praiseworthiness or contemptibility of individuals.[19] The intention of deliberative (and forensic) rhetoric is to generate action, it is not (like history or philosophy) contemplative, nor does it necessarily presuppose a commitment to truth. It is concerned (amongst other things) to discover and recruit pre-existing beliefs in the hearers, beliefs which can be mobilised by the orator to shape the hearers' commitments in the desired way. The *result* is what is important – what is persuasive is what – evidently – persuades, although as an intellectual discipline there are both techniques to be learned and – in Aristotle at least – moral limitations on the means to be used in bringing about persuasion. Rhetorical proof is by words: no weeping relatives in the courtroom or stage props – material evidence like sworn depositions or bloodied daggers.

Politics, where it exists – which is only in deliberative communities – is conducted through rhetoric. Politicians have to persuade, and only what is persuasive persuades. In democratic societies politicians have to persuade a majority. If scientific evidence – or other propositions drawn from specialist discourses, such as theology – is not persuasive to the public, then so much the worse for the evidence. Aligning policy with the evidence may be a fine aspiration, but it cannot be achieved if it requires the public to become scientists before they can be persuaded to adopt such policy. The politician seeking to promote evidence-based policies might well need to find other means of persuasion than the mere evidence on which the policies are based.

Political rhetoric is related in particular and indirect ways to both history and philosophy. The rhetorician's sources, the topics from which he draws his persuasive arguments, are drawn from the history of the beliefs of the community – or at least the version of that history held by the political community. This may, needless to say, be a history far removed from those histories constructed by historians of political thought. Indeed, it exposes a potential bifurcation in what we have been calling HPT. That is, HPT can be the history of political philosophies, or it can be the history of political discourses more widely construed – the history of the languages in which politics has been

---

[19] Rhetoric is deliberative, forensic or appraisive. Aristotle, *Rhetoric* (London: Penguin Classics, 2005), 1.3.3. In this and what follows I draw, as do almost all subsequent formal treatments, on Aristotle.

conducted. And the internal relationship between these is not unproblematic, of which there will be more to say.

Rhetoric relates also to philosophy, Aristotle claimed, in being conducted by an inferior kind of dialectic or formal argument – the enthymeme.[20] An enthymeme is an incomplete syllogism, usually lacking the major premise – which is a truth assumed and provided by the listener; this engages the listener with the argument. Such a premise must be one they already hold – a *topos*, or commonplace of political life.

Consider again, for example, the tabloid-ish story quoted earlier from Herodotus. Here the listener is presented with an incomplete syllogism, the major premise of which is a commonplace thought, initially suppressed, but in this case added as an afterthought: Herodotus' thought runs something like this:

> Abducting young women is not lawful.
> It is stupid to make a fuss about it afterwards.
> [Helen was a young woman.
> The Trojan wars followed from her abduction.
> The Trojan wars were stupid.]

As an argument, this is full of holes. One of the holes is the universal proposition which Herodotus provides afterwards:

No young woman allows herself to be abducted if she does not wish to be.

This claim – that for young women, abduction against their will is an empty category – is actually the logical underpinning for the enthymeme-ish (i.e. incomplete) argument:

Although the abduction of young women is unlawful, it is not worth making a fuss about.

We could tidy up Herodotus's argument to make it more formal, making the major premise explicit (which in rhetoric it would not be). It would then run something like the following:

> No young women permits abduction against her will.
> Helen was a young abducted woman.
> This was not against her will.
> It is always stupid to object, after the event, to things that people are not made to do against their will (even if they are against the law).

---

[20] Aristotle, *Rhetoric*, 1.2.8.

> The Trojan wars were an objection after the event to Helen's abduction.
> The Trojan Wars were stupid.

We might of course want to object to the foundational premise, but that would take us into the realms of (social) science or philosophy proper. For the rhetorician it is enough if the principle is held to be true by the intended audience, for they will then assent to the premises implicitly deduced from it, and as a result the (incomplete) argument will prove persuasive. Indeed, it might well be rhetorically important to suppress the universal premise, since if it is made explicit it might excite objection. In philosophy this would be a good thing, since in philosophy we seek the truth and we want to make explicit and meet all possible objections. In rhetoric, however, we seek to persuade: if we can evade objections, rather than having to overcome them, then this is a good thing. This is, if you like, the realm of Plato's cave, and it is because cave-dwellers are unconvinced by philosophy that philosophers don't rule (just as tabloid readers are unconvinced by evidence, which is why cabinet ministers are constantly tempted to substitute policy-based evidence for evidence-based policy).

If the above, or something like it, is correct, then this sets up a trio of polarities – or possibly (dare one say) a trilarity? – through which to characterise politics and our reflections on it. We could think of these as three nodal points defining the argumentative and discursive space occupied by political language which at the extremes is deployed:

1. to tell its history;
2. to identify necessary features of it or conditions of its employment; and
3. to persuade hearers to action.

These polarities – history, philosophy, rhetoric – are identified in antiquity as distinct intellectual activities. But their identity as distinct activities, it seems to me, is not a contingent feature of that local culture, and certain confusions follow from failing to recognise the epistemic and social properties to be found within each, and of claiming them for, or confusing them with, another activity. Shortly I want to go on and explore these features and some of the relationships between these, but first I want to add a wrinkle.

During the last century and a half, the emergence of professionalised academics conducting both HPT and PP in a context that was more or less – and arguably increasingly – distantiated from politics and public life itself has further altered the situation.[21] HPT and PP are now kinds of meta-political discourses that do not map seamlessly – if indeed at all – onto even intelligent bar-room, dinner-party, or even party-conference discourse about political events. Who amongst us has not experienced the moment of glacial panic on the face of even the most accomplished social inter-locutor that greets the news that you are a political philosopher, or a historian of political thought? But this is not merely a sociological obser-vation. The distance between academic discourse and political life is revealed by the way it affects the meanings or import of statements drawn from one area and articulated in another. In particular, academic truths about public policies change character when intruded into public debate.

For example, the academic observation that economic recession and cuts in public expenditure may be likely to bring about industrial and political unrest can be considered a claim in social science to be evi-denced in whatever way the discipline deems appropriate. However, such a claim made in the course of public debate by a trades union leader is likely to be perceived – and denounced – as a threat. Similarly, an economist's claim that statutory limitation of bankers' bonuses may lead to sub-optimal hiring and an exodus of talent may be an inves-tigable hypothesis. But such a claim made by a banking CE might, again, appear as a threat. Indeed, I can remember Jerry Cohen disqual-ifying the latter kind of argument from consequentialist reasoning to establish egalitarian principles in moral theory precisely *because* it was not a fact about the world, but a moral threat.

The professionalisation of the academy, then, adds a wrinkle to my three nodes, as it were, of political-theoretical discourse – politics/rhetoric, political philosophy and the history of political thought (recognising the tension in the latter between the history of PP and the history of the political rhetoric). Let me now consider some possible relationships between them.

HPT and PP

How might HPT stand then in relationship to current PP? It is a commonplace that the Historical or Cambridge Revolution disrupted

---

[21] S. Collini, 'Afterword', in Castiglione and Hampsher-Monk (eds.), *History of Political Thought in National Context* (Cambridge: Cambridge University Press, 2001).

any easy assumptions about the relationship between the two. Taking history seriously would often, indeed normally, reveal how different from its supposed descendants were theories of the past. Indeed it has been claimed by Quentin Skinner that an awareness of this strangeness was one of the main benefits of historical study, since it emancipated the student from a certain kind of myopia about possibilities different from those currently being articulated.[22] Here was one way, it was thought, in which HPT could influence PP and indeed politics itself, by educating – enlarging the views of – political philosophers or citizens, and by helping them to understand the parochial ways in which different political societies – including their own – constitute themselves or their political thinking.

This is a broad and dispositional effect, but on this view HPT, precisely *because* it reveals the strangeness of historical political thought, might be incapable of producing knowledge applicable directly to PP. Understanding the theological underpinning of Locke's thought broadens our understanding of how legitimacy has been thought of in Western societies. But we surely then cannot – to cite a still disarmingly common aspiration amongst certain academics – seek to apply Locke's theory of legitimacy to liberal society in a Godless world – or at least in a political theory that eschews theistic premises. Such indeed was the explicit message of the founders of the Historical revolution.[23] But equally problematic might be some of the benefits that *were* held out – the recovery of a particular concept – of liberty, say – in hopes of re-introducing it into contemporary PP. I say *might* be, because given the ultimately open-ended character of the *paroles* made possible in a *langue*, these are all contingent matters – contingent, that is, on the logic of the theory or the concept's relationship to the argumentative or intellectual context into which it is hoped to insert it.

That is to say, I take it that it is always conceivable that a concept or argumentative move taken from one historical context *might* be inserted successfully in a different one. The little phrase, 'quod omnes tangit, ab omnes approbatur',[24] extracted from its very specific role in

---

22 Q. Skinner, *Visions of Politics, Vol. I* (Cambridge: Cambridge University Press, 2002).
23 J. Dunn, *The Political Thought of John Locke: An Historical Account of the Argument of the 'Two Treatises of Government'* (Cambridge: Cambridge University Press, 1982).
24 'That which concerns all should be approved by all.'

the Roman private law of trusts, was successfully inserted into the completely different public world of political legitimation in the late medieval and early modern period.[25] But these are in a way exceptional cases (and cases that the intensification of scholarship surely renders less likely). HPT is full of examples of enthusiastic movements to appropriate past thought – the early modern revival of Roman law being the most famous – in which the increasingly sophisticated application of scholarship designed to assist the recovery merely served to expose the historical distance between past and present and in the end revealed the impossibility of the exercise.[26]

HPT and politics

Turning now more specifically to the relationship between HPT and politics, it seems true that not only does the scholarly historical appreciation of a past theory or concepts contained within it often reveal the incongruity of their current applicability within contemporary political *philosophy*, it also commonly reveals their lack of *rhetorical* appeal to wider contemporary political audiences. The idea of the social contract enjoyed a brief revival in the attempts to rein in inflationary wage demands in the late sixties and seventies, but it was merely a rhetorical appeal to social unity in a divided society, and proved incapable of generating articulations of a morally or politically operationalisable kind. It failed to hook into the political reality it addressed.

But it seems implausible to suggest that its appeal would have been any greater had the meanings and valences of the term been more

---

[25] '[The maxim] was only applied to wards and guardians in Roman law, but during the Middle Ages it supported a theory of consent that was a basic element of corporate theory and representative government.' K. Pennington, 'Law, legislative authority and theories of government, 1150–1300', in J. H. Burns (ed.), *Cambridge History of Medieval Political Thought* (Cambridge: Cambridge University Press, 1988), 440ff.

[26] 'The more they worked upon the sources the more convinced the humanists became that much of Roman Law was peculiar to its time and place.' J. H. Franklin, *Jean Bodin and the Sixteenth Century Revolution in the Methodology of Law and History* (New York: Greenwood Press, 1963), 27, and see at greater length D. R. Kelley, *Foundations of Modern Historical Scholarship, Language, Law and History in the French Renaissance* (New York: Columbia University Press, 1970).

precisely focused through the lens of historical scholarship. Whilst the academy can uncover a more or less authentic version of Rousseau's or Hobbes's or Mill's thought, the more 'authentic' it is, the *less* plausible it is likely to be to a (non-academic) modern. Considered as public political arguments, the recovery of historical authenticity surely damages, rather than enhances, the political – that is rhetorical – appeal to modern ears. As Hans Keller, the celebrated music critic, remarked of the authentic performance movement: 'We have period instruments but we do not have period ears!'[27]

At a certain level, the extent to which the above remarks apply depends on the political cultures of particular societies. In some political cultures their very pastness – irrespective of the appeal of their content – can render ideas and arguments unviable. As societies have ceased to be traditional and have become innovative, a process still incomplete in my professional lifetime, the mere fact of a theory or a concept – or a thinker – having a significant status in our past is no longer sufficient to endow them with authority. The invocation (however misguided) of Adam Smith by Margaret Thatcher, and of the Levellers by Tony Benn, were already isolated instances in the 1980s, and I can think of no further British examples since. The predisposition of the democratic public (always drawn, as Aristotle remarked, to novelty) requires political actors – conservative as well as progressive – to vie with each other to present themselves as more innovative. As a consequence, apart from the periodic invocation of a generalised chocolate-box nostalgia, the more precise we are in delineating the local meanings of past theories, the less persuasive purchase they are likely to have on the contemporary mind. In contrast to early modern innovators – who often sought to rhetorically dress their theories up with a historical pedigree – modern revivalists present their offerings from our tradition as innovation, the better to ensure their rhetorical persuasiveness. So, the Conservative moderniser David Cameron's new 'Big Idea' turns out to have been an unacknowledged recycling of the distributivist social teaching of the

---

[27] My case might be thought to be weakened by the observation that since Keller's remark, period performance has become very popular, as modern ears become attuned to period sensibilities and timbres. But if we were to think what the parallel would be in political life, it will be seen that this would be difficult to hold – to recreate a society susceptible to the political arguments of a Locke, would be to recreate seventeenth-century society itself.

Catholic Church as expressed in the ideas of Hilaire Belloc and G. K. Chesterton.[28]

Yet there are other political cultures in which the historical appeal is more rhetorically persuasive and so available to the political actor. In the USA the importance of Founders' Intent in legal philosophy and the presentism of the Founding Fathers in public life exemplifies the ease with which history can be invoked. And a skilled orator such as Barack Obama makes full and unembarrassed use of its resources. But this is already very much a public and not an academic history. It is difficult to imagine a politician being able to make political use of some historical discovery that disconcerted an idealised public history. Most academic historians of political thought find claims about the applicability of Founders' Intent to contemporary society intensely problematic as political philosophy, despite its being an undoubted matter of fact about American political culture.[29]

In sum, whether viewed as 'arguments' or as 'concepts', the more historically constructed, the less plausible the material provided by the history of political thought seems to be. Where political cultures are susceptible to appeals to history, it is the *topoi* to be found in a publicly held history, not in the academy, which are available for political deployment.

There is however another way of reading this relationship between HPT and politics. If certain views of the relationship between a political community and its political-linguistic history obtain, there is another way of thinking about the HPT–politics link which suggests it could be considerably stronger. And this possibility relates to the history of political discourses, rather than the history of political philosophy.

For example, rather than providing discrete *items* for appropriation – concepts or arguments, say – the history of political thought can be construed as providing an understanding of the hermeneutic and cultural-historical roots and structure of the discourse in which our contemporary politics is conducted. Inasmuch as political reality is constituted by the language in which its practitioners describe it and the beliefs it supports, such an understanding, it could be claimed, is not

---

[28] Jonathan Rabin, review of Phillip Blond's *Red Tory: How Left and Right Have Broken Britain and How we can Fix it*, London Review of Books, 22 April 2010, 22.

[29] T. Ball and J. G. A. Pocock (eds.), *Conceptual Change and the Constitution* (Lawrence, KS: University Press of Kansas, 1988), Introduction, section III.

merely of interest to academic hermeneutics, it is an understanding of the very ontology of political modernity itself.[30] Conversely, since political reality comprises sets of beliefs and institutions constructed and perpetuated only through language, and since these beliefs and institutions are historical products, a deep understanding of our politics (and what can be accomplished within it, and how) must presuppose an understanding of the history of its public discourse. This of course must be the history of its public discourse, rather than the history of its star political philosophers, who enter into the picture only to the extent that they figure in the former. As has been argued:

The trick is to encapsulate all this in a story that makes sense to those who hear it, for politics is not inherently or self-evidently coherent. To the extent that it is itself historically continuous, the public discourse of a society performs precisely this function. Its goal is to create, and even sanctify a tradition that tells a people who they have been and are and allows them to ponder who they might become. At this point discursive continuity and academic history can stand as partners in the same enterprise.[31]

This needn't be a totalising or monopolistic story, but it is one that has to be carried on for political identity to be sustained. As Pocock himself has later argued:

it is possible for a sovereign state, a self-governing community, to open up its sovereignty to debate, to render that debate open-ended and ongoing, to debate the history in and on which it is founded, and to proceed to a confrontation and negotiation between two concepts of sovereignty and of history, all this without dissolving the state or abolishing its sovereignty.[32]

But for this to be so, the claim still has to be that the 'history' of political thought that we are dealing with comprises thinking which is constitutive of, rather than external to, the political society that it describes. It is a

[30] Such a view seems to inform J. G. A. Pocock's rigorously historical analysis of the way the English and other inhabitants of the British archipelago have characterised themselves and their internal and external relationships. Focusing both on their conceptions of sovereignty and their historiography, see the essays in *The Discovery of Islands* (Cambridge: Cambridge University Press, 2005), especially 'Sovereignty and history in the late twentieth century'.
[31] G. J. Schochet, 'Why should history matter?', in J. G. A. Pocock, G. J. Schochet and L. G. Schwoerer (eds.), *The Varieties of British Political Thought, 1500–1800* (Cambridge: Cambridge University Press, 1996), 323.
[32] Pocock, *Discovery of Islands*, 259.

history of public discourse that a public would have recognised, even if it had its origins and periodic précis in political philosophy.

Given this, to grasp for example 'the vocabulary of a modern European state'[33] is not to engage in some arcane lexicographical exercise, remote from reality. It is to understand – indeed to delineate the very features of – that reality in which we live. Historically informed political philosophising of this kind – although still a second-order activity – is not something potentially distantiated from political reality, it is rather a formalisation or 'abridgement' of that experienced reality. It is moreover potentially extremely useful to the active politician who, in a democratic culture, is required to deploy the resources of that linguistic culture in order to generate support for his or her policies.

I'm not saying that politicians can only do this through conscious intellectual routes. There are instinctive politicians who accomplish the same through a practical grasp of such resources, through the contingent coming together of a personality with a particular assimilation of experience and a set of circumstances congruently matched to those two chance events – a Machiavellian *occasione*. I once asked a very senior civil servant in the entourage of Margaret Thatcher whether she was conversant with the academic work on economic or political libertarianism on which she seemed so often to be drawing. 'Not a bit of it', he replied, 'it was all pure instinct'. This is not to deny, of course the well-documented roles of Joseph, Letwin et al. in elaborating these instincts and providing them with an academic pedigree (something, of course, that could have been done with other policy orientations as well). My point (and, I think, that of my nameless senior official) was that Thatcher's instincts were already there focusing policy – the intellectual shoring-up arrived after the event. Parts of it had indeed been around a long time,[34] but it was not as a self-conscious exercise in historical recovery that Thatched herself adopted it.

HPT and PP revisited

Could such a relationship – HPT as the broad linguistic repertoire within which specific speech-acts are articulated – obtain between

---

[33] M. Oakeshott, 'The vocabulary of a modern European state', *Political Studies*, 23: 2 (1975), 319–41.

[34] See most recently B. Jackson, 'At the origins of neo-liberalism: 1930–1947' *Historical Journal*, 53: 1 (2010).

HPT and PP? One is tempted to say no. Political philosophers in the contemporary anglophone tradition characteristically consider themselves to be operating innovatively, and according to strictly logical, deductive canons. They nevertheless often deploy arguments, the validity of which depends on an unacknowledged construal of meanings in ways deeply shaped by local academic convention. Continental philosophers, on the other hand – thinking here particularly of francophone work (Ricoeur, Deleuze) – often pride themselves on growing out of and relating to the history of political philosophy, and yet often do so in a way that seems unconcerned with recovering those figures' historical meanings.[35] To the degree that political philosophy has become an academic discipline, the standards by which it is judged have become internal to the discipline. Full-time, career political philosophers recognise features of their productions – elegance, coherence, integration to an existing body of literature – that would have been irrelevant to political argumentation considered rhetorically as part of a public debate, just as those standards do not necessarily map onto the concerns of the historian of political thought.

From the consequences of this narrow-minded professionalism, it is sometimes claimed, the history of political thought can rescue us. This sits oddly with the earlier claim that what the history of political thought reveals to us is the utter strangeness of our historical origins, that the benefit of studying it is akin to that of anthropological study in revealing human (and hence our own) particularity. There is indeed some tension between these two claims, which hasn't stopped them being advanced at the same time, and sometimes by the same people. And there is some tension between the second and the persuasive deployment of arguments drawn from the history of political thought in our own politics. However, this presages another, different and more diffuse, possible relationship between HPT and PP.

That is to say that rather than providing the political theorist directly with categorical and controversial *materiel* for contemporary deployment, HPT's contribution to PP operates through affecting us

---

[35] Ricoeur's *Rule of Metaphor*, for example, devotes a considerable amount of space to the history of metaphor in Western writing; Deleuze's later, substantive work was preceded by, and draws on, a number of studies of individual historical thinkers undertaken in his earlier career: Leibnitz, Hume, Kant, Nietzsche. See P. Ricoeur, *The Rule of Metaphor: The Creation of Meaning in Language* (London: Routledge, 2003).

dispositionally, through challenging the otherwise narrowly based confidence characteristically evinced by the political philosopher, through
affecting our sense of the indeterminacy of reasoning. HPT feeds a certain
scepticism about the claims of PP, without (as do some other scepticisms)
entirely undermining it. Political philosophy often cites its own emancipation from the past, and yet if the former view of history as a dispositional corrective to the stridency of PP is correct, such emancipation may
render it more narrowly grounded, as well as less – not more – likely to be
persuasive beyond its professional membership.

PP and politics

I turn lastly to consider the relationship between PP and Politics.
Political philosophers often consider themselves to be operating in a
political environment – indeed some of them have redefined the political
in order to vindicate the claim. The claim that the political world is
discursively constructed seems often to be accompanied by a further
claim: that there is an unproblematic discursive continuity between the
meta-language of political philosophy and the quotidian world of everyday politics. This assimilates the theoretical world that philosophers
created in the academy to the political one they would influence, and
blurs the distinction between rhetoric and philosophy.

Thus, for example, Chantal Mouffe, in a work devoted to the re-
invigoration of democracy, writes: 'Democratic societies today are
confronted with new challenges they are ill-prepared to answer ...'.
One of the main reasons for this 'lies in the rationalist framework which
informs the main currents of political theory'. In order to 'consolidate
and deepen our democratic institutions' we need to adopt a way of
political philosophising that is more informed by Wittgenstien.[36]

Now the assumption that there is a seamless causal link between
problems of contemporary democracy and the mode in which a tiny
group of academics conduct the distinctly recherché activity of political
philosophising is surely as breathtaking as the assumption that those
problems would disappear if that tiny group conducted their activity
under a different set of assumptions from the one they do. It is the
slipperiness of the 'we', moving as it does from the community of
political theorists to the political community at large, that reveals the

---

[36] C. Mouffe, *The Democratic Paradox* (London: Verso, 2000), 60–1.

supposition of discursive continuity between what philosophers do and what is done – or indeed doable – politically.

Another way in which political philosophy seems to bleed across into politics itself is in the various ways that it seeks to model or emulate what representative citizens could be persuaded to endorse, without actual recourse to persuading them. Yet original choosers, public reason and idealised interlocutory situations cannot (can they?) substitute for the empirical test of what a given public can actually be persuaded to endorse. The rhetorical task of persuading people is an irreducible feature of politics, for which no degree of theorising can substitute. What is persuasive is only what persuades, not what would persuade if . . .

Philosophers only try to understand the world, but to change it you don't need a different kind of philosophy, you need – as Marx recognised – a different kind of activity – rhetoric, and rhetoric is defined not only in terms of its characteristic mode of persuasion – enthymeme, rather than the syllogism – but also in terms of (1) the arena in which it is practised, (2) its aim and (3) its audience. The arena of rhetoric includes the political assembly, public debate, and, in modernity, the various forms of print and electronic media. Its aim is persuasion and the audience is those who constitute the political community to be moved to a decision – to exercise its or their power.[37] Philosophy – the aim of which is truth – cannot destroy or supplant rhetoric (unless the political community becomes philosophers). Philosophy is to be found in the academy, and the condition of the integrity of its practice is its refusal to seek power. Philosophy may, as did Socrates and Diogenes, speak truth to power, but if it seeks power for its truth, it will always be drawn into the realm of rhetoric. Plato and Aristotle, it seems to me, were on to something in insisting on distinguishing between philosophy and rhetoric.

Why and how have we moved away from retaining this distinction? Two axes along which important distinctions have been conflated can be identified. One is the political-private. If the political is not some identifiable public forum, but extends even to the most private and intimate emotional and intellectual corners of our lives, then, of course, even the most private or intellectualised of actions can be dignified as political. Academic actors can delude themselves – and their few readers – into believing that they are performing works of great political

---

[37] Ricouer, *Rule of Metaphor*, 11.

moment by urging (or 'calling for', as the modish locution characteristically has it) the adoption of a different methodology in philosophical
reflection, or claiming to have identified a just foundation through
modelling what a citizen would (and by implication, should) decide is
foundationally just.

To the sceptical speech-act theorist the illocutionary question that
the former exercise raises is 'to whom is the "call" addressed?', whilst
the further perlocutionary question that arises is 'who is going to hear or
take notice of it?'[38]

Implicit in such questions is the second axis, which has collapsed and
contributed to the obscuring of the distinction between rhetoric and
philosophy. This is a failure to think through carefully enough the
implications of the undoubtedly true claim that social and political
entities are discursively constructed. I have no wish to dissent from
this, but it does leave unanswered the further question: within which,
and whose, discourse is the entity constructed? If it is true – as it seems to
be – that late modernity's political academy operates with a discourse,
or discourses, that are dislocated from those of the general population,
and with which our political world is constructed, how exactly are
interventions in the former supposed to be effectual in the latter? The
relationship between the (at least two) discourses is an empirical/histor-
ical one, not a logical or philosophical one. It requires at least some
token effort on the part of the theorist to demonstrate the means by
which the one is supposed to affect the other. Berlusconi's discursive
construction of a favourable political environment for himself had
surely more to do with his control of newspapers, television and other
public spaces – which he achieved through political and rhetorical
means – than with the happy choice of the foundational philosopher
favoured by his right-wing ideological theoreticians.

I've tried to identify three ideal kinds of political-theoretical talk.
First, political philosophy, which attempts positively or normatively
to discern constitutive truths about the political realm. Second, the
history of political thought, which seeks to construct a narrative
about such enterprises, and about the more quotidian languages in

---

[38] Which is not to say that it cannot be done, as the consciousness-raising exercises
of the feminist movement showed in the last century. But this was a widespread
movement which took seriously, in intellectual and organisational terms, the
business of bringing together intellectual insight and personal experience.

which politics takes place. And third, rhetoric, the animus of which is to change the commitments of members of a political community by the manipulation of existing beliefs. Although these are idealised specifications, which I concede are never fully realised or separated from each other in practice, being self-conscious about their identity – about which activity we are engaged in and being aware of their socio-linguistic properties and context – can, I think, help us to practise each of them better, as well as avoid the not always obvious pitfalls of confusing one with the other.

6 | Constraint, freedom, and exemplar: history and theory without teleology

MELISSA LANE

Reading the newspaper early in the morning is a kind of realistic morning blessing.

> (Hegel, Jena journal, published as 'Aphorismen aus Hegels Wastebook')[1]

... the introduction of the parliamentary imbecility, including the obligation upon everyone to read his newspaper at breakfast.

> (Nietzsche, *Beyond Good and Evil*, Part VI, § 208)[2]

Is reading about historical events a blessing or a curse, or even an imbecility? Is it the royal road to political understanding, or a dark and damning diversion from true political principles? Plato invented the new genre of philosophical dialogue a little later than, and in distinction from, Thucydides's invention of the new genre of contemporary historical reconstruction, yet for the inheritors of both, such as Plutarch, and those who read him, such as Rousseau, to reflect on the history of classical Athens and later Rome was an indispensable part of the emerging tradition of political theorising. It is only in light of certain

---

[1] G. W. F. Hegel, 'Aphorismen aus Hegels Wastebook', in his *Werke*, ed. E. Moldenhauer and K. M. Michel, Vol. II (Frankfurt am Main: Suhrkamp, 1970), 547 ('Das Zeitungslesen des Morgens früh ist eine Art von realistischem Morgensegen'). I have given my own translation, finding inaccurate the selections translated in G. W. F. Hegel, 'Aphorisms from the Wastebook', trans. S. Klein, D. L. Roochnik, and G. E. Tucker, *Independent Journal of Philosophyh*, 3 (1979). In this case the notion of reading 'early in the morning' (Morgens früh) is omitted from their rendition of 'Reading the morning paper'.

[2] F. Nietzsche, *Beyond Good and Evil: Prelude to a Philosophy of the Future*, trans. R. J. Hollingdale, intro. M. Tanner (London: Penguin, 2003), 138. The German text is 'vor Allem die Einführung des parlamentarischen Blödsinns, hinzugerechnet die Verpflichtung für Jedermann, zum Frühstück seine Zeitung zu lesen', as in F. Nietzsche, *Werke: Kritische Gesamtausgabe*, ed. G. Colli and M. Montinari (Berlin: Walter de Gruyter, 1967), VI-2.143–4, quoted from the electronic edition, *Nietzsches Werke: Historisch-kritische Ausgabe*, (ed.) M. Brown.

developments, themselves historical, that the significance of history for normative political theory can even be put into question. Those developments have led to a state in which – to caricature, for the sake of emphasis – some theorists read Machiavelli and Hobbes, without feeling it essential to read their own sources such as Thucydides, Livy, Sallust, and Plutarch, while others dispense with all these prior writers in practising a pure theoretical construction or analysis.

The contrast in the epigraphs between Hegel and Nietzsche on the value of the morning newspaper (a form, or at least a source, of contemporary history) dramatises a deeper question about whether and how history relates to value. If history has a direction and a purpose which can be discerned, then that discernment can become a 'realistic . . . blessing' even in the prosaic form of the daily paper. Such providential directionality in history provides direct access to values, whether yet to be realised, as in classical Marxism, or as embodied in the 'end of history', as briefly contended by Francis Fukuyama. But the criticism of Hegelianism, Marxism, and other forms of providential optimism from the mid-nineteenth century onward engendered widespread scepticism about whether history has a direction, at least one clearly discernible by human beings. The significance of history for political theory is called into question insofar as it comes to be believed that history as it bends into the future has no discernible shape, and so no inherent guidance for political understanding.

If values are not securely ensconced in the course of history, then they have to be found or made elsewhere. Kantian self-legislation and its Emersonian and Nietzschean variants of self-creation constitute one alternative. Indeed the late nineteenth century 'return to Kant', recapitulated by Marxist writers such as Eduard Bernstein, represents one precursor of the later revival of Kantianism in anglophone moral and political theory.[3] Here, values are defined and political justification

---

[3] Eduard Bernstein, in 'Is scientific socialism possible?' [1901], collected with other of the articles in which he gradually came to clarify his differences with Marxism, as then widely understood, in H. Tudor and J. M. Tudor (eds.), *Marxism and Social Democracy: The Revisionist Controversy 1896–1898* (Cambridge: Cambridge University Press, 1988). See also the brief remarks in the conclusion to his *The Preconditions of Socialism* [1899], ed. H. Tudor (Cambridge: Cambridge University Press, 1993), 209–10. On the general tenor of the movement 'back to Kant' and its relation to the critique of Marxism, see H. S. Hughes, *Consciousness and Society: The Reorientation of European Social Thought 1890–1930* (Brighton: Harvester Press, 1979 [1958]), 33–104, and M. Lane, 'Positivism: reactions and developments', in R. Bellamy and T. Ball (eds.), *The Cambridge*

proceeds from the beliefs and attitudes of present-day actors. It is only such actors who can formulate the consensus which thinkers influenced by Kantianism, such as John Rawls and Jürgen Habermas, demand, or who can participate in the conversations which deliberative democrats and others modifying the demand for strict consensus require.[4]

Admittedly, history is not altogether irrelevant to political theorists influenced by Kantianism. Rawls's thinking, for example, was profoundly shaped by reflection on the historical experiences of the Reformation, World War II and the Holocaust, and the American civil rights movement.[5] So too the complex theoretical project of Habermas has been oriented by Nazism and the Holocaust, as well as more general reflections on the economics and politics of modernity. Nevertheless, the fundamental standard of both value and justification in this line of thinking is ahistorical. This makes neo-Kantian approaches in political theory the hardest case for whether history matters to normative political theory, or more specifically, to the normativity of such theory – and therefore the test case on which I will focus. While there are many other forms of political theory which are normative in their own ways, such as those propounded by David Miller, Martha Nussbaum, and James Tully, the term 'normative political theory' is for most of this chapter to be understood as restricted to broadly neo-Kantian approaches. Its very existence results from stripping value out of history, locating it instead in a putatively autonomous realm of self-legislation.

History of Twentieth-Century Political Thought (Cambridge: Cambridge University Press, 2003), 321–42.

[4] For an overview of the Kantianism of both Rawls and Habermas – while other crucial influences on their thought must be acknowledged as well – see K. Baynes, *The Normative Grounds of Social Criticism: Kant, Rawls, and Habermas* (Albany, NY: State University of New York Press, 1992). Those rejecting the standard of consensus, while still emphasising forms of conversation, include S. Benhabib and I. M. Young; perhaps their most influential works on this point are respectively S. Benhabib, *Situating the Self: Gender, Community, and Postmodernism in Contemporary Ethics* (Cambridge: Polity Press, 1992), and I. M. Young, *Justice and the Politics of Difference* (Princeton, NJ: Princeton University Press, 1990).

[5] See further reflections on the role of the civil rights movement in Rawls's thought below, as well as Paul Kelly's discussion in this volume of Rawls's reflections on and use of the history of political thought and moral philosophy. For a biographical overview, see T. Pogge, *John Rawls. His Life and Theory of Justice*, trans. M. Kosch (New York: Oxford University Press, 2007), 3–27.

If history offers no master key, and normative political theory embodies the turn to a source of value outside history, then what can be the significance of the former for the latter? To answer once again in broad strokes: that significance is Janus-faced, reflecting the nature of history itself. On the one hand, history embodies constraint, and normative political theorists sometimes turn to it to discover the constraints of modern politics. They do so by asking broadly explanatory questions (though explanation need not be deterministic, it must be determinate to some degree, and any determinateness is at least weakly constraining). History can help theorists to explain the processes of social change and the broad features of the modern world. On the other hand, history has also more recently been viewed as a source of liberation. Insofar as genealogies treat history as contingent, viewing current beliefs and conditions as its contingent products is often thought to be liberating. Here, the non-deterministic nature of history infects even its determinateness: rather than being impressed with the shape and weight by which history has inflected us, we are to be intoxicated by the unbearable lightness of history, by the fact that so much about us could have been otherwise.

In the next two sections of this chapter, I will treat history as constraint, and history as liberation, respectively, asking in each case about how adopting such a view might be significant for broadly neo-Kantian normative political theory. The final section will discuss an older but more recently neglected view of history, as the source of moral exempla. Before turning to these three topics, however, I need to say something more about what I understand the genre of political theory itself to be. In the next section, I will be concerned with 'normative political theory' understood more broadly, in both its Kantian and non-Kantian variants, before returning to the narrower Kantian meaning for the remainder of my discussion.

The nature of normative political theory

Insofar as it is 'normative', political theory is a branch of moral theory considered in its widest sense: it involves the advancing and testing of ought-claims, both prescriptions for actions and claims about how concepts ought to be understood. Insofar as it is 'theory', it positions itself at some remove from actual practice, though the nature of that remove and relation to such practice is a matter of divergence among diverse theorists.[6] Yet insofar as it is 'political', it must be related to the political as a domain of practical predicament. Plato's *Statesman* classifies political expertise as a theoretical science (*epistêmê*) which has practical and architectonic purposes. That seems to me the right starting point – political expertise must be oriented to a comprehensive understanding of political practice – even though Plato's conception of political expertise is inherently oriented to political practice itself in a way that our conception of theory is not.[7] Today, our view is that normative political theorists need not engage in political practice. Nevertheless, they must think about its practice on some level of abstraction for their work to count as *political* theory at all. The practice inflects the theory just as the theory inflects the practice. We are reflective as well as political animals, which makes us (among other things) reflectively

---

[6] Whereas philosophers such as G. A. Cohen and Philippe van Parijs propose normative frameworks which challenge existing intuitions and practices, others such as Michael Walzer and James Tully see the task of political theorists as fundamentally similar to the task of their fellow citizens. See Walzer's call for theorists to see themselves as 'immanent critics' in (*inter alia*) his *The Company of Critics: Social Criticism and Political Commitment in the Twentieth Century* (New York: Basic Books, 1988), and Tully's call for a public philosophy in his *Public Philosophy in a New Key, Vol. I: Democracy and Civic Freedom* (Cambridge: Cambridge University Press, 2009), where he writes: 'Every reflective and engaged citizen is a public philosopher . . . and every academic public philosopher is a fellow citizen working within the same broad dialogue with his or her specific skills'.

[7] The *Statesman* begins by classifying the art of statecraft as 'more closely related to the theoretical sort of knowledge than to the manual or generally practical sort' (259c–d), but then notes that some forms of theoretical knowledge are 'directive' (like the knowledge of the master-builder), whereas others are simply judgemental (like the knowledge of arithmeticians). Statecraft is located among the 'directive' forms of 'theoretical' expertise (259e–260c). The later modulations of method in the dialogue, from the early divisions to the introduction and criticism of a myth to the introduction and execution of the method of *paradeigma*, do not alter these initial classifications. Crucially, however, political expertise is ultimately defined with reference to its ability to judge the *kairos* or opportune moment for each of the other forms of expertise in the city to be exercised (305c–e), and so the statesman as the possessor of political expertise is inherently defined as a political actor, albeit at one remove from the ordinary actors and offices of the Greek *polis* (see esp. 309d). See Plato, *Statesman*, trans. C. J. Rowe, in *Plato. Complete Works*, ed. J. M. Cooper and D. S. Hutchinson (Cambridge: Cambridge University Press, 1997), 294–358, and for commentary, M. S. Lane, *Method and Politics in Plato's Statesman* (Cambridge: Cambridge University Press, 1998), 163–82, and M. S. Lane, 'Emplois pour philosophes: l'art politique et l'Étranger dans le *Politique* à la lumière de Socrate et du philosophe dans le *Théétète*', trans. F. Teisserenc, *Les Études Philosophiques*, 3 (2005), 325–45.

political; the two practices cannot be segregated or insulated from one another. The study of what political agents do becomes normative when pursued in light of what they should do.[8]

In thinking about politics as a domain of practical predicament, we can make use of a wide range of studies of the world. Advances in decision theory and (more controversially) biology may have important ramifications for political theory, even for its normative sub-genre. The purchase that normative political theory needs on the world may come from epistemology, social ontology, and even neuroscience and social science, as well as from history. So while history can be significant for normative political theory in at least the three ways outlined above, and to which I will soon turn, this is not to say that all such theory must be oriented or permeated by history. Indeed, normative political theory may sometimes be able to make important contributions to politics precisely insofar as it is relatively independent of history.[9]

It is worth considering how and why this might be so, as a bulwark against the claim sometimes made that normative political theory without history must be devoid of value in relation to practical politics.[10] Grant that practical politics is always context-specific. It does not follow that for a theory to be useful to it as orientation, that theory must also be equally context-specific. In fact there is no necessary fit between the

---

[8] This is not to say that all normative theory must be ideal theory however; non-ideal theory can also be normative, as Marc Stears emphasises in this volume.

[9] This point is also made by M. Philp, 'Political theory and history', in D. Leopold and M. Stears (eds.), *Political Theory: Methods and Approaches* (New York: Oxford University Press, 1988), 128–49, at 130, and as a speculation about a possible outcome of the 'Cambridge School' of intellectual history (to cordon off historical understanding from a reinvigorated and autonomous normative theorising: a path however not taken by subsequent development within the so-called School) by Richard Tuck, 'The contribution of history', in R. E. Goodin and P. Pettit (eds.), *A Companion to Contemporary Political Philosophy* (Oxford: Blackwell, 1996), 72–89, at 83–4. These are both articles to which I am more generally indebted.

[10] R. Geuss, *Philosophy and Real Politics* (Princeton, NJ: Princeton University Press, 2008), comes close to making this claim, if one conjoins his attack on a certain understanding of 'politics as applied ethics' (6–8) with his insistence that 'If one thinks that understanding one's world is a minimal precondition to having sensible human desires and projects, history is not going to be dispensable' (15). Note however that earlier he lists history alongside sociology, ethnology, psychology and economics (7) – so while he views history as necessary (the claim I question in the paragraph above), he does not prescribe it as the theorist's sole study.

degree of contextual specificity and the measure of orientation which a theory can provide: this is a pragmatic question. A graduation speech which inspires students to dream big may be much more practically effective in shaping their behaviour than one which tracks the discouraging statistics of their unlikely success. A sketchily drawn treasure map may be much more useful than a contextually detailed one in which the relevant features are submerged rather than highlighted.

One example supporting this contention is the influence of Philip Pettit's republican theory of freedom on the policies adopted by José Luis Rodríguez Zapatero as President of Spain.[11] Soon after being elected as leader of the Spanish Socialist Party in 2000, Zapatero laid out the principles by which he would govern if his party were to be elected, in terms influenced by Pettit's 1997 book *Republicanism*, as focusing on reducing domination and enhancing non-domination in political life. Zapatero's election as prime minister in 2004 led to an invitation to Pettit to give a public lecture, followed by a further invitation to conduct a formal review of his government's achievements prior to the next election in 2008. A historically oriented political theorist would likely have counselled Zapatero to eschew controversial moral questions such as rights for women against domestic violence, and rights of gays and lesbians to marry, given the traditional influence of the Catholic Church in Spanish politics. But Zapatero, informed by Pettit's republicanism – which he took to systematise and clarify a tradition of thought which was kin to his understanding of the socialist tradition[12] – made exactly the opposite choice, putting these rights

[11] The review was published as part of P. Pettit, *Examen a Zapatero* (Madrid: Temas de Hoy, 2008), 19–66, alongside other material including the transcript of an interview Pettit conducted with Zapatero in 2006, in which the latter remarks that 'su libro tiene una vocación práctica que me parece extraordinariamente útil para la tarea política' (93). A revised version of that review is incorporated in the overview of the relation between Pettit, Zapatero and republicanism, in J. L. Martí and P. Pettit, *A Political Philosophy in Public Life: Civic Republicanism in Zapatero's Spain* (Princeton, NJ: Princeton University Press, 2010), where the same quotation is translated as '[your book] has a practical side to it that I find extraordinarily useful for political work' (110).
[12] See Zapatero's comment that Pettit's book, *Republicanism: a Theory of Freedom and Government* (New York and Oxford: Oxford University Press, 1997), 'presantaba de una forma clara y sistemática una vieja tradición de pensamiento que no nos era ajena', in the interview published in Pettit, *Examen*, 93, and translated in Martí and Pettit, *A Political Philosophy*, 110, as 'Your book clearly and systematically presents an old tradition of thought that is not foreign to us'.

among others at the top of his legislative agenda, and carrying both sets of measures through.

Pettit's theory may even be said to have functioned as a blueprint for Zapatero's government. This is a term which has been given a bad name by those like Burke and de Maistre, followed by Hayek and Popper, who attacked any idea that society could be remade from head to toe in accordance with a rational plan. The idea of the 'blueprint' became implicated in this rejected rationalism, precisely as part of a conception of social engineering. But social engineering, in a less totalising version, is an inherent part of democratic politics. Political manifestos are, in parliamentary democracies, precisely blueprints. A blueprint is, after all, a practical instrument: it is not the architect's dream-vision, one which might have been sketched without any regard for practicalities, but rather precisely the tool which translates a vision into constructive engineering specifications so that people can assess the value and feasibility of their various proposals as a practical and interrelated whole.[13] Blueprints will reveal very quickly whether the sides of a building don't join up, or that the load-bearing pillars are too slender. Those are useful engineering virtues; that is why, more prosaically, manifesto commitments have to be costed. At the same time, a blueprint may have the virtues of a dramatically new vision: it can translate such a vision into feasible and evaluable terms.

The point here is that history is not the only possible practical guide for political agents. Normative political theory – even issuing in the wrongly despised blueprints – can be a valuable guide in particular for elected politicians. (Administrative policy-makers have less autonomy and are generally more sensitive to, and constrained by, existing public opinion.) This is because theorists and elected politicians alike should sometimes dream big, expanding the horizon of what is taken to be possible. The prevailing social imaginary can sometimes be changed by a cascade of actions and reactions set off by theoretical provocation.[14]

---

[13] And of course, a blueprint for a building which is never built may itself play the role of reshaping our vision, loosening our grip on what is and is not possible and realistic – as in the chapel for mental patients, detailed in the exhibition 'Madness and Modernity' at the Wellcome Institute in London in the spring of 2009. See the catalogue by G. Blackshaw and L. Topp (eds.), *Madness and Modernity: Mental Illness and the Visual Arts in Vienna 1900* (Farnham: Lund Humphries, 2009).

[14] The term 'social imaginary' is drawn from C. Taylor, *Modern Social Imaginaries* (Durham, NC: Duke University Press, 2004). For an example of a

Such visionary activity should not be wilfully disdainful of history, but may learn different lessons from it than conventional wisdom teaches, and may be inspired and guided more by moral principles (such as those embodied in a normative political theory) than by history directly. Visionaries informed by normative political theory may sometimes, at least, outflank historically bound pessimists in the forum of political action.

History as constraint: explanation and normative political theory

If visionary ideals may arise for theorists and politicians independently of history, theorists still have a further role of testing them against the best available account of social explanation. Return then from the domain of practice, to normative political theory as a form of theoretical inquiry and reflection, now again restricted to its broadly neo-Kantian variants. In theoretically reflecting on politics as a domain of practical predicament, what if anything need such theorists know about historical explanation? Should normative political theorists spend their time reading about the multiple forms of masculinity in early modern England, the causes of the Black Death, the history of machine tools or the reasons for and timing of Hitler's invasions of Poland and then of Russia?[15] To answer this question, we need to offer one further characterisation of both 'normative political theory' and 'history' in addition to those with which we began.

The crucial contrast here is that of temporality. Normative theory has not characteristically tended either to index its claims as time-dependent, or to think much about the way in which temporal change would internally alter the political institutions and practices it commends.[16] History, in contrast, is at its core the study of what William

bold theoretical vision aiming to reshape, rather than conform to, historically formed beliefs and values, consider Philippe van Parijs's call for unconditional basic income in his *Real Freedom for All: What (If Anything) Can Justify Capitalism?* (Oxford: Clarendon Press, 1995).

[15] This list pays tribute to what I learned from my former colleagues in the University of Cambridge's Faculty of History, exemplified but not exhausted by the references in these cases, respectively, to Alex Shepard, John Hatcher, and for the last two, Adam Tooze.

[16] I say more about time and political theory in M. Lane, 'Political theory and time', in P. Baert (ed.), *Time in Contemporary Intellectual Thought* (Amsterdam and New York: Elsevier, 2000), 233–51. Here the work of John Rawls is a notable exception: his emphasis on stability in Part III of *A Theory of Justice* (Cambridge, MA: Belknap Press of Harvard University Press, revised edn 1999) was actually

Sewell calls 'social temporalities', dynamics and rhythms, each of which has its own timing and which interact in complex and unpredictable ways.[17] Some historians content themselves with ever-more-rich and minute descriptions of phenomena; others ask schematic questions based on statistical analyses. In between are those who ask big questions about the nature of social development through time, but who are sensitive to the ever-reflexively changing identities of the persons and groups they study, and to the multiple and endlessly rich ways in which those persons and trajectories can be characterised. What value might there be from bringing the temporally riven and the self-consciously atemporal together?[18]

The most important gain lies in enriching the social ontology and causality assumed by normative political theory. Such theory tends to talk about 'moral agents' and 'citizens'. It is too easy to forget that these are moderate evangelicals or children of immigrants, that they are NASCAR fans or custodians of family trusts. But rich description for rich description's sake, which occurs in both disciplines – many normative political theorists gain plaudits for occasionally interweaving apostrophic mention of such identities, just as many historians gain plaudits for ever-more-subtle characterisation of the minds of early modern witches – quickly palls. To be productive, such finer-grained social categories and identities need to be harnessed to a subtler account of social change.

Social science might seem like a better bet at this point for political theory to draw on: surely social science is the place to turn to find categories and theories of social change? Yet the very elusiveness and

an invitation to dynamic feedback analysis of the effect of his principles on their own sustainability.

[17] W. Sewell, *Logics of History: Social Theory and Social Transformation* (Chicago and London: University of Chicago Press, 2005). Danielle Allen brought this book to my attention in her lecture 'Do Ideas Matter?', one of four Bristol Blackwell Lectures in Greece, Rome and the Classical Tradition delivered at Bristol University in April–May 2008. I subsequently learned much from discussing it with members of the Cambridge Reading Group in American Intellectual and Cultural History.

[18] My claim is not that normative political theory is in fact immune to temporality; as Marc Stears has reminded me, it may be committed to particular ways of thinking about time and 'progress', as discussed in B. Honig, 'Emergence', ch. 2 of her *Emergency Politics: Paradox, Law, Democracy* (Princeton, NJ: Princeton University Press, 2009), 40–64. My claim is rather that those engaged in the normative political theory enterprise do not characteristically see it as such.

complexity of the narrative explanations of social change in history are a valuable caution for political theorists. History reminds theorists that the trajectories of change are much more subtle, unpredictable, and manifold, than any theory or set of categories has yet been able fully to explain. And categories like periodisation – generating for example the frequent invocations of 'modernity' in neo-Kantian political theorists – cry out for historical reconsideration.[19] The constraints embodied in historical explanations are flexible and non-deterministic, yet they can provide political theorists with a richer and subtler canvas on which to practise normative theorising.

There is another way in which an immersion into historical worlds and historical study can enrich normative political theory. This is not in terms of explanation itself, but a looser underpinning of sheer erudition. History in this vein reminds us that the world is a stranger place than we readily imagine – that there are more things on heaven and earth than are imagined in our philosophies. E. P. Thompson spoke of his purpose in writing *The Making of the English Working Class* thus: 'I am seeking to rescue the poor stockinger, the Luddite cropper, the "obsolete" hand-loom weaver, the "utopian" artisan, and even the deluded follower of Joanna Southcott, from the enormous condescension of posterity.'[20] Normative political theory is too often guilty of unconscious condescension to past thinkers and to past societies. It is easy to delude ourselves that our distinctions are newly minted, our problems or concerns unprecedented.

It took historians to point out, for example, that the millehnial enthusiasm for studies of globalisation and political theory as something new was ignoring the waves of globalisation which had gripped the world periodically and unevenly since prehistory: and in particular, for example, the fact that the world economy and society was more globalised, by many measures, in the nineteenth century than it is today.[21] Equally, moral concern for others as individuals has not been

---

[19] See for example the thoughtful discussion of periodisation in C. Maier, 'Consigning the twentieth century to history: alternative narratives for the modern era', *American Historical Review*, 105: 3 (2000), 807–31.

[20] E. P. Thompson, *The Making of the English Working Class* (London: Victor Gollancz, 1980; first edn 1963), Preface, 14.

[21] See for example the fascinating set of essays on 'archaic globalization' and other earlier forms of globalisation than the modern one, in A. G. Hopkins (ed.), *Globalization in World History* (London: Pimlico, 2002).

the exclusive property of secular analytical thinkers. Until the final dismantling of most formal colonial governments in the mid-twentieth century, the language of missionary burden and duty to care for those abroad was primarily religious and often imperialist.[22] Forgetting that history makes it too easy to assume a pristine virtue or novelty for normative political theory, they evaded hard questions about the implications of those strands of it which are committed to cosmopolitanism or toleration.

The humility consequent upon historical erudition need not trip us back into a vision of unchanging concepts and questions. On the contrary, seeing both where similar concerns have arisen (but in radically different contexts) and where genuine novelty lies (such as the world's one superpower now being its greatest debtor) will help normative political theory to get a grip on the questions it might best ask. Such recognition of novelty reminds us that history is always Janus-faced: each form of constraint also produces a form of freedom. It is to an emphasis on history as freedom that we now turn.

History as freedom: genealogy and the implications of contingency

A traditional metaphor for history has been the practice of archaeology: history as the recovery of a cross-section (and sometimes of a reconstructed whole) of layered past events and beliefs.[23] More recently, however, historians have become enamoured of the notion of genealogy, a notion developed by Friedrich Nietzsche and in his wake by Michel Foucault. Whereas archaeology can slice into the synchronic strata against which speakers act, a diachronic form of inquiry is needed to capture the changes in the extensional applications over which

---

[22] See for example M. B. Oren, *Power, Faith, and Fantasy: America in the Middle East, 1776 to the Present* (New York: W.W. Norton & Co., 2007), a reference I owe to Robert Kargman.

[23] Both John Pocock and Quentin Skinner have invoked the image of archaeology for their own historical work. Skinner's genealogical turn has not displaced archaeology entirely – the images and language of which he continues to use at times even in texts also declaring their adherence to genealogy. See also M. S. Lane, 'Doing our thinking for ourselves: method and politics after Quentin Skinner', *Journal of the History of Ideas*, forthcoming, in which much of the text of this section will also appear, with permission from Cambridge University Press and Pennsylvania State University Press, respectively.

evaluative terms can be aptly used. This is the subject matter of genealogy as recently adapted by Quentin Skinner, for example, and constitutes what he identifies as the usual mechanism by which 'concepts' may
be loosely said to change (a mechanism which he points out most often
involves not changes in the 'concepts' themselves, so much as changes in
their application, as a result of and bringing about new social perceptions and attitudes alike).[24]

Having been fashioned to serve the philosophers of the future who
will be able to reshape their lives as works of art, Nietzschean genealogy
has always been associated with power and freedom, even while the
meaning of freedom (and the rejection of a certain view of free will) is
itself reshaped by that genealogy. Although the early reception of
Michel Foucault's works raised concerns about whether its implications
for politics were deterministic and constraining, his own practice as a
political activist together with the shifts he engendered in the understanding of freedom largely quelled those early criticisms.[25] Recent
theoreticians of genealogy share their forebears' emphasis on contingency in defining it as a practice. Mark Bevir remarks that 'Nietzsche
searches for the contingent accidental sources of a belief [in any moral
principles]', while also contending more broadly that nominalism,
contingency, and contestability are central features of genealogy:
'Genealogy reveals the contingency and contestability of ideas and
practices that hide these aspects of their origins.' Tyler Krupp asserts
that 'Genealogy narrates the contingent path of historical unities ...'
and that 'However contingency is understood, it stands in stark contrast
to teleological narrativised history'.[26]

---

[24] See especially 'Moral principles and social change', and 'The idea of a cultural
lexicon', in Skinner, *Visions of Politics, Vol. I: Regarding Method*, 145–57 and
158–74 respectively.

[25] M. Bevir, 'What is genealogy?', *Journal of the Philosophy of History*, 2 (2008),
263–75, at 271.

[26] Bevir, 'What is genealogy?' 266; T. Krupp, 'Genealogy as critique?', *Journal
of the Philosophy of History*, 2: 3 (2008), 315–37, both quotations at 319. Bevir
however observes that genealogy has no critical purchase on any idea or practice
'which recognizes its own contingency' (275). This goes some way toward
acknowledging the debunking dimension of genealogy, which is an important
aspect of its use by Nietzsche. Yet as George Kateb has pointed out in oral
discussion of these topics, it is not contingency alone which effects that debunking
move: this must also involve the reversing or undoing of value, something which
neither Bevir nor Krupp emphasises in their accounts.

Most practitioners of Nietzschean-Foucauldian types of genealogy today assume or contend that genealogy in engendering an awareness of contingency will also engender freedom, in the form of the power to carry out social change. That link has been summarily asserted by James Tully thus: 'a history or genealogy of the formation of these specific languages and practices ... has the capacity to free us to some extent from the conditions of possibility [taken for granted or given as necessary in our present practices]'.[27] We should ask, however, whether contingency simply and necessarily equates to freedom. While contingency in a certain sense is necessary for practical freedom (as Aristotle knew, there is no point in deliberating about things that cannot be otherwise), it is a mistake to suppose that it is alone sufficient.[28] To suppose so is to fall into a version of the old nature–culture dichotomy: because and insofar as something is culture, not nature, it is in our power to change it. Apart from the crudity of that dichotomy, it is a mistake to think that because some aspects of our social life may be historically contingent in the sense that they could have been otherwise (perhaps not even in the sense that they have ever actually been otherwise), they are necessarily now within our power to change. Feminist debates in the 1970s as to the origins of patriarchy sometimes fell into this trap. Even if we were able to diagnose its origins, that would not necessarily imply either that we have the power to change it now, or that the lever to do so depends on those origins. Surely one point of genealogy is that much more has intervened between origins and the present to complicate that relationship.[29]

Given that the connection between contingency and freedom is not necessary, can an argument be made to connect them? Some important,

---

[27] Tully, *Public Philosophy*, Vol. I, 17.

[28] Liya Yu has drawn my attention to Hannah Arendt's striking remark that 'The opposite of necessity is not contingency or accident but freedom', in H. Arendt, *The Life of the Mind* (New York: Harcourt, 1981), 60. Arendt continues on the same page: 'Everything that ... happens to mortals for better or worse is "contingent", including their own existence'. The implication seems to be that while contingency is a fact of the human condition, it is not this sheer fact but the human freedom to think and act with which we respond to it that is to be celebrated.

[29] There is also the vexed question of whether history can truly be viewed in the light of contingency, given that the conditions and causes were at least sufficient for things turning out as they did; this is the problem on which Tolstoy meditates in *War and Peace*, and which Skinner acknowledges in the following remark at the end of *Liberty before Liberalism* (Cambridge: Cambridge University Press, 1998), 119–20: 'There were obviously sufficient conditions of this outcome, but I have tried to show that it can nevertheless be viewed in the light of a choice.'

if briefly stated, claims by Quentin Skinner enable us to reconstruct a possible argument here. Skinner uses the language of liberation most strikingly in his introduction to the first volume (*Regarding Method*) of his *Visions of Politics*. An understanding of the past, he writes, enables us to see 'how far the values embodied in our present way of life, and our present ways of thinking about those values, reflect a series of choices made at different times between different possible worlds'. 'This awareness', in turn, 'can help to liberate us from the grip of any one hegemonic account of those values and how they should be interpreted and understood.'[30] The theme of liberation is repeated in the last line of the chapter, glossing the 'political plea' 'to recognise that the pen is a mighty sword' which can be used to 'undermine' as well as to 'underpin' our practices: 'We may be freer than we sometimes suppose.'

In these pages, Skinner is best understood as arguing not that recognition of contingency *eo ipso* bestows the power of change, but rather along the following, more complicated, lines:

1. Genealogy liberates us from assumptions, giving us more mental options than we previously had, so enhancing our freedom to think (I will call this mental freedom, as a shorthand for freedom in the domain of thinking).
2. In then contributing to our own culture's discourses, we can intervene so as to modify ('undermining' rather than 'underpinning') the languages in which those assumptions are embedded, and this multiplication of our options for engaging with existing languages enhances our freedom to act (I will call this performative freedom, as a shorthand for freedom in the domain of physical action).

Both mental and performative freedom call our attention to specific domains in which freedom can be exercised. Mental freedom can be experienced in any form of regime and with any personal status: I might enhance my mental freedom by reading genealogies, while arbitrarily imprisoned incommunicado and deprived of writing materials by a

---

[30] All the quotations in the latter part of this paragraph come from Skinner, *Visions of Politics*, Vol. I: *Regarding Method*, 6–7. These sentences are adapted from the concluding discussion of Skinner, *Liberty before Liberalism*, 117, where a different sentence stood in the place of the one to which this note is attached: 'Equipped with a broader sense of possibility, we can stand back from the intellectual commitments we have inherited and ask ourselves in a new spirit of enquiry what we should think of them.'

repressive regime. Performative freedom, by contrast, will differ in different regimes, insofar as it is produced by and against any given set of sociolinguistic structures. Neither however is equivalent to republican freedom. I may have the mental freedom to denounce political servitude in my thought, as well as the performative freedom to denounce it by a demonstration on the streets, even if I am subject to arbitrary imprisonment as soon as I do the latter.

We find an early clue to Skinner's notion of mental freedom at the end of his influential article of 1969, 'Meaning and understanding in the history of ideas'.[31] In the concluding paragraph there, Skinner observed 'that our own society places unrecognized constraints upon our imaginations', and that 'the historical study of the ideas of other societies should be undertaken as the indispensable and the irreplaceable means of placing limits on those constraints'. Here he did not see history as engendering performative freedom directly, but only as 'placing limits' on our imaginative 'constraints', such that the mental freedom thereby gained can enhance 'self-awareness itself'.[32] Mention of performative freedom emerged later, as a persisting image of archaeological inquiry came to be accompanied in his writings by the image and language of genealogy.

Skinner came to observe that there is a difference between 'the unexceptionable claim that any agent who is engaged in an intended act of communication must be limited by the prevailing conventions of discourse, and the further claim that he must be limited only to *following* these conventions'.[33] Bound by the need to use existing languages and recognisable speech-acts to make even the most global dissent understood, language – in particular 'the normative vocabulary available to us' – is 'one of the constraints on our conduct itself', even as our performative freedom lies in our ability to operate within that constraint.[34] We cannot know in advance whether our speech-acts will find either immediate or eventual uptake, or whether others will

---

[31] Q. Skinner, 'Meaning and understanding in the history of ideas', *History and Theory*, 8 (1969), 3–53; also rpt. in J. Tully, *Meaning and Context: Quentin Skinner and his Critics* (Princeton, NJ: Princeton University Press, 1988), 29–67, and with changes in Skinner, *Visions of Politics, Vol. I*, 57–89.

[32] Skinner, 'Meaning and understanding', 53, for both this and the preceding quotation.

[33] Q. Skinner, 'Some problems in the analysis of political thought and action', as rpt. in Tully, *Meaning and Context*, 97–118, at 105.

[34] Both quoted phrases are in Q. Skinner, 'The idea of a cultural lexicon', in *Visions of Politics, Vol. I*, 158–74, at 174.

respond to the ripples which our *parole* leaves on the surface of the *langue*. Such freedom-cum-constraint extends to the various dimensions of linguistic change which Skinner has identified in more recent work: changing social beliefs and theories; changing social perceptions and awareness; and changing social values and attitudes.

Yet here we come to a further difficulty. Skinner insists that 'no one is above the battle'. This dictum should not be understood to imply that there is no role for ideas within the battle, only that the role of ideas is always *engagé*.[35] It does, however, seem to suggest that the performative acts of the historian are on a par with, and of the same kind as, those of her subjects: which in turn would deny history any distinctive ideology-puncturing and liberating role. If the historian is simply advancing another ideology (in her case about the past), it is hard to see how history can have a distinctively liberating value to bequeath to any theoretician seeking such in its study.[36]

Admittedly, Skinner sometimes seems to reject this implication, suggesting that the intentions of the historian are in fact qualitatively different from those of her subjects: she is seeking to reconstruct *wie es eigentlich gewesen war*, not to prosecute any purpose (we might say ideological purpose) of her own. Thus he sometimes speaks of the fruit of the study of history as 'one of the best means of preventing our current moral and political theories from degenerating too easily into uncritically accepted ideologies'.[37] Yet are we not all, inevitably, what Skinner elsewhere calls 'innovating ideologist[s]'?[38] Indeed, Nietzsche already pointed out in his essay 'On the uses and disadvantages of history for life' that it is not possible for the historian to avoid serving the interests of

---

[35] In a seminar held at Princeton University on 21 October 2009, however, Skinner asserted that as genealogists 'we stand above the battle' (according to my notes of the seminar: there was no formal transcript). The centrality of battle in Skinner's work is highlighted by James Tully, 'The pen is a mighty sword: Quentin Skinner's analysis of politics', in Tully, *Meaning and Politics*, 7–25, esp. 24–5.

[36] The problem is similar to the question asked by H. Hamilton-Bleakley in her discussion of Skinner, of how his own practice as a historian relates to his precept: H. Hamilton-Bleakley, 'Linguistic philosophy and *The Foundations*', in A. Brett and J. Tully, with H. Hamilton-Bleakley (eds.), *Rethinking the Foundations of Modern Political Thought* (Cambridge: Cambridge University Press, 2006), 20–33.

[37] Q. Skinner, 'Interpretation', 126, a point which he footnotes as being 'much influenced by' A. MacIntyre, *Against the Self-Images of the Age* (Notre Dame, IN: University of Notre Dame Press, 1971), esp. viii–ix.

[38] Skinner, 'Some problems', 111.

(his) life in some form or other, even in writing the most severely anti-quarian kind of history.[39] If all history is ideology, then while studying it may save the normative political theorist from falling prey to the current ideologies captivating her culture, will she not simply be catapulted into another ideology promulgated by the historian? In that case, how can history liberate the imagination and potential action of the theorist, as opposed to simply providing another form of imaginative enslavement?

I propose that the elements of a solution can be found in John Pocock's elaboration of the nature of the professional role of the histor-ian. In his essay, 'The historian as political actor in polity, society and academy', Pocock points out that while political debate about a society and its past is continuous throughout the society, not reserved to a special class of historians, nevertheless the professional guild or acad-emy of the latter makes a distinctive contribution to that debate. While the historian (or indeed the theorist) may, *qua* citizen, '[become] aware that the same story can be differently told by the protagonist and the antagonist', what she 'acquires [is] the capacity to declare', *qua* histor-ian, that 'there are an indefinite number of ways of telling and retelling any story'.[40] That is, the standards of discussion among the historians are such as to emphasise the contingency of their own answers, and this professional emphasis is a special contribution made by the republic of letters to the republic (or polity of another kind) as a whole. Whereas many citizens will be wholly invested in their political outlooks in a way which ignores or denies the contingency of those outlooks, the histor-ian's role is to remind them of the multiplicity and contingency of the histories we tell and the theories which take them as foundations. In doing so, the historian holds certain ideologies up to the light of critical scrutiny, even though she may at the same time be subject to others of which she is not aware. Her role in the political battle of ideas is a special one: not on a par with the role of other actors, but akin to the role of an umpire or regulator, entitled to assess claims made by others, even though

---

[39] F. Nietzsche, 'On the uses and disadvantages of history for life', *Untimely Meditations*, trans. R. J. Hollingdale, intro. by J. P. Stern (Cambridge: Cambridge University Press, 1983), 57–123; original text in Nietzsche, *Werke* (both *Kritische Gesamtausgabe* and the electronic *Historisch-kritische Ausgabe*), Vol. III-1.

[40] J. G. A. Pocock, 'The historian as political actor in polity, society and academy', *Political Thought and History: Essays on Theory and Method* (Cambridge: Cambridge University Press, 2009), 223 and 224 respectively for these quotations; the point in the previous sentence here is made by him there on 225.

unable to guarantee the absolute merit of her own claims. She is still in the battle, but she is not a fighter in it in the same way that ordinary fighters are, even though her role may also be controversial and contested.

Thus the solution to the problem of ideology is the following: while the historian may purvey ideologies unwittingly, this does not detract from her professional role of ensuring that she does not – insofar as she is or can be conscious of her relation to ideologies – 'accept' them 'uncritically'. By practising her craft, the historian can make a distinctive contribution to the mental freedom of her reader, and so provide the tools for a greater performative freedom, even though as an actor in history she must acknowledge herself also to be prone to ideology (and may have more active ideological purposes also). Pocock reminds us further that no one is fully in control of her own intentions: 'History consists largely of unintended performances.'[41] Thus a given history may serve to dismantle the current hegemony yet at the price of serving to construct the next. The historian may liberate us while at the same time, intentionally or not, enslaving us: again a Foucauldian point. This highlights the distance between categorical republican liberty (one is either a free person or a slave) and performative liberty (one is always under constraints and subject to ideology, even as one chooses how to perform). One is tempted to say that we perform our own history but do not perform it just as we please. In choosing to study history with the aim of liberating themselves from mental assumptions and so liberating themselves for certain new theoretical and (perhaps) practical performances, normative political theorists can find such liberation so long as they acknowledge that no form of liberation is free from constraint.

History as exemplar: classical practices and contemporary analogues

We do not perform our own history just as we please, but we do perform it ourselves. That dictum, adapted from Marx above, points finally to a third and now unfashionable role of history in its significance for normative political theory: its function as a storehouse of examples of actions and of lives. This function too has sometimes been thought to have become defunct as a result of the discovery, or assertion, discussed at the outset

---

[41] J. G. A. Pocock, 'The concept of a language and the *métier d'historien*: some considerations on practice', *Political Thought and History*, 87–105, at 98.

of this chapter: that history has no inherent direction and so licenses no necessary values. The practice of past generations of schoolchildren, taught to read Livy and Plutarch in order to imagine themselves as austere statesmen, able and willing to defend political principle against wayward democratic or plebeian mobs, has come to seem naive. We today do not live in a classical republic; there are no transhistorical moral standards which make the behaviour of antique men relevant to our predicaments.

This general reaction is however fallacious. For history's function as a store of moral exempla of characters and actions is logically independent of the question of historical teleology. This suggests that it is not teleology as such, but rather the rise of social history and the history of the *longue durée* (the former at least associated with a Marxist historical-materialist perspective, but outliving its specific teleological story), which has made the study of the actions of individuals (in particular, 'great men') seem antiquated and irrelevant. If individuals are largely irrelevant to the course of history, then it would be deluded to study their biographies in order to model oneself on them. Individual role models are no longer to be found in the drama of past societies (in which individuals wrongly took themselves to be significant in shaping events) but perhaps rather in the role of the historian or social scientist itself, the objective scholar who subordinates himself to the demands of his subject matter, or for the theorist, in the attempt to comprehend rather than to act.

Against this rejection of biography and moral examples, however, we can again appeal to the point that political theory must be the theoretical study of politics as a practical predicament. The condition of practice is one which demands individual action even when that action is informed by complex causal understandings as to how limited the significance of the action may be. Theoreticians may not aim to inform practice directly, but they cannot help the fact that they may be read or studied by those engaged in political action (as Pettit found himself being read by Zapatero). As such, the question of the role of the individual as agent will inevitably arise. And here the study of historical agents – who faced the demands of agency, however great the constraints on their performances, and the unintended consequences of their actions – cannot help but be instructive. History displays both the constraints on individual agency and the examples of individual agents deciding how to act in the face of those constraints. Neither teaching is complete without the other. If political action is inescapably normative – which is to say, inescapably involving a moral dimension – then the theorising of political action must attend to the practical predicament of moral agents deciding how to act.

So historians need to continue to write biographies alongside other forms of historical inquiry, and political theorists need to read them. These biographies may be informed by the thinking of social history: they may be group or generational biographies, for example, or studies which focus on the lives of the marginal and overlooked. But there is also a case for continuing to read the lives of individual 'great men' and 'great women': for continuing to read Plutarch alongside Natalie Zemon Davis or Carlo Ginzburg. Precisely because ancient statesmen, for example, may have had different assumptions about how political change takes place or about what their role as leaders should require them to do, studying their lives can inform the political theorist's understanding of constraint as well as liberating them from certain assumptions. And insofar as political theory bears on practice, the study of individuals aware that they are acting politically at any level – 'high' or 'low' – is relevant to understanding the normative demands such agency inherently involves.[42]

There are two further wrinkles to this story, or elements in this defence. First, all agents will act with and against the backdrop of some folk-knowledge of history (whether or not they conceive history as linear but non-teleological in the way that most people have come to do today). It is only on the basis of a certain story about the causes of World War I that the founders of the League of Nations made the decisions that they did. The same holds true for theorists: it was only the basis of a certain understanding of the nature and causes of the Holocaust – an understanding gleaned from historians like Raul Hilberg, who was informed by Franz Neumann's *Behemoth*, a work itself shaped by an understanding of classical political theory – that Hannah Arendt came to theorise as she did about the nature of totalitarianism.[43] Theorists who don't read history will nevertheless rely on history – what they remember of it from school or assume of it from contemporary chatter. Both history and normative theory are present as background assumptions in the culture, and so the wise theorist or social scientist will interrogate those assumptions. It is as bad for political theorists who don't read history to

---

[42] See the discussion of leadership, drawing on historical examples, in
N. O. Keohane, *Thinking about Leadership* (Princeton, NJ: Princeton University Press, 2010).
[43] Again a point drawn to my attention in this context by Adam Tooze.

rely on the ideas of some defunct historian, as it is for economists who don't read economic theory to rely on the ideas of some defunct economist.[44] Indeed, given the interpenetration of the normative and the historical in both political theory and economics, it is bad for either to be ignorant of the full development of both.

The second wrinkle is that historical ideas which may seem to have been conclusively left behind in the past can nevertheless be brought into the present by agents who use their performative freedom to do so. As John Pocock has pointed out, although historians resist what he calls 'historiosophy' (the ancient view of history as a source of wisdom, related to my use of history as a source of moral examples) on the grounds that history carries no message, nevertheless 'The history of political thought must consist, in significant measure, of actors doing things that historians of political thought insist that *they* should not do.' That is, agents are constantly prone to drawing on past (sometimes dramatically or archaically past) concepts to inform present practice.[45] We may study the past for the sake of its liberating alterity, only to discover that it unexpectedly becomes our contemporary once again. History as the medium for political agency extends to the imitation of the past as well as to the understanding both of its (partial) explicability and of its (partial) alterity.

Conclusion: an example of the role of examples

I turn in conclusion to an example which brings together our three themes of history as significant for normative political theory as constraint, as liberation, and as moral exemplar. This is the role played by the example of the nineteenth-century abolitionist movement against slavery, and by the Reverend Martin Luther King Jr, in informing John Rawls's theorising about public reason. Rawls originally thought of public reason as limited to arguments drawing on a political conception of justice,

---

[44] Keynes' dictum was: 'Practical men, who believe themselves to be exempt from any intellectual influences, are usually the slave to some defunct economist': see his *The General Theory of Employment, Interest, and Money* (New York: Houghton, Mifflin, Harcourt, 1964), 383. I was reminded in discussion of an earlier draft of this paper at the Annual Meeting of the American Political Science Association, 2008, that Keynes refers in the preceding sentences to 'the ideas of economists and political philosophers' – that is, to theorists rather than to historians. For this reason I have drawn the point as a parallel in the present text.

[45] J. G. A. Pocock, 'Quentin Skinner: the history of politics and the politics of history (2004)', in *Political Thought and History*, 123–42, at 140.

excluding appeal to wider comprehensive doctrines such as religious beliefs which are not shared by all reasonable members of a society. However, he then confronted the example of the abolitionist arguments against slavery, which were steeped in religion, together with King's religiously infused appeals for civil rights, and came to acknowledge the power which religious appeal gave such arguments in the public sphere of American politics. These examples of how moral appeal in America actually, historically, worked, led Rawls to rethink his normative theory to formulate an 'inclusive' account of public reason. In the publication of 'The idea of public reason' in *Political Liberalism* and in his subsequent writings, he admitted religiously or comprehensively informed arguments to public reason so long as the values and claims they are used to defend can also be stated in terms limited to the political conception.[46]

In this case, an understanding of the constraining logic of social change (in other words, a historical explanation) was found also to be liberating, at least mentally liberating, and to prescribe a more liberal form of practice (insofar as history taught that social change often occurred differently from the way the theorist had first assumed). In other words, a moral example drawn from history served to reshape a normative theory. History is not the only way in which normative political theory can support its claims, as was established earlier in this chapter. But it would be a foolish theorist (and a foolish politician) who would ignore it. A political theorist who reads no history is not likely to write significant theory, even though history should not be all that she reads or the sole influence shaping what she writes.[47]

[46] John Rawls, 'The idea of public reason', in *Political Liberalism* (New York: Columbia University Press, 1996), 212–54, at 247–54. Rawls notes (250 with n. 39) that King Jr was able to appeal 'to the political values expressed in the Constitution correctly understood' (as in *Brown v. Board of Education*), whereas the abolitionists had no such settled constitutional doctrine available to them.

[47] Previous versions of this chapter, or of other papers which have been incorporated into it, were presented at a round table of the Annual Meeting of the American Political Science Association (2008); the King's College Philosophy Reunion (2009); and a conference on 'Quentin Skinner: From Method to Politics' held at The Center for the Humanities of the Graduate Center of the City University of New York (2009), at all of which useful comments were received from fellow speakers and audience participants. More general thanks for comments and discussion are owed to Joel Isaac, Nan Keohane, Michael O'Brien, Philip Pettit, Quentin Skinner, Adam Tooze, Liya Yu, and to the editors of this volume, Jonathan Floyd and Marc Stears, for their insight and patience.

7 | History and reality: idealist pathologies and 'Harvard School' remedies

ANDREW SABL

My topic in this chapter is realist or non-utopian political theory. My question is why this kind of political theory must depend, as its partisans often claim it must, on history. Realism can name many different positions. My focus here will be on the kind of realism produced by what I shall call the 'Harvard School'. This is the kind of political theory *cum* political science that flourished at that university in the 1960s and 1970s and persisted, with decreasing prominence, through the 1990s. It was associated with such figures as Carl Friedrich, Samuel Huntington, Michael Walzer, Harvey Mansfield, Louis Hartz, Samuel Beer and Karl Deutsch (and more recently with thinkers educated at or influenced by Harvard, such as Jonathan Allen, John Dunn, Rogers Smith, Bernard Yack, Stephen Holmes, Frederick Whelan and, more equivocally, Nancy Rosenblum). It drew on a canon of liberal and non-liberal realists from Thucydides and Machiavelli through Montesquieu, Hume, the authors of the *Federalist*, Tocqueville (sometimes obsessively), and culminating in Weber; and bore a sneaking, reluctant admiration for Nietzsche.

Realism in this sense sought to understand and vindicate liberal, democratic institutions not only through canonical and analytic political theory but also through an interlocking group of inquiries that cut across political theory and political science but invoked a remarkably consistent set of assumptions. Political inquiry should assume the standpoint of agents, but benefits agents most not by lecturing them but by illuminating political contexts or situations. Interests, conflict, and power are permanent and fundamental components of politics. Instrumentalist modes of justification, which derive judgements or recommendations from considerations of what will achieve or has achieved the ends of political actors, are both politically salutary and normatively sound. Because democratic institutions are not always universally popular, and their decisions are typically thought illegitimate by someone, they must sometimes be established and defended by force and must enforce their decisions through coercion. It is the weak and powerless who most need 'restraining norms and conventions' (backed, of course, by properly organised power). Any political theory worth the name must deal forthrightly with 'the empirical complexity of the real social world and of actual political situations'. A prudent political theory should reject moralism, but not morality. Finally, ideal theory is at best a one-sided and at worst a vain enterprise.[1] (To answer an obvious question: Harvard's Government department, the seat of the realist school, overwhelmingly defined itself against the rising Rawlsian tradition, and against the Philosophy department, rather than in accord with it.)

One assumption of the Harvard School, which helps explain its lack of continued influence, was that its approach was so natural as to require neither explanation nor defence. Only Judith Shklar produced, scattered through her work, something approaching a defence of Harvard realism in one of its modes. Shklar was never 'representative' of any school, and her work's moral commitments – its focus on cruelty, on despised minorities, and on those without power – were not endorsed by all members of the Harvard School and were actively opposed by many. In what follows, I shall stress those aspects of her work that did accord with Harvard realism, while leaving for another occasion those that did not. (In particular, I shall not explore Shklar's alleged belief that the chief purpose of history was to teach about the evils and horrors of the twentieth century and to instil gratitude for current liberal institutions – a serious exaggeration in any case.[2])

---

[1] This list is condensed from Frederick Whelan's more comprehensive account in *Hume and Machiavelli: Political Realism and Liberal Thought* (Lanham, MD: Lexington Books, 2004), ix and 289–377; the quotations above are from pp. 314, 303. My list of central figures and canonical works differs somewhat from his. Late in the writing of this chapter I discovered that Katrina Forrester plans a systematic study of the Harvard School. An early sample is her 'Hope and memory in the thought of Judith Shklar' (unpublished paper at the time of writing). It echoes some of the themes discussed here, though of course with a greater focus on Shklar's particular concerns.

[2] Among many other examples of this reading of Shklar see B. Williams, 'The liberalism of fear', in G. Hawthorn (ed.), *In the Beginning Was the Deed: Realism and Moralism in Political Argument* (Princeton and Oxford: Princeton University Press, 2005), 52–61; G. Kateb, 'Foreword' to S. Hoffman (ed.), *Political Thought and Political Thinkers* (Chicago, IL: University of Chicago Press, 1998), viii. For challenges to this view (to my mind, refutations) see D. Thompson, 'Foreword' to J. Shklar, *Redeeming American Political Thought*, ed. S. Hoffman and D. F. Thompson (Chicago, IL: University of Chicago Press, 1998), ix–xi; J. Dunn, 'Hope over fear: Judith Shklar as political educator', in B. Yack (ed.), *Liberalism without*

Harvard School realism, as imperfectly elucidated here, has distinct advantages over a more purely or idealistic 'normative' theory, and those advantages are due to its continual and pervasive reliance on history. The second of these two claims, like all exercises in the moral psychology of intellectual inquiry, is necessarily more speculative than the first. That said, there is reason to believe that the kind of realism canvassed here does require history as other kinds might not. Political realism in the broad sense of relative freedom from fantasy or illusion does not require history; it can be learnt through personal experience in government, politics, or social movements, or simply by reading newspapers.[3] Moreover, one particularly common charge against ideal theory – that it cannot help us decide among concrete alternatives in real-world situations – can at least in theory be solved by the kind of division of labour between ideal theory and social science described by Adam Swift, albeit on fairly heroic assumptions regarding each party's ability and willingness both to do its respective duty and to co-operate with the other.[4] But the particular advantages canvassed in this chapter – a salutary bridging of the is/ought distinction, an inoculation

Illusions: Essays on Liberal Theory and the Political Vision of Judith N. Shklar (Chicago and London: University of Chicago Press, 1996), 45–54; A. Sabl, 'The party of memory and the party of will: Judith Shklar and democratic history', comments delivered at the American Political Science Association Annual Meeting, round table on 'The Significance of History for Normative Political Theory', Boston, MA, 29 August 2008; and Forrester, 'Hope and memory'.

[3] In an often-repeated story, Samuel Huntington, asked to describe his 'method', replied: 'The *New York Times* and a cup of joe [coffee]'. From my recollection, Shklar also regarded these methods as necessary for political theory, though not sufficient.

[4] See A. Swift, 'The value of philosophy in nonideal circumstances', *Social Theory and Practice*, 34: 3 (2008), 363–87. Swift's proposal could, in theory, address the complaints that ideal theory fails to acknowledge the constraints of economics and administration, which render perfect enforcement of rights infinitely costly, and those of politics, in which politicians can only make policy to the extent that they play the political game as the larger society demands. See respectively on these concerns C. Farrelly, 'Justice in ideal theory: a refutation', *Political Studies*, 55 (2007), 844–64, and M. Philp, 'Political theory and the evaluation of political conduct', *Social Theory and Practice*, 34: 3 (2008), 389–410 and *Political Conduct* (Cambridge, MA: Harvard University Press, 2007). Indeed, one can see in the abstract how history would do worse than social science in this regard: it would not teach us about current constraints, and indeed might promote a spurious sense that all things are possible now that past constraints have been overcome. Against this, and against an earlier version of Swift's proposal, see M. Stears, 'The vocation of political theory: principles, empirical inquiry and the politics of opportunity', *European Journal of Political Theory*, 4: 4 (2005),

against the urge for system, an appreciation of the true, practical and agent-centred, basis of political morality, and a serum against the ideal-theory tendency to mistake comparative mythology for systematic research – do seem to require a combination of reflection on particular narratives, attention to experience, and emotional immersion in unfamiliar political surroundings that only history is likely to provide in convenient form.

Political bridging: between is and ought

The first thing Harvard School realism can teach is how to bridge is and ought in politics. In moral philosophy, Alasdair MacIntyre has famously denied the common doctrine that no statement of what is can ground a claim of what we ought to do (and has denied that Hume, in particular, ever maintained this doctrine). While Kantian assumptions can indeed ground a rigid distinction between is and ought, absent those assumptions 'bridge notions' such as 'suits, pleases ... wanting, needing, desiring, pleasure, happiness, health', and 'everyone's long-term interest' connect is to ought in perfectly intelligible ways. For instance, if it turns out that something that was thought to be in everyone's interest is not – and this is at least partly a factual question – it ceases to be worth pursuing.[5]

Politics is not ethics, and the same 'is' statements cannot build normative bridges in one as in the other. For one thing, as game theorists note, in situations of collective action we cannot choose outcomes, only strategies.[6] Doing what we wish everyone would do, or what we 'value',

328–31, which articulates John Stuart Mill's arguments for why these two functions should be combined in the same person and in a single activity of political theory, rather than divided. At the very least, those familiar with modern social scientists might entertain scepticism that they have any interest in specifying feasible alternatives for purposes of practical choice – let alone a proven ability to do so.

[5] A. MacIntyre, 'Hume on "is" and "ought"', in *Against the Self-Images of the Age* (Notre Dame, IN: University of Notre Dame Press, 1978), 120, 114.

[6] 'In philosophical action theory, the actions are simple ones such as flipping a switch to turn on a light. In real life, our most important actions are not so simple. They are inherently interactions. We have reasons for taking our actions, but our reasons may not finally be reflected in the results of our actions even if hope for specific results is our reason for our choice of actions ... [D]epending on what you do, I may do very well or very badly'. Russell Hardin, *Indeterminacy and Society* (Princeton and Oxford: Princeton University Press, 2003), 2–3.

is often no more likely to achieve the collective result that we would prefer than flapping one's arms is likely to produce flight. Yet political theory, like moral theory, would benefit from eroding the is-ought distinction. A variety of political inquiries bridge questions of political reality and questions of what political agents should do. These inquiries include 'political development' (the study of regime change and stability and their social preconditions), moral psychology, comparative political culture and institutions, constitutional design, studies of leadership and executive power, the ethics of war and peace, and political rhetoric. All of these inquiries, not coincidentally, held great appeal to Harvard realists, and continued to be taught there when neglected elsewhere.[7]

These inquiries are, to be sure, worth pursuing primarily for their own sake, in order to yield interesting and useful political knowledge. For current purposes, however, they also bridge the empirical and the normative in one of two ways: by casting doubt on assumptions about the world that normative theory relies on, or by casting doubt on whether normative theory retains its point or effectiveness, given new empirical discoveries. Very briefly: political development casts doubt on the implicit premise of normative political thought that normative consensus is either necessary or sufficient for liberal-democratic 'stability' (understood either empirically or in the Rawlsian sense of the alleged capacity of some moral beliefs to reproduce themselves). Moral psychology, the new name for what was once called 'discourses on the

---

[7] One might call these crossover realist studies the 'JA66 School', after the Library of Congress classification that includes key works by David Apter, Brian Barry, Arthur Bentley, Maurice Cranston, John Dunn, Carl Friedrich, Samuel Huntington, Michael Laver, Austin Ranney, David Runciman, and Dankwart Rustow – and, astonishingly, the old syllabus for Harvard's 'Government 1' course, *c.*1940. I suspect this category of having been constructed by a librarian who had attended Harvard. Mark Bevir has noted that of all US subfields of political science, only political theory has retained a historical approach, which to a great extent severs it from empirical political scientists who practise formal and ahistorical approaches. See M. Bevir, 'Introduction' to *Encyclopedia of Political Theory*, 3 vols. (Thousand Oaks, CA: Sage Publications, 2010), 1:xxxiv. The fact that many of Harvard's 'empirical' political scientists retained a historical and institutional focus long after most departments had adopted quantitative and formal methods is no doubt both cause and result of the persistence of a Harvard realist School that could straddle theory and empirical study. For that matter, Harvard was focused on the history of political theory – its general exams were exclusively 'canonical' – long after other political theory departments had fractured into contemporary schools.

passions',[8] questions whether valid arguments are the usual occasions
for people changing their beliefs, much less their actions. Comparative
political culture provokes us to explain, if we can, why settled points
on which 'we' ground normative discussion should be regarded as
normative for us, when others would find them baffling or invalid,
and whether institutions that are present in some reasonably decent
democracies but not others can rightly be regarded as normatively
essential or exemplary of democracy's deepest values.[9] Constitutional
design forces clarity on just how much we are willing to gamble on the
proposition that ideals drive conduct. To study executive decision is to
study recurrent claims that morality as such must sometimes yield to
necessity; to study leadership, the gentler concept, is to study persuasion
and compromise, political virtues not usually reckoned as moral ones.[10]
The ethics of war and peace raise similar questions of necessity, as well
as suggesting that communal solidarity may be an unwelcome precondition for individual security. That the study of rhetoric is unsettlingly
both practical and moral does not need argument.

What these inquiries have in common is that they can only be done
well by taking on a perspective very different from one's own. That
rhetoric and comparative political culture appear in the above list shows
that history is not logically necessary for this. But there are several
reasons to suppose that history will play this role more typically and
more durably.

To begin with, most human beings are, to cite an accurate cliché,
narrative creatures. Outlooks very different from our own are hard to
take seriously without a story about where they come from: about the
paths by which we ourselves have come to take for granted things that
are questionable, and by which reasonable others have come to think
differently. The alternative is typically a forensic attitude – the 'rebut-
ting objections' of the philosophy paper – that has two obvious flaws.

---

[8] This was, and is, a particular speciality of Shklar and her students. For a defence
of its importance see J. Allen, 'The place of negative morality in political theory',
Political Theory, 29: 3 (2001), esp. 346–7.

[9] I am alluding especially to judicial review, whose essential character is assumed by
Rawls and most of his followers but considered baffling and eccentric in other
countries. This emphasis has been named as partly responsible for Rawls's limited
acceptance, until recently, in Britain. See J. Horton, 'Rawls in Britain', *European
Journal of Political Theory*, 1: 2 (2002), 157.

[10] On this see Philp, *Political Conduct*.

First, one's actual or imagined opponent will often share one's social assumptions: Cicero's masterly preparation of his opponents' cases provided no distance from the customs of his ancestors. Second, forensic preparation, i.e. logic and empirics devoid of sympathy, typically provides cynical distancing from the opponent's position (and sometimes one's own as well), rather than an appreciation of it; one masters the other side's arguments without questioning one's determination to vindicate one's own. (That the Catholic Church used to appoint Devil's advocates in trials for sainthood is not evidence that it gave the Devil a fair hearing.) The only remedy is a principled omnivorousness: an effort to drink in as many different political studies as possible, with a concentration on whichever kinds one can stand the most of, for the sake not of scholarly system but of perspective.

Beyond this, history more than other genres is commensurate with the philosopher's search for permanent insight. Lynn Hunt has argued that accounts of torture (such as Voltaire's *Treatise on Tolerance*) and epistolary novels were responsible for the triumph of ideas of universal human rights; Richard Rorty has advocated 'the novel, the movie, and the TV program', not to mention 'the journalist's report, the comic book, [and] the docudrama' as modern equivalents.[11] These authors, however, portray such genres as effective at one thing, crucially important but very narrow: making us appreciate that people different from us have real human lives, that cruel things done to them matter as much as if they were done to us (or more realistically, that they matter at least a little, enough for us to care).

But the portrayal of an abuse is no more than that; attention paid to it is a matter for action, not reflection.[12] History, in portraying the durable persistence of unaccustomed evils, and the long-running but (always) initially unsuccessful attempts to combat them, forces rethinking of whether we might be not merely inattentive to injustice but wrong about what it is and where it comes from. The same quality

[11] L. Hunt, *Inventing Human Rights* (New York: W.W. Norton, 2007); R. Rorty, *Contingency, Irony, and Solidarity* (Cambridge: Cambridge University Press, 1989), p. xvi. The reader should not laugh at the list. Brian Wood's graphic novel *DMZ: On the Ground* (New York: DC Comics, 2006), by portraying a near-future New York City as the bombed-out front in a civil war, does more to make war's horrors vivid to an American audience than any documentary I can imagine.

[12] Allen makes a similar point in *Negative Morality*, 340, 355–6.

that explains why journalism, documentaries, and television programmes grip the average person explains why they bore the average
theorist: their immediacy. Everyone knows that practical ethics has low
status among theorists. The usual explanation is that it represents
theory rather than practice, but perhaps the real reason is that trying
to solve current or pressing problems would involve deliberately
expending mental effort studying things that one hopes will soon disappear. When a practical problem is of long standing and unlikely ever
to be solved, it has fairly high theoretical status: consider distributive
justice, global inequality, or multiculturalism. No satire is intended
here. It makes excellent sense for some people – and professors of political
theory seem good candidates – to approach the real world through paths
that are not those of the activist and the journalist. History contains
the kind of thing that can appeal to minds used to disdaining the
impermanent.

A certain kind of genealogy may hold a privileged place in this
project. Geuss's subversive faction within the Cambridge School coun-
sels engagement with facts and engagement with past thought for much
the same reason: both force us to think outside current prejudices and to
reject the project of 'generalizing one's own local prejudices and repackaging them as demands of reason'. If one definition of normative theory
is 'judging what is actual relative to what is possible', only immersion in
history lets us actually grasp the second half: 'One of the great uses of
history is to show us what, because it has in the past been real, is a
fortiori possible.'[13] This is political or ideological genealogy, aimed at
broadening our view of what political and social action might achieve.
In his own study of the public–private distinction, Geuss applies the
same approach to intellectual genealogy, and aims at broadening our
ideas of what past moralists found it possible to think.[14] But however
attractive, this project faces the usual tension between what people most
need and what they will voluntarily seek out. Those most complacent
in their normative assumptions are unlikely to seek out genealogies,

[13] R. Geuss, 'Neither history nor praxis', in *Outside Ethics* (Princeton, NJ:
Princeton University Press, 2005), 39. Presumably, an engagement with 'facts'
and social science gives us a firm idea of what is actual; normative political theory
by itself cannot do that either.

[14] R. Geuss, *Public Goods, Private Goods* (Princeton, NJ: Princeton University
Press, 2001).

alternative histories of political and moral thought. (Perhaps one may hope, in Kuhnian style, that their students will.)

Another approach to genealogy works with the grain of theorists' anxieties, rather than against it. Normative theorists who live by one belief may still harbour inchoate doubts that its opposite has been put to rest. Shklar once compared Rousseau, Nietzsche and Freud to Hesiod as practitioners of 'psychological invocation'. Genealogical histories of political thought, like Hesiod's reconstruction of Greek mythology (which Shklar finds 'subversive' and suffused with 'bitterness' compared to Homer's less politically anxious portrait of 'amoral, happy warriors'), appeal to our sense that morality has been written by the winners, and has set up as heroic what should be criticised, in ways that we feel but do not yet understand. The history of political thought can play much the same role – with the crucial difference that it aspires to tell genealogical stories that are not, or not only, mythical; that respect the 'limits of the given'.[15] Here, the many strands of Harvard realism have an active appeal, not just the admonitory, corrective one that their tone sometimes implies. To those schooled in an established tradition who have come to doubt that the tradition can be quite as authoritative as its mandarins believe, scholarship that explores how the tradition is path-dependent, culturally specific, the product of intellectual entrepreneurship, or limited (despite its self-portrait) to recent times, is not troubling at all but both fascinating and encouraging.

---

[15] J. Shklar, 'Subversive genealogies', in *Political Thought and Political Thinkers*, 140, 137, 136, 154, 156. Shklar's reading of Hesiod is, by her own tacit admission, idiosyncratic, shared by few of her contemporaries (139). Hesiod's portrait of gods who act on power, lust and jealousy, as opposed to motives we would think just, was not an unusual one in Greek antiquity. Shklar's comparison to Genesis, brief enough but perhaps implicit throughout, may explain her point, which is one of opposition to system and comforting answers: 'It has been said that religion makes pain sufferable ... Hesiod's myth is only one way of coping among many. But it is an exceptionally intellectual way, a model of and for philosophy. By opening an avenue to the truth that lies at the very foundation of all experience, it appeals to minds not only in revolt against the structure of actuality, but also unable to rest with any obvious solution to its most tormenting paradoxes. The Book of Genesis is not adequate to these demands.' Shklar goes on to compare those who 'want remedies, who want "to do something"' 'to those who prefer ritual to philosophy, prefer assuaging "anger and doubt" to expressing and exploring it' (141).

Against the psychology of system: hope through narrative

Precisely this self-subverting logic helps explain why Harvard realism produced no system that could serve as a contemporary canon, and proposed no programmatic research programme as unambiguously worth pursuing. (This is another reason for its obscurity: Harvard founded no 'School' of theory that could field a team in academe's factional struggles, and naively tended to regard freedom from faction as an intellectual virtue.) The previous section explains why this makes sense. To the extent that realism teaches that no system of thought is immune from critique, genealogy and the suspicion that it reflects the interests of those in power, neither of these teachings, nor any other to which realism might aspire, can consistently claim systematic validity. Here I will suggest why the Harvard realist also has reasons for not mourning the absence of system – or rather, psychic resources for rejecting the anxious desire for its presence.

Shklar wrote that 'the liberalism of fear does not rest on [Kant's] or any other moral philosophy in its entirety. It must in fact remain eclectic.'[16] It is common for realists, whether liberal ones or those more supportive of power, to assert a link between realism and moral pluralism.[17] Neither logically entails the other. Many realists place, or seem to place, one value (peace, the 'balance of power', liberty, stability, security, justly earned fame, the avoidance of cruelty) consistently above others; many moral pluralists are not realists in politics, or even particularly interested in politics.[18] Still, I would claim – following Frederick Whelan – an elective affinity between realism and pluralism. In asserting the importance or

---

[16] J. Shklar, 'The liberalism of fear', in *Political Thought and Political Thinkers*, 12.

[17] See the account in Whelan, *Hume and Machiavelli*, 339. By pluralism Whelan means what Rawlsians call 'intuitionism', the denial that conflicts of value can be settled by appeal either to single yardsticks or to lexical rules.

[18] Swift maintains that moral pluralism provides reason for ever more 'formal or conceptual analysis yielding precision about the various values at stake, how they relate to one another, and so on'. But he then goes on to say that comparing two states that differ across multiple values also requires 'substantive or evaluative judgments about the relative importance or value of the different values at stake' – and gives neither a single example of someone who has arrived at such through analysis nor a single methodological suggestion for how one could. He is in the odd position of arguing that only fact-independent moral philosophy can settle these questions, while providing no reason to think that it can take the first step towards doing so. See 'The value of philosophy in nonideal circumstances', 369.

validity of that affinity I am making a normative, liberal claim: the best kind of realism should be eclectic with respect to its stories of moral foundation, and the most compelling application of moral pluralism to politics involves a kind of realism.

History plays a crucial role here. Liberalism tends to become more realist as it becomes more historical, since history 'implies groundedness in the complexity of the real world'.[19] But this again might beg the big questions: why realism should seek a grounding in history (rather than, say, formal models, which can certainly represent a vertiginous complexity), and why moral pluralism should welcome its reception by realists, as opposed to some of its other allies (e.g. lovers of literature, or of ancient tragedy).[20] The hidden premise seems, by which I mean ought, to be the following. We are prone to too much system in political morality because system drowns out the value claims of those we would prefer to ignore. Who systematises, rationalises. We are used to the critical or radical version of this claim: Enlightenment reason excludes the Other. There is also a conservative version: those who are uncomfortable with tragic choices, imperfect compromises, the necessary exertion of power, or the dependence of domestic tranquillity on international security, are able to ignore such questions by immersing themselves in an intellectual or moral community whose system simply rules such questions out of order.[21] The culprit in both cases is often taken to be an overrating of Reason. But the urge for system may have a more fundamental origin: the desire for continuity, for a set of thoughts that will persist when the thinker is gone. If so, the link between realism and eclecticism or pluralism will be essentially privative. Rather than asking why realism is eclectic, we can ask why idealism is systematic. Realism

---

[19] Whelan, *Hume and Machiavelli*, 304.

[20] Allen suggests two moral reasons why theories of 'negative morality' that put cruelty first, as Shklar does, might practise eclecticism and be distrustful of system: first, because negative morality insists that we give higher priority to our direct awareness of injustice than to settling on a justification of justice; second, because systems may justify a callousness towards the untheorised, customary prohibitions that prevent the greatest evils. See 'Negative morality', 350, 354. While I endorse those reasons, my purpose here is to stress the claims of Harvard realism generally, not just the specific subset of it that overlaps with negative morality.

[21] Whelan implies a similar argument with respect to political theory; in moral theory see J. Kekes, *Against Liberalism* (Ithaca, NY: Cornell University Press, 1997).

may find in history resources, which idealism lacks, for combating the psychic need for system.

No respectable social scientist or natural scientist thinks that his or her system truly (i.e. fully and accurately) describes the world. The goal is to radically simplify the world so that human intellects, which evolved in environments in which cosmology and microbiology conveyed little survival value, can partly grasp it and, in limited ways, affect it. Most working scientists have nonchalantly adopted historicising philosophies of science. They acknowledge that the paradigms they currently accept capture part of the world while ignoring other parts, and that a future generation will marvel at why what was omitted seemed to us less important than what was explained. Only in moral theory are universality and architectonic unity still taken to be values. We are comfortable with 'light is a wave' being an approximation, extremely useful for everyday purposes but inaccurate as a full description of what light is (or even of what we know about it). We are less comfortable with 'a decent society must allow political dissent' having this status. Of course, it *does* have this status, as any student of toleration knows. What one society thinks a symbol of freedom, another will see as a symbol of oppression (headscarves); what one society sees as a clear and present danger, motivating justifiable exceptions to liberal norms (Japanese-Americans during World War II, minarets in present-day Switzerland), another will see as no danger at all, a central case of when those norms should be applied.

Now, admitting such imperfections and exclusions in no way undermines the basic liberal commitment to dissent (or equal votes, regular elections, independent courts, or what have you), any more than advances in quantum physics will stop my eyeglasses from working. A Kuhnian approach to political morality would rule out Whiggish progress on the smallest scale, but not the largest. It is fairly certain that future generations will cherish some values that we ignore, and ignore some that we cherish. But it is far from impossible that the overall number and importance of values that we ignore may decline, and that some core principles and practices that prove their moral and political worth may more or less endure (in altered shape).[22] We have no idea how the shape of future

---

[22] Here I dissent from the radical conclusions, though not the conceptual approach, of Raymond Geuss, *History and Illusion in Politics* (Cambridge: Cambridge University Press, 2001).

geological science will differ from what we now have; to do so we would already have to know things yet to be discovered. But there is no particular reason to doubt, though it is always possible, that a category like 'earthquakes' will still be of interest to future geologists; after all, it seems likely to track the fairly permanent human interest in keeping off the rain and therefore in living in houses that do not fall down. Nor is it unlikely that money, time, and psychic energy put into predicting earthquakes and discovering their causes will yield discoveries that future historians of science will see present-day 'geology' as having contributed to, and that will reduce the number of people harmed by earthquakes. That the concepts and principles in whose terms future breakthroughs will be formulated might be totally unfamiliar to us now does not at all rule out substantive progress.[23]

The same ought to apply to political theory, and will apply if we are comfortable with history. That our concepts and research programmes will change radically over generations does not rule out our promoting a substantive result that furthers recognisable analogues to the kinds of political interests we care most about. That future research will look very different from ours in no way implies that current research is wasted. No desired degree of liberalism, or any other criterion of political worth, is ruled out by the above picture – provided that we do not care what these things are called and are not wedded to a particular dogma regarding how they fit together. (To this extent Harvard realists, though not particular opponents of the Cambridge School, have tended to wonder why its conclusions are thought to matter so much. Almost all the concepts of political language might change beyond recognition without this ruling out the possibility of long-term progress, with plenty of interruptions and imperfections, in managing various political predicaments. Tricks and technologies can be transmitted over time even as the language of the instruction manual changes. Put differently, words matter less than the effectual truth.)

The reason normative theory still resists the analogy to scientific theory is that we who devote our lives to political theory, as opposed

---

[23] I take this to be consistent with Kuhn. 'Later scientific theories are better than earlier ones for solving puzzles in the often quite different environments to which they are applied. That is not a relativist's position, and it displays the sense in which I am a convinced believer in scientific progress.' T. S. Kuhn, *The Structure of Scientific Revolutions*, 2nd edn (Chicago, IL: University of Chicago Press, 1970), 206.

to messy political practices, do not want the worth of our political orders to be a matter of degree. We are anxious that they be perfect; we do not want to live under a regime that does evil towards a few citizens but (one hopes) not too many, across some dimensions but not others. Political theorists do not, for the most part, disagree about this anxiety – only about its consequences. The mainstream view in normative theory is that the search for ever-more accurate and systematic ideal theories is good: the search both motivates reformist ambitions and, crucially, indicates which direction they should take.[24] A more marginal, Nietzschean view is that this search is very dangerous, since the demand for perfection is likely to promote not reform but the rationalisation of imperfections, perhaps to the point of demonising those whose claims challenge perfection. The latter view has much to be said for it – and again, it can be articulated in commonsense, only mildly Nietzschean, versions. Here the key liberal-realist text would be Shklar's *Faces of Injustice*, which urges the view that injustice is as basic a political category as justice, that mainstream theory tends to take up the standpoint of injustice's likely perpetrators rather than its victims, and that realising this will lead us to listen more closely to the concrete, possibly non-theoretical claims of those whom a 'well-ordered' society leaves out.[25]

The Nietzschean critique commonly suffers, however, from its own psychological defects: it asserts truth but provides no comfort. When faced with demands for greater system, Nietzscheans typically respond with mockery, with an odd, postmodern moralism (system promotes a domination that is vaguely assumed, though without warrant, to be bad, or else is insufficiently reverent for life), or a grim demand that their opponents embrace chaos. These stances seem to give us less to live for than the progressive, rational story of the mainstream view.

---

[24] Thus A. J. Simmons, 'Ideal and nonideal theory', *Philosophy and Public Affairs*, 38: 1 (2010), 5–36. Like Swift, Simmons asserts that ideal theory is required in order to direct our actions in second-best cases, while giving neither examples nor methodological suggestions that would provide reason to believe it ever has done this, or can.

[25] J. N. Shklar, *The Faces of Injustice* (New Haven, CT: Yale University Press, 1990). Shklar tended to read Hawthorne along with Nietzsche in making this point. See, e.g., 'Hawthorne in Utopia', in *Redeeming American Political Thought*, 35, and *Ordinary Vices* (Cambridge, MA: Belknap Press, 1984). She writes, in the latter, 'nothing but cruelty comes from those who seek perfection and forget the little good that lies directly within their powers' (39).

A similar message may be more hopeful, however, when recast into the narrative or agent-centred language of a realism influenced by history. In that language it would say: the current state of things may be adequately good, in fact may be getting better in a non-linear way, but given the imperfection of all human institutions, there is always more to be done, and potential excitement in the task of doing it.

Rationalist histories of freedom and autonomy uniquely provide hope for the future only if one defines hope as the belief that reason will do our political work for us. History – here emphatically *not* intellectual history, but accounts of actual things that happened – can, on the contrary, sustain non-rationalist accounts of contingent human progress. Realist histories of interest, power, and agency within institutions – the history of labour and social movements, political histories that retain a sense of agency and strategy, military and diplomatic history – show that the possibility of action and praiseworthy accomplishment under conditions of uncertainty and (retrospectively obvious) moral blindness is not only thinkable but demonstrable. Historical actors, who have never had perfectly adequate moral theories, have somehow been able to achieve a great many things that most of us – including those who aspire to possess such theories – regard as good. Not the supposed 'lessons' of history, but its actual stories are what matter for this purpose: they give realists psychological space that non-realists lack.

Political morality: agency, situation, and practical commitments

The narrative or agent-centred approach to political theory, however, does more than comfort: it illuminates truths. Those who regard political ideas solely as the causes or results of other ideas will miss insights into the moral and political world that those who see them as shorthand for what people have aimed at or valued in politics will see clearly.

The kind of history that can be normative or practical is the kind that centres on agents. But to be truly practical in a complex social world it must not be simply monumental or exemplary, but sophisticated in its view of agency. Action takes place within cultural, social, and political constraints. This is social science shorthand for the practical statement that real-world agents must take account of what they and other agents believe, which resources those agents do and do not have at hand to draw on, and what they (and not just the initial agent) would like to accomplish. Both Montesquieu and Hume have been read as offering such histories: revealing 'our permanent traits in a variety of circum-stances', or adding a sense of 'situation' to the eighteenth-century English obsession with judging character.[26] Human nature may or may not be constant, but it does not much matter: to understand past actions, and draw lessons for present ones, we must study the interplay between choice and circumstance. Contextualism is all-important in such history, but not the kind of contextualism we are used to in political thought. What matters is not the conceptual but the political context.

To the extent that we are still political theorists, and not politicians or political historians, our interest in studying such things will still be theoretical. Understanding that political slogans or ideals are dead metaphors for past programmes will remind us why we cannot easily do without them. The 'rule of law', for instance, seems a tired liberal ideology, if taken out of context; it seems less so if regarded as a concrete political mechanism 'to protect the ruled against the aggression of those who rule'.[27] And if the kind of history that draws attention to agents in practical historical situations can resurrect the appeal of neglected doc-trines, it can also undermine the current appeal of some over-hyped ones. It might seem that some normative positions remain immune to historical purchase. MacIntyre admitted that his bridge categories could not touch an ethical theory that insisted that moral judgements could rest only on other moral judgements; the same must logically be true of political theories. But history can force people who claim to hold a position to face up to what its adoption has meant in practice, or else to explain their grounds for believing that the practical effect it has had in the past would not occur in the future. History, wielded by realists, results not in logical refutation of what a theorist claims, but in justified contempt for theorists who affirm a principle yet disavow the results of believing it.

[26] J. N. Shklar, *Montesquieu* (Oxford: Oxford University Press, 1987), 66; J. J. Burke Jr, 'Hume's *History of England*: waking the English from a dogmatic slumber', in R. Runte (ed.), *Studies in Eighteenth-Century Culture*, Vol. VII (Madison, WI: University of Wisconsin Press for the American Society for Eighteenth-Century Studies, 1978), 235–50. The exact mode in which Hume combined agency and situation will be discussed in my forthcoming book on Hume's *History* as political thought.

[27] Shklar, 'Political theory and the rule of law', in *Political Thinkers*, 24; compare Shklar, *Montesquieu*, 68.

Consider philosophical anarchism, scepticism towards the existence of political obligation. The realist would demand that its proponents, if they claim to intend something normative, defend the superiority of actual anarchism, and the non-governmental coercive forces that would operate under anarchism, to a modern government that rules through laws and relies on a sense of obligation to obey them. To such arguments Shklar replies:

It might well seem that the liberalism of fear is very close to anarchism. That is not true, because liberals have always been aware of the degree of informal coercion and educative social pressures that even the most ardent anarchist theorists have suggested as acceptable substitutes for law. Moreover, even if the theories of anarchism were less flawed, the actualities of countries in which law and government have broken down are not encouraging. *Does anyone want to live in Beirut?* The original first principle of liberalism, the rule of law, remains perfectly intact, and it is not an anarchistic doctrine. There is no reason at all to abandon it. It is the prime instrument to restrain governments.[28]

Let us unpack that. The philosophical anarchist believes that coercion by governments is morally indefensible because it infringes on moral autonomy. From an agent-centred perspective, i.e. a perspective that judges a normative statement according to whether one would want to adopt a strategy that relied on it, theorists who believe this should admit no obligation to obey the law on the part of themselves *or others*. The consistent philosophical anarchist should endorse a state in which he or she must actually rely for personal security not on coercive authority but on fellow citizens' practical reason or respect for moral dignity. The example of Beirut lays bare a claim that in philosophical language is clear but would never be admitted: philosophical anarchists want the lack of obligation to apply only to themselves, so they are free to break

---

[28] Shklar, 'Liberalism of fear', 18 (internal citation omitted; emphasis added). That many have in fact wanted to live in Beirut in times of civil war does not affect Shklar's rhetorical point. Those who stayed in Beirut had overriding reasons for doing so, whether straightforward and admirable (jobs, possessions, the desire to stay with family and neighbours), regrettable but understandable (revenge), or blameworthy (religious or ethnic fanaticism). The question facing the philosophical anarchist is whether he would *in principle* and absent other considerations prefer a Beirut-like world in which political obligation is not generally acknowledged to one in which it is.

laws they think immoral, while enjoying the safety deriving from others' continued acknowledgement of obligation.[29]

A concrete historical case will render this more vivid. David Hume in his *History of England* mentions a time under King Edward I (Longshanks) in which the clergy asserted immunity from the civil law's jurisdiction, and from the realm's general taxation power in particular. Edward, rather than making a normative argument – which at the time would have meant a religious argument aimed at winning over the Pope, the ideal-theoretical arguments for civil power being as yet undeveloped – called the clergy's bluff through 'what might be called a legal lock-out, a harsh, though logical, answer to a refusal to give aid in time of national need'[30]:

[H]e told the ecclesiastics, that, since they refused to support the civil government, they were unworthy to receive any benefit from it; and he would accordingly put them out of the protection of the laws. This vigorous measure was immediately carried into execution. Orders were issued to the judges to receive no cause brought before them by the clergy; to hear and decide all causes in which they were defendants: To do every man justice against them; to do them justice against no body. The ecclesiastics soon found themselves in the most miserable situation imaginable. They could not remain in their own houses or convents for want of subsistence: If they went abroad, in quest of maintenance, they were dismounted, robbed of their horses and clothes, abused by every ruffian, and no redress could be obtained by them for the most violent injury. The primate himself was attacked on the highway, was stripped of his equipage and furniture, and was at last reduced to board himself with a single servant in the house of a country clergyman. The king, mean while, remained an indifferent spectator of all these violences; and

---

[29] One might protest that philosophical anarchists differ from political anarchists: the former claim that there is no political obligation independent of moral obligation, but have no objection to obeying laws (e.g. against assault or murder) that track morality. Practically speaking, the distinction does not stand. Anyone tempted to commit assault or murder is presumably impaired in his moral reasoning, or subjectively denies the moral duty. Yet we would not welcome the results of his also rejecting legal obligation. If political anarchism is the doctrine that the murderer should be restrained by social sanctions or private power, philosophical anarchism is the doctrine that a potential murder victim's best course of action is to appeal to the practical reason of the murderer.

[30] M. V. Clarke, *Medieval Representation and Consent* (London and New York: Longmans, Green & Co., 1936), 263.

without employing his officers in committing any immediate injury on the priests, which might have appeared invidious and oppressive, he took ample vengeance on them for their obstinate refusal of his demands. ... [T]here was scarcely found one ecclesiastic in the kingdom, who seemed willing to suffer, for the sake of religious privileges, this new species of martyrdom, the most tedious and languishing of any, the most mortifying to spiritual pride, and not rewarded by that crown of glory, which the church holds up, with such ostentation, to her devoted adherents.[31]

Hume suggests elsewhere that barons in the thirteenth century should have been treated in much the same way. If they failed to support the king's justice, they should have been cast out from its protection. Those who live by autonomy and anarchy should be left to die by it.[32]

Finally, an ethics of circumstance, rooted in history, tends to produce over time a salutary irony regarding what normative theory can accomplish. History that simultaneously aims at intelligible agency and a realistic portrayal of historical circumstance will end up explaining how apparently callous, reckless, or even tyrannical actions in the past in fact often (though not always) made sense to the actors, given the circumstances of the time and the moral assumptions that were common in society. History, approached in a certain way, leads us to realise that the sympathetic but morally and intellectually limited agents of the past will someday be us. Many of the things we do, and congratulate ourselves for doing, will seem to future generations perhaps understandable but in hindsight quite obtuse. This in no way entails relativism. We can judge some circumstances better than others: while food

---

[31] Hume, *The History of England from the Invasion of Julius Caesar to the Revolution in 1688*, 6 vols, William B. Todd (ed.) (Indianapolis, IN: Liberty Fund, 1983), Vol. II, 115–16 (internal citation omitted).

[32] Describing Peter, Bishop of Winchester, in effect the first minister in 1235, Hume writes: 'The estates of the more obnoxious barons were confiscated, without legal sentence or trial by their peers; and were bestowed with a profuse liberality on the Poictevins [that group of foreigners, which included Peter himself, who were very prominent in Henry III's administration]. Peter even carried his insolence so far as to declare publickly, that the barons of England must not pretend to put themselves on the same foot with those of France, or assume the same liberties and privileges: The monarch in the former country had a more absolute power than in the latter. It had been more justifiable for him to have said, that men, so unwilling to submit to the authority of laws, could with the worse grace claim any shelter or protection from them.' Hume, *The History of England*, Vol. II, 18 (internal citation omitted).

riots during a famine are intelligible, no famine, and therefore no reason to riot, would be better. We can hope for improved canons of reason – less superstition, decreasing respect for ascriptive distinctions – that may be durable and welcomed by future ages. We can certainly expect that improved political knowledge will widen the sphere of possibilities that people may consider. Hume stresses that toleration, freedom of the press, and strict observance of habeas corpus were considered poor statecraft in the time of Charles I; every political decision-maker since that time knows better.[33]

But attention to circumstance does undermine a certain mode of normative theorising that proceeds as if putting forth an ideal theory had a necessary and strong relationship to bringing about a society that embodies it. History provides few examples of non-religious thinkers who reasoned so compellingly to moral conclusions that those whose practices flouted those conclusions immediately stopped doing wrong. Normative reform typically works indirectly: through modes of political action that are intelligible at the time and appeal to prevailing interests and opinions; by altering customs so that new ways of living become matters of habit rather than saintliness; or through institutional design that gives the ambitious and greedy an incentive to pursue wealth and power in more socially productive ways.[34] This approach can still be normative, and can involve very specific counsel – just not the same counsel that normative theory without history would imagine. There is often a single right thing to do in a given situation, or rather a thing that must be judged right given the limits of what an actor can legitimately be expected to know. And one thing we can say with near certainty is that looking for guidance to an ideal theory, rather than to what the agents

---

[33] See A. Sabl, 'When bad things happen from good people: Hume's political ethics of revolution', *Polity*, 35: 1 (2002), 73–92.

[34] Though there is no time to discuss it here, one neglected difference between realists and idealists in political theory seems to lie in the former's willingness – not shared by the latter – to take people's existing desires, passions, opinions, or interests as *prima facie* worthy of respect, as objects that are rightly accommodated or taken into account (perhaps because doing so is democratic, or consensual) rather than merely denounced to the extent that they fail to track a given ideal. The question is not whether the theorist should try to proceed democratically in practice, as most ideal theorists agree they should, but whether the fact that people unanimously oppose proposal X provides substantive reasons *for the theorist* to doubt the normative worth of X.

in a given situation actually value, is not going to be that thing. 'Candor is not a political virtue in a democracy; successful persuasion is.'[35]

Avoiding the intellectually worst: realism versus speculative fiction

Realism is often said to be concerned with discerning and avoiding the worst political evils, rather than promoting the highest goods.[36] It might also be said that it discerns and avoids two *intellectual* vices endemic to the kind of normative theory that flees from reality: a tendency to mistake repeated, communal speculation for evidence, and, conversely, an inability to let any amount of real-world evidence interfere with speculation.

While idealist theory may aspire to a role and vocation that is independent of empirical statements of feasibility, it is hardly shy of making such statements in a particular style. In fact it specialises in what might be called the empiricism of the subjunctive: confident assertions about what would occur if things were very different from any state of affairs ever observed. The very idea of a 'realistic utopia' defines the 'practically possible' through 'conjecture and speculation'. In particular, we are to imagine 'people as they are' but 'constitutional and civil laws . . . as they would be in a reasonably just and well-ordered democratic society'.[37] The criteria of well-ordering are familiar: the 'political conception of justice' is universally accepted and a matter of common knowledge; society's basic structure embodies that conception; and citizens have a 'normally effective sense of justice' that lets them understand those common principles of justice and motivates them to follow them.[38] (As many have pointed out, this last criterion is roughly equivalent to what Rawls elsewhere calls 'strict compliance'.[39]) Now, this is a

---

[35] Shklar, *Ordinary Vices*, 136.
[36] Shklar, 'Liberalism of fear'; Whelan, *Hume and Machiavelli*; Allen, 'Negative morality'.
[37] J. Rawls, *The Law of Peoples* (Cambridge, MA: Harvard University Press, 1999), 12–13; compare Rawls, *A Theory of Justice*, revd edn (Cambridge, MA: Belknap Press, 1999), 397–8.
[38] J. Rawls, *Justice as Fairness: A Restatement*, ed. E. Kelly (Cambridge, MA: Belknap Press, 2001), 8–9.
[39] Rawls, *A Theory of Justice*, 125; Rawls seems to treat a well-ordered society and strict compliance as equivalent assumptions on 216.

'considerable idealisation':[40] put more simply, a well-ordered society has never existed, and no group of people has ever practised strict compliance. These are not laws or constitutions in the sense of any that human beings have experienced, i.e. conventions incrementally adapted over time to the pervasive absence of strict compliance and of agreement on political justice. While our ideal theory is to take into account 'general facts of moral psychology', these are (on Rawls's view) the *only* empirical facts – if empirical they indeed are – that matter.[41] Historical evidence regarding social and political institutions is not relevant. Such institutions are, after all, designed under the assumption of human imperfection, not strict compliance.

---

[40] Rawls, *Justice as Fairness*, 9.

[41] Rawls in early work repeatedly lists the 'general facts of moral psychology' as the only inquiry that need constrain reflection on ideal principles of justice. As long as we know those, the deliberations of those in the original position are 'no longer guesswork'. See *A Theory of Justice*, 123 and compare pp. 126, 157, 405 and esp. 153. Rawls, in *Political Liberalism* (paperback edn, New York: Columbia University Press, 1996), 86–7, explains that moral psychology is 'Philosophical not Psychological': not part of the 'science of human nature' but 'a scheme of concepts and principles for expressing a certain political conception of the person and an ideal of citizenship'. Moral psychology is, in other words, a subset of ideal normative political philosophy. In later work Rawls adds 'political sociology' to the relevant considerations. But at no point does Rawls consider such sociology the kind of thing to which empirical evidence is relevant. Moreover, Rawls appeals to political sociology in support of a surprisingly limited and moralised set of claims: the doctrine of reasonable pluralism in various of its facets (*Political Liberalism*, 193, 389, 390; *Justice as Fairness*, 177 and esp. 33–6); the importance of the burdens of judgement (*Justice as Fairness*, xvii); the alleged civic-educational importance of judicial review (*Justice as Fairness*, 146–7); and in passing some (plausible) statements of the institutions necessary for social and economic inequality (*Political Liberalism*, lvii). In *Political Liberalism*, xlvii–xlviii, Rawls admits that talk of political sociology does not represent an 'attempt to prove, or show' that his key normative goal in that work, that of a reasonable overlapping consensus, is capable of being achieved; in *Political Liberalism* at 205 he denies that a serious disagreement regarding the political sociology of constitutional design can provide a 'fundamental' objection to a normative theory; in *Justice as Fairness*, at 137, he denies that 'political sociology' in the sense of 'the political, economic, and social elements that determine [a regime's] effectiveness in achieving its public aims' is relevant to a consideration of that regime's 'ideal description' (in particular, any evidence that welfare states in their actual operation are ineffective in achieving their goals should not be rebutted but rather ignored as irrelevant to our moral determination to try harder). All that notwithstanding, the parties to a reasonable scheme are to 'accept' various 'facts' of political sociology in the apparent absence of evidence for or against them (*Justice as Fairness*, 90 n 11; *cf.* 101).

All this is fine as a theory of value in the social realm, which is perhaps how Rawls intended it. But those who study the theory cannot always resist the temptation to write of speculation as if it resembled experience. According to John Simmons, 'if we compare the operation of societies ordered by competing principles of justice while assuming strict compliance with those principles, the *different effects we observe* can reasonably be taken to be wholly the responsibility of the different ordering principles themselves' (emphasis added). Such comparison, he argues, teaches us more about the relative worth of different principles than more realistic assumptions would, since it yields a clear signal free of noise. 'If we try to evaluate principles in terms of how societies governed by them would operate with a "normal" amount ... of noncompliance, *we will likely find ... that our evaluations yield* quite indeterminate results' (emphasis added).[42] But the language of experiment could not possibly be apt here. When comparing two societies under the assumptions of strict compliance, we have not 'observed' anything. Such societies are after all *imaginary*, not real. Similarly, the attempt to 'evaluate' and compare hypothetical societies with arbitrarily varied levels of noncompliance does not yield 'findings'.

This is not a mere verbal tic. It leads to claims being made that could not possibly be substantiated. According to Simmons, approvingly glossing Rawls, '[I]nstitutions that embody different conceptions of justice will *predictably* affect differently the degrees of support (and, ultimately, compliance) that those institutions can expect from their subject populations' (emphasis added). We can predict no such thing. There never having been a well-ordered society, the number of things we can predict about such a society is zero, with the level of confidence we can place in any idle speculations about it also being zero. Ideals whose preconditions and effects have never been observed are legitimately a basis for hope and striving, but not for causal claims. The attempt to mimic social science while abstracting from history obscures what should be obvious. Literary criticism applied to speculative fiction does not constitute observation. Widespread agreement among a group of people who practise such criticism constitutes a literary faction – not a basis for reasoned decision or prediction, and certainly not a 'result'.

---

[42] Simmons, 'Ideal and nonideal theory', 8, emphases added.

This confusion regarding the status of the conclusions that emerge out of ideal theory is matched by equal confusion regarding the assumptions that go into it. Prevailing forms of normative theory operate without robust accounts of their premises. Reflective equilibrium, as has often been noted, presumed that prevalent intuitions – within a carefully chosen circle – were adequate. Later normative theory has presumed that the conclusions of earlier normative theory are adequate, perhaps infallible. There is no purchase for questioning the aptness of the whole project, or the possible faultiness of the initial premises. (One Rawlsian philosopher to whom I once proposed this worry responded, 'But a premise to me just means the conclusion of a previous argument.' Indeed.)

In contrast, political theorists who are both strongly normative and readers of history are rarely at a loss for arguments over first principles. That this style of theory is often ideological is a common and often accurate accusation. But few notice that it guarantees a professional virtue. If ideology involves an account of how the world is, an account of how we ought to act, and an account of how the first part bears on the second,[43] ideological claims are (even to some who begin the process under Party discipline) automatically porous to arguments on all these counts. When a claim in political theory has a touch of ideology to it, new evidence about how things are, new claims about causal mechanisms in politics, or new doubts, based on historical experience, about the viability of a political regime can weaken it.[44] To this extent ideology could not be more different from ideal theory. While both may provide hope, only the former provides a sense of when a fondly cherished hope should be abandoned in favour of another that is less idle.

A normative theory that professes immunity to history and that aspires to draw normative statements only from other normative statements (the standard normative theory position, present in both Kant and Mill[45]) can claim only the level of truth or validity that accrues to

---

[43] Here I follow Alasdair MacIntyre, 'The end of ideology and the end of the end of ideology', *Against the Self-Images of the Age*, 6.

[44] Geuss claims that many political theories have been refuted in much this way. His further claim that Rawlsians should ask whether current inequalities in liberal societies in turn refute Rawls requires the assumption that current normative theory has some influence on society – which Geuss concedes may not be so. See the chapter 'Neither history nor praxis', in *Outside Ethics*.

[45] On the latter see Stears, 'The vocation of political theory', 328–9.

any other theory that is all but impervious to refutation (or its Kuhnian equivalent: generational replacement as future researchers find that it fails to solve the problems that interest them). And that level would seem to be low. A theory that derives moral statements solely from other moral statements would seem *logically committed* to saying that a new argument can refute the theory only if it has three qualities: (1) it shares all important normative premises with the theory, i.e. follows the progress of the theory with respect to all important conclusions except the latest one (since otherwise there would be no shared premises from which to argue); (2) it contains *a priori* arguments that disprove all the theory's latest conclusions; (3) those arguments are not merely suggestive or speculative but compelling. These qualities are unlikely to appear together.

Here I am claiming that the relationship of history to any normative theory that claims to aim at truth is one of necessity. There is no philosophy, no true openness to argument and refutation, outside history – or at least some empirically grounded inquiry that does everything that history can do, and I believe that to be a null set. Many criticisms can be levelled at Harvard realism, most of which come down to excessive pragmatism (in the everyday, not the philosophical, sense). One could accuse the School of being too willing to accept existing circumstances, too prone to privilege order over justice, too distrustful of human hopes and aspirations, too statist (even in the way in which it tries to assert ordinary citizens' liberty and equality in the face of state power, i.e. through constitutions and institutions rather than social movements), too willing to tolerate the love of power and manipulation rather than searching out ways of keeping out of power those who love these thing too much, or at least of systematically preventing their abusing power (perhaps at the cost of restraining their strategic flexibility). All these criticisms have some validity applied to Harvard realism generally, though much less when applied to Shklar in particular.

But to fault realists' reliance on history for rendering their theories too 'contingent', for admitting the possibility that a whole field of theoretical reflection may be overtaken by events, would be to attack their School at its point of greatest strength. The fear that a normative theory based on history will be contingent or lack definitive justification is essentially a fear of pursuing a project that may be extinguished when it outlives its usefulness. It may be compared in all seriousness to the fear of death: the fear is natural, and even functional for survival (of an animal or a theory), but the attempt to evade it by erasing the thing feared is not sane.

One of the protagonists of Don DeLillo's *White Noise*[46] overcomes the fear of death by taking pills that eliminate that fear. The pill is habit-forming, one builds up a tolerance, and it has a side-effect: inability to distinguish fantasy from reality.[47]

---

[46] Don DeLillo, *White Noise* (New York: Viking, 1985).

[47] I would like to thank for invaluable comments Carmen Pavel, the editors of this volume, and the participants at the Oxford 'Rethinking History and Political Theory' workshop (September 2009) and the APSA round table on 'The Significance of History for Normative Political Theory' (August 2008).

8 The new realism: from modus vivendi to justice

BONNIE HONIG AND MARC STEARS

Introduction

Political theorists periodically go public to fault their subdiscipline for its flaws. As the chapters of this volume demonstrate, the critique is often that political theory is too ahistorical, abstract and removed from the political realities theory is supposed to help us understand. Caught up in canonical texts, gripped by ideal questions never asked by real politicians, like 'what is justice?' or 'which is the best regime?' or 'how are subjects formed?', political theory is said to list too far to one side, becoming all theory, no politics. On the other hand, when political theorists correct the imbalance and turn to complex historical case studies or the practicalities of daily life, they are accused of abandoning the big questions and grand narratives that dignify their mode of inquiry and distinguish it from mere journalism. Both timeless and timebound, it sometimes seems that political theory can do no right.

In the 1970s, Rawls's *A Theory of Justice* was welcomed because it made the case for systematic political theorising, after decades of political theory's confinement to canonical textual interpretation or the small, seemingly soluble questions of analytic philosophy. But to everything there is a season. Within ten years of the publication of *A Theory of Justice*, political theorists had already begun to worry about the cost of such systematic approaches, citing in particular their remove from the real world of actual politics. The most recent such self-castigation comes to us from Raymond Geuss, in a series of books including *Outside Ethics*, *History and Illusion in Politics* and *Philosophy and Real Politics*, in which he makes the case for what he calls 'realism'.[1] He is not alone.

---

[1] See R. Geuss, *History and Illusion in Politics* (Cambridge: Cambridge University Press, 1999); R. Geuss, *Outside Ethics* (Princeton, NJ: Princeton University Press, 2005); R. Geuss, *Philosophy and Real Politics* (Princeton, NJ: Princeton University Press, 2009).

Others, too, calling themselves realists, have seen in political theory's interests in canonical texts, critical inquiry, system building, and norm-generation a fool's errand that tells us nothing about the real world and, indeed, takes 'flight from reality', as in the title of a book by Ian Shapiro. For Shapiro, the problem is mostly political science's greater fidelity to models than to the realities they are supposed to illuminate. For Jeffrey Isaac, the problem is political theory's absorption by rarefied debates about arcane topics while the world stumbles around without the compass that political theory in more engaged ages sought to supply (though Shapiro, too, pillories the subdiscipline's affection for 'gross concepts').[2] Here, political theory is Nero fiddling while Rome burns. For Geuss, the problem is political theory's takeover by philosophy, which has drawn the subdiscipline into analytic and systematic approaches that operate at some remove from historically situated realities, deride the art of the possible, and promote abstract unrealities of reason, consensus, or right while abjuring the study of power and violence. By contrast with such abstract approaches, says Geuss, a realist will 'start from an account of our existing motivations and our political and social institutions (not from a set of abstract "rights" or from our intuitions)'.[3]

Those actually existing motivations, as Geuss sees them, are less than noble. Historical reflection on politics, he argues, demonstrates that people seek power and crave security. Power, decision, violence and the stabilising influence of the state are key elements of political life. Geuss's realism leads him to reject political theorists' longstanding quest for justice and to embrace in its place the less ambitious, supposedly more realistic end of modus vivendi arrangements, albeit dressed in the language of 'legitimacy'.

Having chastened the aspirations of political theory, Geuss endorses pessimism as a trait of historically informed realism: co-operation, solid-arity, symbolisation, hope, and optimism are sidelined by Geuss, cast as 'unreal', 'ideal' or hopelessly 'optimistic'. But, contra Geuss, realism need not necessarily be pessimistic. In this chapter, we argue that a realist account of politics may find in the experience of political action

---

[2] See I. Shapiro, *The Flight From Reality in the Social Sciences* (Princeton, NJ: Princeton University Press, 2007) and J. Issac, 'The strange silence of political theory', *Political Theory*, 23 (1995), 636–52.

[3] Geuss, *Philosophy and Real Politics*, 59.

inspiration to fight for such ideals, rather than set them aside. Realists may also find in history and experience reason to press beyond modus vivendi arrangements to legitimacy and justice. Closer attention to history and to politics teaches us that we may be more not less ambitious in our politics, and more idealistic than Geussian realism allows. These possibilities become clearer when we read Geuss in connection with two other thinkers who call for a historically informed political theory: Bernard Williams and James Tully. Taken together, in contestatory context, Geuss, Williams and Tully inspire an alternative realism – a truly new realism we call 'agonistic' realism.

Bernard Williams, whom Geuss characterises as a fellow realist and who shares many of Geuss's assumptions about politics and the real world, was not as pessimistic as Geuss.[4] Williams wrote in a way that appeals to our moral integrity, not our rational self-interests, and he had high aspirations for collective life. Rather than make do with a mere veneer of legitimacy over a modus vivendi arrangement, Williams sought to hold our sets of arrangements to higher standards. Politics may always involve calculation, trade-off, cowardice and more, but these are not the entirety of it. He insisted that ethics is properly concerned with care for one's integrity, and that such care for integrity is no less a feature of actual moral experience than are the other traits, privileged by realists. Similarly in politics, where Williams openly described himself as a realist, he urged us to acknowledge that decision, power, and violence are some of what goes on in politics but also to accept that establishing a fuller sense of legitimacy is, in fact, the central challenge faced by each and every regime. Indeed, we might think of Williams's argument on behalf of legitimacy in politics as the corollary to his argument on behalf of 'integrity' in ethics. We may not always achieve or cherish it properly, yet integrity and legitimacy are the postulates of ethical or political life, and we ought to strive to care for and preserve them. Thus, as may already be clear from this, the mood

---

[4] Speaking of the non-utopian character of Judith Shklar's liberalism of fear, for example, Williams said: 'It is conscious that nothing is safe, that the task is never ending. This part of its being, as Judith Shklar said, is resolutely nonutopian. But that does not mean that it is simply the politics of pessimism which has not collapsed into the politics of cynicism ... it can be, in good times, the politics of hope as well.' See B. Williams, *In the Beginning Was the Deed* (Princeton, NJ: Princeton University Press, 2005), 61. For more on Shklar and Williams, see A. Sabl's essay in this volume.

of Williams's work might best be described not as pessimism, but as cautious optimism.

We round out our consideration of alternative realisms by turning to James Tully. Tully does not call himself a realist but he, no less than Williams and Geuss, also calls for political theory to begin with history and the realities of political life. He too rejects the ahistorical abstractions of philosophical approaches and the high normativity of much deliberative democratic theory. He faults them not just for abstraction, however, but also for the power they exercise. 'Elite political theory', as Tully calls the various rational, universalist or abstract approaches he criticises, mistrusts the plural demoi of politics, seeks to constrain or inform or instruct popular will rather than attend to it, and argues deductively in a way quite removed from the daily realities of lived experience, rather than inductively and in touch with political realities. Worse yet, abstractions like 'rights' and 'sovereignty' serve the interests of hegemony when they fold citizen-subjects into (post-)colonial prioritisations of order over freedom, state institutional stability over self-governance.

For Tully, justice, freedom and self-governance are not abstractions and they are no mere ideals: that we may think they are is testimony to the sad success of elite political theory and realists, who often cast freedom and true self-governance as chaotic and dangerous, or unlikely and 'ideal'. In fact, Tully insists, practices of freedom and justice are a lived reality, often autonomous and stable. The realities of freedom are more visible when we build our theoretical positions inductively rather than deductively, and attend to what Tully calls the 'rough ground' of politics, where we see not just violence, self-interest, political chicanery, and instability, but also action in concert, mutuality and non-violence. The latter are no less real than the so-called realities to which realists like Geuss seek to confine our attention. If realism means a commitment to describing what we see, then surely realists must concede that politics includes violence and consensus, agreement and strife, murderousness and reasonableness. Real politics shows we are incited by political engagement into rationality and violence, practicality and fantasy, war and solidarity. And if we attend to these realities, we may find ourselves inspired to strive for more than modus vivendi and more even than legitimacy. We may seek justice.

In what follows, we trace how each of these three thinkers deploys realism to advocate for a political theory of modus vivendi, legitimacy, or justice. First, we outline Raymond Geuss's claim that stories of legitimacy pose grave dangers in politics, especially when they are taken in their own terms, divorced from the interests of power that always, in Geuss's view, under-gird them. Geuss claims Bernard Williams as an influence but, as we argue second, Williams insisted, contra Geuss, that legitimacy must be taken seriously as an aspiration in politics. Legitimacy may always remain insecure or undecidable – possibly authentic, possibly a mask for power interests – but it is a resource for a decent politics nonetheless, in Williams's view. Third, we turn to James Tully's far less cautious optimism. For Tully, there is, in fact, no conflict between realism and some of the bolder ideals of politics. Indeed, he urges us to move from realist premises to a politics oriented beyond both modus vivendi and legitimacy, to focus instead on freedom and justice. Finally, in conclusion, we review each of these approaches and propose an alternative new realism, an 'agonistic realism', that contains elements of each of these contending views, drawing on Tully's ambitious optimism while taking seriously Geuss's and Williams's more cautious or pessimistic assessments of the prospects of political life, the need for stability, and the task of preparation for ongoing political struggle.

Raymond Geuss: from modus vivendi to legitimacy I

Politics, Raymond Geuss argues, is about power, 'its acquisition, distribution and use'. The implicit universalism of this sentiment stands in odd contrast to Geuss's own declared 'contextualist predilections' but, at the same time, the simplicity of the position is gripping.[5] Without direct attention to power and its distribution – what Geuss describes as the Leninist question of 'who, whom?' – political theory can offer little guidance to those who need it. Geuss's essential objective is to restore the tradition of ideology critique in which the task is to use historical reflection to demonstrate how all political practices, including the practice of political philosophy itself, are always inherently in the service of power. To 'think politically' should always be 'to think about agency, power, and interests, and the relations among these' and 'a theoretical approach with no place for a theory of power is not merely deeply deficient but actively pernicious, because mystifying'.[6] For Geuss, then,

---

[5] Geuss, *Philosophy and Real Politics*, 96–7, 25 and 90.   [6] *Ibid.* 94.

realists 'strongly reject the exaggerated moralization of politics', because such exaggerations hide the perils of political life.

This concentration on the politics of power inflects all elements of Geuss's realism, shaping both the explanatory and prescriptive dimensions of his work. Nonetheless, Geuss stakes his claim to being no mere realist, by insisting that his theory is not a crude version of realpolitik, such as those he attributes to International Relations Theory or some versions of Marxism. Those crude realists, Geuss outlines, refuse to accept the importance of ideas, visions, and aspirations in politics, reducing everything to pre-packaged state interests or to the material self-interests of economic class. But Geuss contends that his own fuller realism appreciates the essential role of ideas in political life. He points in particular to the importance of ideas in 'stories of legitimacy'.[7]

A 'realistic understanding' of politics, he continues, necessarily connects politics 'with attempts to provide legitimacy not simply for acts of violence, but for any kinds of collective action, such as deciding voluntarily to build a new road or change to a new unit of measurement (as was done during the French Revolution), or for that matter for any arrangements that could be seen as capable of being changed, controlled, modified or influenced by human action.' All politics, in other words, requires its 'legitimatory mechanisms', which include 'mechanisms for changing beliefs, or generating new ones', for without those mechanisms, and without the stories of legitimation they convey, it would be impossible for political agents to build the coalitions necessary for concerted action let alone to sustain them across time.[8]

Where his realism breaks with aspirations towards legitimacy, however, is in his insistence that stories of legitimation in politics are ultimately offered in order to secure only one thing: power.[9] For Geuss, the process of legitimation is never *above* but always rather historically located *in* the fray of political struggles. Attempts to demonstrate the 'legitimacy' of particular courses of action are thus 'a part of real history, like most of the rest of life'. Accounts of legitimacy thus necessarily differ radically across time and space, depending on the contours of the precise struggle for power of which they are a part. Put another way, aspirations towards, or stories about, legitimacy never solely assess or evaluate

---

[7] See R. Geuss, *Politics and the Imagination* (Princeton, NJ: Princeton University Press, 2010), 31–42.
[8] Geuss, *Philosophy and Real Politics*, 35.   [9] *Ibid.* 34–6.

power, or seek its reform or restraint: they are rather always just another way to procure power.

The vast majority of political philosophers today miss this central point, Geuss contends, and as a result find themselves entangled in ever more abstract and idealistic discussions of the 'true' nature of legitimacy and how best to achieve it. This leads in part to a simple waste of time, with political philosophers developing schemes of 'truly' legitimate politics which are so divorced from the historical realities of politics as to be of no use whatsoever. Beyond that, however, the unwillingness to admit that every story of legitimacy serves some interest in power leads to the worst excesses of politics, connecting together such otherwise dissimilar historical events as the French revolution, Soviet communism and Nazism.[10]

When he turns to matters of political prescription, therefore, Geuss demands that political theory should confine itself to the only proper question that results from an emphasis on the continual competition for power: that of how human beings are capable of living together in a relatively orderly and peaceful way despite their instincts to control and dominate each other. Realists, he explains, should cleave to the 'basically Hobbesian insight' that 'political philosophy' is at its best when it concentrates on the 'variety of ways in which people can structure and organise their action so as to limit and control forms of disorder that they might find excessive or intolerable'.[11] Because conflict, disorder, and competition for dominance are the essence of human interaction, political thinking should always focus on the avoidance of the dangers that follow from these features. There is, of course, a paradox here. For Geuss, politics is partly understood as simple competition for power, often in its crudest, most dominative form, but a particular kind of politics – state politics – is also occasionally lionised as the means by which humans create order out of the most unlikely of material. This is the Hobbesian project, in other words, whereby the horrors of anarchy are avoided through a particularly limited kind of political aspiration focused largely on the controlling power of the modern state.

Geuss explicitly denies much of this. As Patchen Markell observes, Geuss is keen to present his own realism as compatible with the spirit of political radicalism.[12] He is, after all, an intellectual child of the

---

[10] Geuss, *Outside Ethics*, 13. [11] Geuss, *Philosophy and Real Politics*, 22.
[12] See P. Markell, 'Philosophy and real politics', *Political Theory*, 38 (2010), 172.

Frankfurt School, author of the book, *The Idea of a Critical Theory*.[13]
And so we may hear Geuss, the critical theorist, when Geuss the realist
insists that realism, as he understands it, 'does not deny that humans
have an imaginative life that is important to them, aspirations, ideals
they wish to pursue, or even moral views that influence their behaviour'.[14] But the 'even' in the last clause should put us on our guard. For
Geuss's texts are full of such distancing devices which demonstrate
that he is wary of the moralising passions, hopes, and dreams that
beset real politics. It is the task of the political philosopher to ensure
that the visions behind these dreams are always debunked, dismissed
either as 'illusions' bereft of 'real' implications or as temptations to
frightening forms of dangerous excess.[15] Here the echo is more to
Popper than to Adorno.[16]

Geuss's own historical referents testify to his wariness of idealism in
politics. In *Outside Ethics*, Geuss revels in what he calls the 'steely
realism' of Thucydides who showed us that 'hope' in politics is 'almost
inevitably deluding and its power overwhelmingly destructive'.[17] Indeed,
it is this very argument which Geuss takes as evidence that Thucydides's
history is 'realistic, values truthfulness, and is lacking the shallow optimism of later philosophy'.[18] At other times, Geuss makes the argument in
his own voice, rather than through his sources, as when he says: 'Rites,
rituals, and ceremonies' can be misinterpreted as being part of the very
stuff of politics, their content revealing the intentions, aspirations, beliefs,
and commitments of those who practise them. On the contrary, says
Geuss, the self-described realist who knows better, they are instead
clearly 'attempts to deal practically with phenomena that are the locus
of extreme states of anxiety', phenomena which themselves always orient
us fundamentally back to questions of power and powerlessness.[19]
Religion too is firmly rejected. It is somehow 'unreal', belonging essentially to the past. It is true, Geuss admits, that some religious longing still
finds political expression in even the most 'modern' of societies, but, he
continues, 'there seems little to congratulate . . . on this'. 'Religious belief

---

[13] R. Geuss, *The Idea of a Critical Theory: Habermas and the Frankfurt School*
(Cambridge: Cambridge University Press, 1981).
[14] Geuss, *Philosophy and Real Politics*, 9.   [15] *Ibid.* 11.
[16] On the varieties of post-war realism, see M. Stears, *Demanding Democracy:
American Radicals in Search of a New Politics* (Princeton, NJ: Princeton
University Press, 2010), ch. 4.
[17] Geuss, *Outside Ethics*, 221 and 224.   [18] *Ibid.* 225.   [19] *Ibid.* 138.

in 2005', he concludes, 'would have to be even more wilfully obscurantist than it was in 1805 because it requires active suppression of so much of humanity's active stock of knowledge.'[20]

Thus, Geuss's 'realism' is at some distance from the rich texture of the actual lived experience of real citizens and of the historical record of such experiences, both of which Geuss claims to wish to reconnect with political philosophy. Which is more 'real'? To treat aspirations towards legitimacy as mere mechanisms for domination? Or to see in them ongoing struggles for improvement within the political? Or both? If the last, we may grant that such struggles are always contingent, and contested, but still see in them evidence that the mere maintenance of peaceful order is not the only good to which politics is or should be directed.

Fortunately, Geuss's is not the only realism on offer. For those who remain interested in that project of reconnecting to the real, there are other options. We turn now to consider the work of two other political realists, Bernard Williams and James Tully, each of whom moves some distance beyond Geuss to endorse some of the more positive aspirations of political and collective life. For both, political ideals are powerful and welcome elements of political life, not per se part of a threatening or foolishly unrealistic 'idealism' or utopianism in politics.[21]

Bernard Williams: from modus vivendi to legitimacy II

Raymond Geuss says his reading of 'real' politics is inspired by Bernard Williams and there are several reasons he might see Williams as an ally. Throughout his scattered political writings, Williams, too, indicted the easy idealisations of analytical liberalism[22] and he, too, opposed the sort of wishful thinking that too often distracts political philosophers from the harsh realities of political life. He said it was crucial to steel oneself against what he called 'the subversion of the wish',[23] by which he meant that when we focus on how we *wish things were*, our efforts to

---

[20] *Ibid.* 152.

[21] It should be noted, of course, that utopianism is properly a subject for realists as well. On the real impact of utopianism in politics see D. Leopold, 'Socialism and Utopia', *Journal of Political Ideologies*, 12 (2007), 219–37.

[22] Geuss, *Outside Ethics*, 219–33.

[23] B. Williams, *Truth and Truthfulness: An Essay in Genealogy* (Princeton, NJ: Princeton University Press, 2002), 267.

develop clear-sighted analyses of politics are often subverted. We offer theories based upon what we want to be true, or what we believe our audiences want to hear. This is an empty optimism, Williams argues, and we should replace it with attention to the starker realities of ethical and political life as revealed by historical reflection.

In the realm of political theory, Williams took as his conceptual starting points the ineliminability of value conflict, the continual prospect of 'real loss' in our moral and political lives, and the unavoidable contingency of human identity. Like Geuss, he also insisted on the uselessness of both idealised abstraction and the pursuit of certainty and system in ethics and politics. 'We know that the world was not made for us, or we for the world', Williams explained. We know 'that our history tells no purposive story, and there is no position outside the world or outside history from which we might hope to authenticate our activities'.[24]

Unlike Geuss, though, Williams steadfastly refused to draw pessimistic conclusions from these realist premises. Both his philosophy and his own political endeavours were full of a spirit of aspiration. 'Social reality', Williams insisted, '*can* act to crush a worthwhile, significant, character or project', but it is our task both as individuals and as members of collectives to strive against precisely such outcomes.[25] Historically and philosophically informed political activity – what Williams called 'reflection in concrete historical terms'[26] – would inspire consideration as to how to overcome tyranny, to strike against injustice, to attain and maintain freedom for even the most disadvantaged in our midst, all whilst never giving way to utopian or wishful thinking too removed from the real world to be practical or so removed as to be dangerous.

For Williams, the study of history served two essential purposes. First, as with Geuss, it put us in mind of the dangers of the 'subversion of the wish', by constantly reminding us of the 'complete contrasts between what people say, plan, think, and hope, and the often hideous and unpredictable outcomes of events'.[27] It reveals that partiality, partisanship, and power are all ever-present in political life. But, second,

---

[24] B. Williams, *Shame and Necessity* (Berkeley, CA: University of California Press, 1993), 164.
[25] *Ibid.* 165. Emphasis added.
[26] B. Williams, *Philosophy as a Humanistic Discipline* (Princeton, NJ: Princeton University Press, 2006), 159.
[27] Williams, *Truth and Truthfulness*, 153.

and equally importantly, Williams saw in history a reason not to despair. History reminded us of the positive possibilities of politics, of the moments when things go well, when domination is overthrown and injustices put right. Williams found in history encouragement to act, as well as not to act, to aspire, as well as to fear. History not only inoculated us against the subversion of the wish, it could also incite in us the wish for some subversion.

Many interpreters have been distracted from this more optimistic orientation towards politics by Williams's resolutely anti-foundationalist insistence on the historical contingency and ineliminable variability of even our deepest moral beliefs. To these readers, such commitments seem to warrant a realism like that of Geuss: on what grounds are we to seek 'justice' or 'progress', if our moral beliefs are solely the products of our local environment and historical setting? On what grounds can we hope to employ those beliefs critically, and use them to plan for a better future than the one that we now find ourselves facing? How, indeed, could Williams conceive of a 'better' future at all when everything, including our very notions of 'better' and 'worse', is itself inexorably shaped by contingency, and constantly subject to disagreement?[28]

Williams had two responses. The first emerged from his continual insistence on the integrity of our own moral experience. 'What we are left with if we reject foundationalism', Williams insisted, 'is not an inactive or functionalist conservatism that has to take ethical ideas as they stand.' On the contrary, once our 'ethical thought is ... made historically and socially realistic', we are provided with 'a possibility of deploying some parts of it against others, and of reinterpreting what is ethically significant, so as to give a critique of existing institutions, conceptions, prejudices, and powers'.[29] In other words the very plurality of values that Williams embraced and that drives some critics to distraction because it seems to give up on the fundamental task of ethical theory (to identify and rank the values that should orient moral life) is itself a source of promise.[30] In that plurality lies the

---

[28] M. Nussbaum, 'Tragedies, hope, justice', in D. Calcutt (ed.), *Reading Bernard Williams* (London: Routledge, 2009), 219, 220, 235. See too S. Benhabib, 'Feminism and postmodernism', in L. Nicholson (ed.), *Feminist Contentions: A Philosophical Exchange* (London: Routledge, 1995), 17–34.

[29] Williams, *In the Beginning Was the Deed*, 37.

[30] As Williams continued, 'there is no inherent conflict among these three activities: first, the first-order activity of acting and arguing within the framework of our

possibility of conflict and incommensurability but also the possibility of the sort of internal critique that vouchsafes integrity in ethics.[31] Williams did not believe that ethical reflection ever provided final or fully systematic answers to the question 'what should I do?' There would always be disappointments and remainders, decisions to be made amidst conflicting impulses and values; in this way, the argument contrasted with Rawls's 'reflective equilibrium'. But Williams was certain that, at its best, such reflection could – indeed clearly *does* – provide answers that in some way work for us – as individuals, as members of a given society, as collectivities.

For Williams, politics is our imperfect response to those moments when an inner conversation between our intuitive ethical outlooks, clear analytical reflection on those, and a consideration of their historical and present location in social reality, suggest it is time to act for change or maintenance of which we can be proud, even if we know, especially in reflective moments, that such pride may be temporary because things may yet go awry. This awareness does not take away from our dedication to – or even our self-realisation in – the moment of political engagement.

Williams's realism appears to have drifted closer to Geuss's once again however, once he turned to the history of political change and the means by which such change is sought. If the history of moral and political revolution tells us anything, Williams argued, it is that political transformations do not come through dispassionate reason-giving or through the development of a broad and stable consensus. 'For liberals' ideas to have won an *argument*,' Williams explained with reference to the great eighteenth-century revolutions, 'the representatives of the *ancien regime* would have had to have shared with the nascent liberals a conception of something that the argument was about, and not just in

ideas; second, the philosophical activity of reflecting on those ideas at a more general level and trying to make sense of them; and third, the historical activity of understanding where [those ideas] came from'. Instead, he insisted, 'the activities are in various ways continuous with one another, with each providing the resources for potential critiques of the other'. See Williams, *Philosophy as a Humanistic Discipline*, 194.

[31] In the mode of reflection, we may be asking, in other words, whether we have thought our actions through thoroughly enough or whether we are acting in a way consistent with other fundamental beliefs we hold dear. In the mode of genealogy, we may be asking whether we want to act in accordance with principles we just happen to have inherited as a result of historical accident or might we prefer to disavow them?

the obvious sense that it was about the way to live or the way to order society. They would have had to agree that there was some aim or value which liberal ideas served better, and there is not much reason, with change as radical as this, to think that they did agree.'[32] Instead, change came about by one group winning a battle, or series of battles, of some sort, or simply by outliving their opponents (an argument also made by Thomas Kuhn, in the *Structure of Scientific Revolutions*[33]). Change thus requires the deployment of a host of political tactics and strategies, including some of which we may disapprove. Indeed, 'the circumstances in which liberal thought is possible have been created in part by actions that violate liberal ideals'.[34] A troubling finding for most liberals, perhaps: but not for realists.

In sum, although Williams wished to maintain a role for aspiration in his politics, he was always conscious of the unavoidably crude, even brutal mechanisms of power politics. But he was not pressed by this into pessimism: 'A hopeful [political] story does not need a morally edifying' account of political practices, he insisted. Indeed, quite to the contrary: 'The need for an interpretation of the past to be hopeful offers no publication funds to Pollyanna.'[35] Slavery was abolished, the 'rights of man' promulgated, votes for women obtained, not by reasoned per-suasion and careful argumentation, and not even out of the best of motives, but rather by partisan political actors pursuing contrasting agendas in passionate and arduous political contestation. Still, their objectives were improvements and their actions brought them into being.

This is not to say, however, that Williams simply thought that 'might was right' in politics, or less that 'anything goes' in the realm of political action. Two particularly striking constraints emerge in his work, both of which are entirely absent in Geuss and both of which take Williams beyond modus vivendi to legitimacy. First, individuals and collectivities are enjoined constantly to reflect on their actions and implications in the actions of others. Ethical integrity should never be compromised lightly, Williams insisted, and protecting it demands of us a willingness to be introspective about our actions, before and after. Violence on this

---

[32] Williams, *Philosophy as a Humanistic Discipline*, 190.
[33] T. Kuhn, *The Structure of Scientific Revolutions* (Chicago, IL: University of Chicago Press, 1962).
[34] Williams, *In the Beginning Was the Deed*, 25.
[35] Williams, *Truth and Truthfulness*, 267.

account is never, or at least very rarely, straightforwardly 'justified', and is always lamentable. After all, 'only those who are reluctant or disinclined to do the morally disagreeable when it is really necessary have much chance of not doing it when it is not necessary'.[36] This is not the sentiment of a *mere* realism, but rather the mark of an alternative – more agonistic – realism, one that knows how things often are but also insists we can do better.

Second, Williams also thought that change that had been brought about by power alone should always be subject to another test, a test that he believed was in some important sense external to the change itself. This he actually called 'legitimacy' or, more precisely, the 'Basic Legitimation Demand' (BLD).[37] According to the BLD, there has to be *something* else going on in order to explain why it is acceptable for one party to seek to impose itself on the other above and beyond the brute success of the powerful party. This was not to go as far as to say, *pace* Rawls or Habermas, that behind every coercive act there had to be a 'reason that the other party could accept', or even to say that 'each side must have listened and responded to the demands of the other' before they employed coercive force. But it is to say that 'if one comes to know that the *sole* reason one accepts some moral claim is that somebody's power has brought it about that one accepts it, when, further, it is in their interest that one should accept it, one will have no reason to go on accepting it'.[38]

While clearly attractive, Williams's move away from the modus vivendi politics embraced by Geuss to a realist politics that takes seriously the demand for legitimacy introduces a problem to which Williams was not alert. The insistence on this kind of test marks an important turning point in Williams's realism, and reveals some crucial tensions and weaknesses in his work. First, it is hard to see how Williams could have responded to an exasperated realist of Geuss's school, who would insist that *all* efforts at legitimation are best understood as parts of the struggle for power itself, shaped by the contours of particular and contingent struggles of the day. We have suggested that history itself provides a response, with its many instances of hopeful and successful political action on behalf of legitimation and solidarity, not all of which are

---

[36] B. Williams, *Moral Luck* (Cambridge: Cambridge University Press, 1981), 62.
[37] See Williams, *In the Beginning Was the Deed*, 3–5.
[38] Williams, *Truth and Truthfulness*, 231.

aptly redescribed in realist terms as mere power politics, as we shall see again, on Tully's account, in a moment. But Williams does not make this move.

Second, it is difficult to see what would count as evidence that 'the *sole* reason one accepts some moral claim is that somebody's power has brought it about that one accepts it', and that 'further, it is in their interest that one should accept it'. Williams's criterion is meant to secure the possibility of a legitimation that is not reducible to the realism championed by Geuss. But the criterion encounters a problem neatly avoided by Geuss when the latter focuses only on outcome – are the arrangements stable – and not on legitimacy – are they imposed? The question of imposition is complicated: As Williams himself would surely have acknowledged, most of what ordinary people do believe is a result of having been socialised into a form of life by others who may or may not have had self-serving reasons for promoting what are now dominant beliefs or viewpoints. This is implicit in Williams's remark that liberal arrangements are not the products of liberal arguments but rather, often enough, of illiberal actions. But with his criterion, Williams ventures close to a rationalism he otherwise rejected when he insisted, as he did, elsewhere and often, on the commingled qualities of rational and emotional life.

It may be that this curiously rationalist conception of legitimacy comes of Williams's continual effort to balance his commitments to pluralism, contingency, and open-endedness with a quest for stability, safety, and security in the face of uncertainty. In addition to inspiring and motivating action for change, Williams also thought political philosophy should always ask 'how much conflict of value' politics 'can and should absorb'.[39] There were limits on the amount of subversion that one could wish for, he explained, and those limits emanated from considerations stretching far beyond the avoidance of domination and the pursuit of ethical integrity. Paradoxically, given its origins in the quest for legitimacy, it is in this quest for reassurance that we once again hear echoes in Williams of a more pessimistic strand of realism. In other words, although the call for legitimacy itself marks a crucial difference between Williams and Geuss, it emerged from a notably similar concern above all to prioritise stability as a political good.

---

[39] Williams, *Philosophy as a Humanistic Discipline*, 164.

Like Geuss, Williams was drawn to the Hobbesian insistence that the 'first political question' has always to be that of 'securing of order, protection, safety, trust, and the conditions of cooperation'.[40] Indeed, history itself was said to demonstrate that these goods were both the most important and the most vulnerable in human lives, independently of what other ends individuals or collectivities wished to pursue. Concrete historical reflection, in other words, was said to reveal a single 'set of problems' which should be seen as 'peculiarly defying our understanding and revealing our ignorance: the problem, that is to say, of how to live together'.[41] At times, indeed, Williams went as far as to imply that such reflection revealed that the *only* 'undeniable actualities' of political life are the 'horrors of torture and war' that follow from failure to address these problems properly.[42] Here Williams converges with what Judith Shklar termed the 'liberalism of fear', a position with which Geuss, too, openly identifies. The liberalism of fear, Williams argued toward the end of his life, was in a 'unique' position compared to other political traditions because it spoke directly to the 'only certainly universal materials of politics: power, powerlessness, fear, cruelty'. 'It', and presumably it alone, 'is conscious that nothing is safe', that the task to maintain peace, order, and security, is 'never-ending'.[43] For all of his insistence on hope and aspiration, Williams insisted that our political passions had to be at least partially restrained by, and always tuned in to, our continual consciousness of the need for security.

Williams's realism is defined by this tension between, on the one hand, advocacy of a free-flowing, open-ended, agonistic politics, attuned to both the possibilities and the dangers of expressive, (dis)orderly action, and the insistence on a more cautious, safety-seeking, pessimistic pursuit of stability and order. We might see these as signs of his devotion to both Nietzsche and Hobbes; both realists in a way, but each positioning his realism on a different affective register. In Williams, this tension suggests a certain longing for security (and a stable legitimacy) in the face of a value pluralism and value contingency that make him nervous but that he also endorses on behalf of a vitalism that he prized. At its best, he thought, a security-oriented politics should enable and treasure value pluralism and contingency, rather than seek to limit or homogenise them.

[40] Williams, *In the Beginning Was the Deed*, 3.
[41] Williams, *Philosophy as a Humanistic Discipline*, 179.
[42] Williams, *In the Beginning was the Deed*, 55.   [43] *Ibid.* 59–60.

Williams knows that the only stability to be found in the human world is that which we build for ourselves. Perhaps for this reason, he seems finally to put in with Hobbes and with Hobbes's own peculiar variant of legitimacy in politics. The priority of order and security provides Williams's account of politics with a solidity and predictability that would otherwise be lacking. A similar move is evident in his moral theory where moral agents face plural and conflicting values, even incommensurability and tragic choice, but are not themselves described as plural, conflicted subjects. Instead, they are subjects possessed of integrity, a core identity that defines them and orients their choices with a certain predictability in an unstable and sometimes tragic world that assaults them, if at all, from outside.

Throughout his work, Williams argued in this way. He compartmentalised, periodised and temporalised, casting historical periods and conceptual outlooks as internally plural but hermetically sealed off from each other, as for example in his discussion of the transition from the *ancien régime* to liberalism, where he insisted no one in the *ancien régime* could have thought like a liberal, in his discussion of the founding of the United States, where he contended that the republic's very existence acted as a final break with a feudal, illiberal, inegalitarian past,[44] in his discussion of the all-encompassing dominion of liberal ideas today, and in his fanciful examples against Utilitarianism, which assumed the safety and stability of 'home' and cast the dangers of instability to distant elsewhere, such as Latin America.[45]

Again and again in Williams's realism, then, the potential chaos of radical pluralism is anchored in an architecture of time and space that stabilises things and enables the priority of order prized by Williams. The agon is tamed, thereby, without recourse either to the idealisations of a moralised consensus or to the brutal and thoroughgoing pessimism of a Geuss. Such strategies of temporalisation, spatialisation and legitimation limit the pluralism that Williams champions and that seems so wild by contrast with the Kantian and utilitarian approaches he opposes. It is worth asking, therefore: does Williams here yield to the very weakness he worried about in others – the subversion of the wish?

---

[44] See Williams, *Philosophy as a Humanistic Discipline*, 193.
[45] See B. Honig, 'Difference, dilemmas and the politics of home', in S. Benhabib (ed.), *Democracy and Difference* (Princeton, NJ: Princeton University Press, 1996), 257–77.

Williams was not wrong to think that people wish for order, nor, indeed, to think that it is very often through order that the worst political excesses are prevented. But he was wrong to generalise that assumption and to insist that the essential purpose of politics was the avoidance of evil, and not also about the pursuit of something else. He was also wrong to neglect the issue of how much evil is tolerated or ignored because of the fear of instability, or the inability to contemplate a different stability, one with more 'slack in the order' as William Connolly once put it, for example. Stability can be conceived of in many ways: an agonistic equilibrium, for example, might take the risk of what looks like instability from a liberal perspective on behalf of more substantive political arrangements that allow for their own contestation. The alternative is to entrust ourselves to liberal institutions that claim to be minimal and above the fray of politics, while nonetheless disciplining their subjects into certain modes of rationality and behaviour that incite resistance but render it inexpressible, casting it as idiosyncratic or irrational.[46]

In the realm of ethics, one of Williams's outstanding contributions was to call attention to the status of regret as a moral emotion and to the importance of attending to the remainders of moral systems, like Kantianism and Utilitarianism, that claim to resolve moral conflicts without remainder. Williams's theorisation of remainders in relation to moral dilemmas ought to inspire us to attend as well to the political remainders of stability and belonging. The good of national belonging in the US, for example, has come at the price of great evil to many: to African Americans, historically treated as chattels by institutions of juridical slavery, to undocumented workers today subjected to a different apparatus of juridical inequality which conflates their very being with criminality, and to aboriginals, whose perseverance in the face of extermination policies makes clear the costs of the home-orientation of national politics.[47] The first-order principle of politics – stability – turns out invariably to be less stability-granting than we think, for reasons Williams himself adduces – it is purchased by actions mired in force and

---

[46] On Rawls's implication in this strategy, see B. Honig, *Political Theory and the Displacement of Politics* (Ithaca, NY: Cornell University Press, 1993), ch. 5.

[47] See R. Smith, *Civic Ideals: Conflicting Visions of Citizenship in US History* (New Haven, CT: Yale University Press, 1997) and for critical commentary, B. Honig, *Democracy and the Foreigner* (Princeton, NJ: Princeton University Press, 2003) and M. Stears, 'The liberal tradition and the politics of exclusion', *Annual Review of Political Science*, 10 (2007), 85–101.

coercion, which as any realist (and any psychoanalyst) should lead us to expect, often boomerang back on those who try to take advantage of their power.

James Tully: from legitimacy to justice I

For all of the differences between Geuss and Williams, in the final instance both of their realisms are anti-utopian, measured rather than expansive or ambitious. The world of politics is not the world of theory, they insist. Thing go wrong, contingencies abound, practices are plural, fraught, contested. It is (sometimes) best to do least, or at least to do less than a theorist or idealist might advocate doing. For Geuss, any alternative approach to political life threatens to expand the ambit of politics dangerously and unreasonably; it invites the passion of the fanatic. For Williams, there is more point in aspiration than Geuss allows. Legitimacy is a real possibility and it provides a standard by which we can assess and evaluate power. But here too, ultimately the turn is to a postulated safety and security. For Williams, then, legitimacy offers an escape from the instabilities of political conflict, a turning against the potentially ceaseless demands of competing interests and outlooks.

James Tully's perspective is almost entirely other. Unlike Williams and Geuss, Tully's historically grounded alternative does *not* see politics as the sole property of the state. As he contracts political theory's focus on the state's ambit, he makes room to attend to other scenes of politics, often squeezed out or marginalised as unimportant by political theorists on opposed sides of every other issue: liberals, deliberativist universalists, and realists.

At first, Tully's arguments might not seem to stretch realism beyond its concentration on modus vivendi or legitimacy. Indeed, his overall strategy as outlined in *Public Philosophy in a New Key* initially appears to place him nearer to Geuss than to Williams. For just as Geuss seeks to revive the tradition of ideology critique, revealing the power interests lurking behind high-sounding appeals to legitimacy, so defamiliarisation and exposé are Tully's preferred approach. Tully sees power and inequality as intimately involved in the maintenance of the apparently safe, secure, and familiar political institutional arrangements that other theorists (including Williams himself) often promote as stable and well-ordered.

Like Geuss, Tully is particularly critical of putatively universal theories of legitimacy which, Tully argues, disguise particular, partisan projects. Since the Enlightenment, Tully insists, it has been 'assumed that there [is] some definitive ordering of legitimate political associations' and that, consequently, the 'role of political philosophy' is to work out the 'definitive theory of justice or the definitive democratic procedures of legitimation in which citizens themselves could reach final agreements on the just ordering of their associations'.[48] Such accounts, however, deny the inevitability of ongoing disagreement and dispute which are, in fact, constant and crucial elements of political life.[49] Nor is the denial without consequences: claims to universality, certainty, and immutability have been powerful weapons in the hands of some, and especially in the hands of the colonising peoples and states who came to North America equipped with stories of the inevitability and universal desirability of a very particular account of the legitimate form of political life. Those stories helped to promote and legitimate brutal, exclusionary and dominating patterns of political rule and genocide.[50]

Despite these apparent similarities with Geuss's realism, however, the more optimistic nature of Tully's historically grounded realism emerges when Tully turns to offer potential solutions to the dangers that politics presents. In Tully's practice, we defamiliarise established habits of thought not – as with Geuss – in order to resist the siren call of aspiration, but precisely in order to press upon ourselves the need to find new and unsettling ways of thinking and acting. When Tully criticises universalist aspirations to legitimacy, therefore, he does so to undo their depoliticising effects and to call attention to alternative practices of freedom that unsettle the normal order rather than guarantee its stability. Unlike both Williams and Geuss, artificial stability is *not* a first-order good for Tully, nor is it the condition of any possible politics. Indeed, for Tully, the focus on stability in political theory and practice displaces politics and serves to guard privilege and maintain injustice. Where Geuss and Williams see conflict as inevitable and so move toward solutions focused on the good of stability, either through modus vivendi or legitimacy, Tully is struck by the harms of stability itself, which diminishes and disguises conflict while claiming not to.

---

[48] J. Tully, *Public Philosophy in a New Key II: Imperialism and Civic Freedom* (Cambridge: Cambridge University Press, 2008), 97.
[49] *Ibid*. 97.   [50] *Ibid*. 16–42.

Tully does not allow the reality of conflict to force him to relinquish more aspirational aims. He seeks *more* than mere stability or even legitimation. He seeks 'just agreement'.[51] His aim is to promote an ongoing, transformative dialogue of equal parties in contention with each other. He wants those parties to recognise that they are bound by a sense of shared fate, mutual respect, and common future and a shared past that is marred but not exhausted by relations of domination and acts of injustice.

Tully, too, turns to history to make his case. But whereas history offers constraint for Geuss and Williams, it offers promise to Tully. In work on inter-cultural dialogue between Euro-Canadians and Canadian Aboriginals, for example, Tully sees not only genocide and domination, but also a history of *mutuality* that has been deliberately erased from Euro-Canadians' cultural memory, as part of the colonial project. That mutuality, he argues, however, is no less real than the violence and domination on which we have since come to focus. For Tully, therefore, efforts to create inter-cultural dialogue today could learn from the first contact between Europeans and Aboriginals. Lines of power and dependence were murkier then than in the later colonising period – without the hospitality of the Aboriginals, the Europeans might not have survived – and the treaties that resulted promised a politics of almost unparalleled equality and common interest. Canada, he concludes, was 'founded on an act of sharing that is almost unimaginable in its generosity'.[52] Making the generosity unimaginable has been the task of decades of official history and elite political theory. Making it *reimaginable* is the task of Tully's new realism.

Tully's counter-narration of Aboriginal and Canadian history is, therefore, descriptive – as always called for by realism – but Tully finds in the historical account an alternative to the domination and raw power politics that later intervened in the colonising period and that realists tend to assume characterised the whole of the first people's/ settler relationship. Tully's nascent new realism is therefore committed to politics as the art of the possible, but it is not degraded by that commitment, because the possible is immense. That is why Tully can be both a realist, and full of gratitude, optimism and a sense of possibility

---

[51] *Ibid.* 238.
[52] J. Tully, *Public Philosophy in a New Key I: Democracy and Civic Freedom* (Cambridge: Cambridge University Press, 2008), 244–5.

and renewal, even though he is intent on identifying and responding to sedimented injustices that he knows can be only, at best, alleviated or recognised but never fully repaired.

There remain grave difficulties here, however. Tully is persuasive when he portrays the practices of early Canadian treaty-making on which he pins so much hope, drawing our attention to their mutuality, generosity and creativity. But it remains arguable that such treaties were also instruments of domination, as Geuss would surely have it, even European lures into the colonisers' net. At the very least, there were surely elements of both power *and* mutuality, reciprocity *and* suspicion, pragmatism *and* domination at work in the actual practices that led up to the signing of treaties and then in the work those treaties did in solidifying inter-cultural relations into settled patterns of (in)equality.

Taiaiake Alfred argues the point in exactly this way, even casting the Nisga'as' Final Agreement of 1998 as 'a strategy of assimilation', as Tully himself points out.[53] But although Tully cites Alfred, he does not pursue the point further. When Tully focuses on the treaty and not the violence, on the mutuality and not the instrumentalisation, he may inspire. But in so doing he narrates and emplots in a certain partial and contestable way, no less than Geuss does. Tully draws our attention to some elements rather than others, seeking to avoid the pessimism to which so much realist political theory seems to gravitate almost inexorably. When Tully theorises inter-cultural dialogue in Canadian politics, he may even direct our attention away from some of the actualities to which he says he is committed.[54]

Tully seems also to assume as a condition of negotiation the very thing we cannot assume in real politics: the mutual respect whose absence is the reason we need negotiation in the first place. Perhaps Tully's point is that if we adopt the manners specified by respect and recognition, we may come to experience more authentically the trust and civility whose absence the principles are designed to redress. However, when Tully says that with recognition and then dialogue 'consent can *replace* coercion

---

[53] Tully, citing *Peace, Power, Righteousness* in *Public Philosophy in a New Key I*, 275.
[54] Notably, he does insist that inter-cultural dialogue is not an ideal speech situation (*Public Philosophy in a New Key I*, 240), but he also develops his account of recognition obligations out of what he claims are implicit recognitions already granted (234) and in so doing seems to follow Habermas's strategy of identifying immanent norms from our communicative practice.

and conflict', he seems to be a bit dazzled by his own ideal.[55] The risk here is that Tully ends up normativising the real, presuming that the ideal standards to which he rightly aspires can be found and drawn upon in the 'real' world. In this, he mirrors Geuss's realism, rather than interrupting it.

Tully addresses these very concerns at the conclusion of his *Public Philosophy in a New Key*, when he turns to what he believes history tells us of the possibility of citizen transformation even in the face of grave injustice and inequality. Through individual and collective effort, he insists, it is possible to glimpse a political life that might otherwise escape us.[56] Citizens should strive to model themselves on those who have best represented the ideals of dialogue and equal interaction with others in the past. If they do that, he implores, then history tells us that they will – or at least might – succeed; they might recapture the spirit of inclusive dialogue, however elusive it may appear to be.

It is to Mahatma Gandhi that Tully turns to make this argument. Gandhi's politics, Tully argues, offered a form of 'civic organization and uncompromising non-violent confrontation and negotiation with those responsible for imperial relationships', and it did so not with the intention of securing modus vivendi, legitimacy, or an alternative form of domination, but rather 'with the aim of *converting* them to non-violent, democratic and peaceful relationships'. Gandhi and his followers did this by conducting themselves 'constructively'. They sought to live *as if* they already existed in the 'alternative world' that they wanted to 'bring about', eschewing violence, coercion, domination, and power, and offering instead a 'singular style of civic life' in 'personal practices of self-awareness and self-formation'. This 'as if' solves the paradox of politics in which we can bring about change only by living as if we have already brought it about when we have not yet done so.[57]

---

[55] Tully, *Public Philosophy in a New Key I*, 239. For the inspiration behind this idea, see L. Wittgenstein, *Philosophical Investigations* (Oxford: Blackwell, 1997), 81, 104.

[56] In this way, if not in others, Tully's work echoes Kant, who insisted that the gap between ideal and reality, or theory and practice, can best be rectified by better aligning practice – the real – with the demands of theory, rather than by abandoning theoretically valid ideals. See Kant, 'On the common saying: "This may be true in theory but it does not apply in practice"', reprinted in H. S. Reiss (ed.), *Kant: Political Writings* (Cambridge: Cambridge University Press, 1991), 61–92.

[57] For analysis of the paradox, see B. Honig, *Emergency Politics: Paradox, Law, and Politics* (Princeton, NJ: Princeton University Press, 2009). For critical commentary on this move, see Stears, *Demanding Democracy*.

'These are the daily practices of becoming an exemplary citizen', Tully concludes, and by focusing on their performance in real history we should learn to have optimism, even faith, in the possibilities of a new politics.[58] History's exemplarity is brought in to alleviate the paradox of the present moment.[59]

With this argument, Tully mobilises a certain contestable account of Gandhi to inspire actors on the contemporary scene. But attention to other elements of Gandhi's politics presses us in a different direction, toward a more radical or agonistic realism than that developed by Tully. Crucially, key elements of Gandhi's politics are missing in Tully's account. These concern most of all the nature of the opponent and of the circumstances in which the struggle for justice always – or at least often – takes place. Gandhi was well aware that particular kinds of action were more appropriate in the face of some challenges rather than others, both in strategic and principled terms. Of the Palestinians, for example, he wrote in 1947/8: 'I wish they had chosen the way of non-violence in resisting what they rightly regarded an unwarrantable encroachment on their country', but 'nothing can be said against [their] resistance in the face of overwhelming odds.'[60] For Gandhi, it was necessary sometimes just to *oppose*, and not to seek to mend or convert, or even see the question from the other's point-of-view.

Similarly, modes of personal transformation that were available to those engaged in the just struggle themselves were also always, in Gandhi's view, affected by the nature of the injustice to which they were addressed. The fight against colonialism, Gandhi thus believed, required not just training in open-mindedness, generosity of spirit, and a capacity for dialogue; it also demanded a relentless fearlessness and a sense of the profound dangers that politics presented. It was only by developing a deep-rooted courage, for example, that one could face up to, and then begin to resist, the degradations and symbolic violence constantly perpetuated by the false universalisms of the occupier.[61] Yet this courage is a crucially different – even contrasting – characteristic to those that might be demanded at another moment, a moment when the

[58] Tully, *Public Philosophy in a New Key II*, 308.
[59] For more on the idea of exemplars, see Melissa Lane's chapter in this volume.
[60] M. Gandhi, 'A non-violent look at conflict and violence', *Harijan*, 26 November 1938.
[61] See M. Gandhi, *An Autobiography: The Story of My Experiments with Truth* (Boston, MA: Beacon, 1957). We thank Brandon Terry for this point.

most horrific of political evils had been overcome and new political possibilities presented themselves.

In some ways, Tully is, of all the realists, the most attuned to the circumstances of injustice and exclusion in the contemporary world. And his optimistic, hopeful portrait of political engagement surely inspires, in a time when inspiration is sorely needed. Yet the picture he paints – a picture that prioritises the possibilities of dialogue, of reason and of a coercion-free politics – may leave us unprepared for other dimensions of political struggles that Tully himself recognises are ongoing. 'Be the change you want to be' is sometimes excellent political advice, but as Gandhi knew, a contextual political judgement may occasionally direct us to act otherwise. Tully's departure from other realists' faux minimalism essentially consists in dedicating himself to the preparation and training on which good democratic politics always depends, as when Tully notes, for example, that a certain 'kind of respect needs to be cultivated' among parties to the inter-cultural dialogue.[62] Such training may meet the needs of inter-cultural dialogue, in which the terrain of mutuality and respect is already mapped out, even if not fully actualised. But sometimes justice and equality must be fought for in ways for which Tully's respectful subjects of mutuality, trained for inter-cultural dialogue, may find themselves woefully unready. We cannot, as Williams knew, expect to get liberal outcomes by liberal means, nor social democratic outcomes by social democratic means. The forceful, violent actions by way of which certain victories are won, may not be ones we want to advocate for, but as political theorists committed to some form of realism, we may not neglect their place in the political world. Attending to these elements of political life prepares us for some of the difficulties of *fighting*, as we also need to do in current contexts, for justice and equality.

Agonistic realism: from legitimacy to justice II

The realisms we have traced in this chapter all reject the ahistorical, abstract, false universalisms of most contemporary political philosophy. They differ dramatically, however, as they move along a clear trajectory, mapped here, from modus vivendi to justice. For Raymond Geuss, history's lesson is that politics revolves around power – in its

---

[62] Tully, *Public Philosophy in a New Key I*, 243.

crudest Leninist sense – and that stories of legitimacy are likely to
remain vital components of the strategies that those seeking to dominate
deploy and to which we should constantly be alert and of which we
should be properly sceptical. For Bernard Williams, instead, historical
reflection reveals that the quest for legitimacy can operate as a check,
offering a mode of evaluating the politics of power, in order to protect
us from the most unruly or oppressive elements of our plural and
conflictual lives. For James Tully, in contrast, the history of colonialism
reveals that, often, this search for stability masks dangers and coercions.
Instead, we should be attentive to historical moments such as the first
contacts between Europeans and Aboriginals which demonstrate that
contrasting groupings are capable of finding, and often have found,
mutually satisfactory arrangements capable of actions in concert that
are not exhaustively marked by injustice and coercion. We can experience something similar now and not have to settle for either oppression
or perpetual unceasing antagonism if only we practise citizenship and
exchange in the right spirit.

Each of these pictures of the historical realities of politics is, of course,
partial. Pictures always are. But in this case there is an irony, for the
partiality of the political picture presented by these realists would leave
citizens/subjects crucially unprepared for the real challenges of political
life. This is most clear in Geuss's and Williams's realisms, both of which
leave us unprepared in two ways. First, they obscure the dangers of
stabilisation, especially the moments in politics where the state seeks to
reassure us that it is acting in the name of stability by marginalising the
voices of those who feel the time is right for subversion because the
terms of the current order's stability exact too high a cost for some.
Second, Geuss and Williams hide from view the moments when politics
achieves more than we might expect, the times when new collective
goals are set and reached, when the previously excluded are genuinely
invited in, or succeed in inviting themselves in, where coercion is
replaced by or somehow lands us in fair agreements that last a while.

Tully's realism is also marked by some of these defects. Even though
Tully keenly alerts us to both of these phenomena and, in that regard,
offers a realism that is a significant improvement on the others, Tully is
unfortunately silent in two other regards. First, he fails to prepare us
for the sorts of confrontation in which those seeking mutual dialogue,
freedom, and justice find themselves facing violence, resistance, and
rejection. Tully's theory and his examples cast little light on the nature

of such opponents, on the particular strategies that might have to be deployed, or on the qualities of character that might have to be developed in order occasionally to *overcome* rather than to convert or transform those rivals.[63] Second, Tully fails to explore how even when some in struggle do develop exemplary qualities of character such as those that Tully demands – qualities of openness, mutuality, generosity, and consensual exchange – they might nonetheless be parasitic for their success on those who do not. Might it not be the case that every Gandhi needs a Bhagat Singh, every Martin Luther King Jr a Malcolm X? On this point Williams perhaps is better than Tully, because Williams, as we saw earlier, does not disapprove of the fact that liberal arrangements are not the products of liberal arguments but rather, often enough, of illiberal actions.

The struggle to build a more just order requires attention *both* to the aspirational politics of many-sided exchange, to which Tully is so well attuned, and to the harsher politics of 'who, whom?' to which Geuss has done so much to draw our attention. Diminishing coercion on behalf of a more just, inclusive, consensual practice is, it seems to us, clearly desirable, but a politics oriented to replacing coercion with consent leaves those who seek justice and equality ill-prepared for (some of) the battles ahead.

This is why we need an alternative realism. That realism, which we call agonistic realism, maintains many of the common elements of Geuss's, Williams's, and Tully's visions. It shares the sensitivity to the lived experience of historically located political actors, the denial of the usefulness of the abstract universal, the alertness to the politics of power and exclusion. But an agonistic realism also crucially differs on some key points. Maintaining the spirit of optimism, of aspiration, and of justice evident in Tully, agonistic realism seeks to prepare subjects more fully for the often violent contestations of political life. Indeed, an agonistic realism notes with some concern the *absence* of such contestation: have real recognition and mutuality been actualised? Or is this an oppressive regime? Williams might reach for the BLD here, but the agonistic realist does not turn to such criteria to decide the real reality.

---

[63] C. Mouffe offers one sort of analysis in *On the Political* (London: Routledge, 2005) and Stears offers another in *Demanding Democracy*, esp. ch. 5.

Here we have the final element of an agonistic realism; it takes nothing for granted, not even the 'real'. In other words, agonistic realism is committed to the essentially contested character of even the 'real' itself. Agonistic realism assumes that the critique of realism in art, developed by Lyotard, is applicable as well to realism in politics: According to Lyotard, the problem with aesthetic realism is that it reaffirms the illusion that we can seize hold of the real, that photographs or television or other media can be windows to the *real* world. But, Lyotard insists, the truth is that the real is itself often an effect. And for this reason we need continuing, perpetual artistic dissent and the promulgation of ever newer forms of artistic endeavour to avoid complacency and even terror.[64] As Catherine Belsey explains in her gloss on Lyotard, the problem is not just that the picture we get from realists is inaccurate, as if a better description of the real would suffice and correct our vision. It is rather that realism protects us from doubt. It offers a picture of the world that we seem to know, and in the process confirms our status as knowing subjects by reaffirming that picture as true. In sum, art here is confirmatory. Its message is that things are as we think they are.

Each of the political realisms we have analysed here finds such misleading reassurances in their own pictures of the real. For Tully, the reassurance comes from the attention he gives to moments of great optimism, mutuality, and reciprocity. The 'real' here is the occasion of 'first contact' between Aboriginals and settlers, or Gandhi's ability to mobilise without coercion. For Williams, similar solace is found in the closed spaces of stable polities, where the state is able to secure peace and order in an otherwise troubled world and where settled opinion is able to prevail, constraining dangerous, destabilising pluralism as it does so. Even for Geuss, the real reassures, if paradoxically this time. When Belsey explains that realist art generates a sense of security by scaring us, she provides tremendous insight into Geuss's project, which seems so frightening but is nonetheless attractive. Such attraction resides not only in its gripping simplicity, as we suggested earlier, but also in its capacity to frighten us when it makes clear that though our

---

[64] J. Lyotard, 'Answering the question: what is postmodernism?' in I. Hassan and S. Hassan (eds.), *Innovation/Renovation: New Perspectives on the Humanities* (Madison, WI: University of Wisconsin Press, 1983), 329–41.

ideals may be moot, or even pernicious, our embrace of the real is promising indeed.[65]

Does this mean agonistic realism rejects the real it aims to encounter and mobilise, turning its back as it does so on the reassurances that others seem to crave? Not at all. Instead, it is not a question of being for or against the real. It is rather, as Jacques Derrida says, a matter of deconstructing the binary between artifice and actuality while nonetheless avoiding the fall into some sort of idealist rejection of the real. Such a rejection denies the actuality of 'violence and suffering, war and death', and casts these as 'constructed and fictive ... so that nothing ever really happens, only images, simulacra and delusions'. Rather than partake in such denial, 'we must keep in mind', said Derrida, 'that any coherent deconstruction is about singularity, about events and about what is ultimately irreducible in them'.[66] As we also know from Derrida, such singularity can be powerful in its impossible exemplarity for the future. As agonistic realists try to rebuild our futures together, we do well to look to the events of history, and to the essentially contested realities of our own time, in order to inaugurate or maintain futures worth having.

[65] C. Belsey, *Poststructuralism: A Very Short Introduction* (Oxford: Oxford University Press, 2002), 101–2.

[66] See J. Derrida, 'The deconstruction of actuality', 1993 interview reprinted in translation in *Radical Philosophy* (1994), quoted in C. Belsey, *Culture and the Real* (London: Routledge, 2005), 59.

Relative value and assorted historical lessons: an afterword

JONATHAN FLOYD

In this final contribution to our volume I should like to do two things: first, to introduce a concept which seems to me an implied requirement of many of the arguments developed by our gathered authors; second, to briefly reflect upon what further lessons might be drawn from their chapters, especially once those chapters are viewed alongside each other, with common trends and patterns thereby coming to the fore. The two parts are relatively independent of each other, so readers who find themselves uninterested in the first should feel free to jump ahead to the section entitled 'Further thoughts and assorted historical lessons'.

Relative value and the ranking problem

In our introduction to this volume, we pointed out that, judging from the contents of our collected chapters, what emerges more than anything else from consideration of the significance of history for political philosophy is the need to orientate work in our subject between, on the one hand, universalistic and contextualist positions on the nature of political morality, and, on the other, idealistic and pessimistic positions on the nature of political possibility. The challenge thus posed is that of how to strike the right balance between these four extremes, or, if one prefers a different metaphor, that of how to how to find the right pair of positions on the two spectra which exist between them. And of course, as we have seen throughout this volume, different scholars have different ideas about how we ought to go about doing just that. My intention here though is not to wade back into this argument directly. Instead, what I want to do is point out a problem which, it seems to me, has to be addressed once one recognises that there *is* this difficulty regarding how to balance political philosophy between these four extremes, and which is going to remain, almost regardless of whatever balance one recommends between them.

206

The best way of getting at this problem is to begin by setting out the four simple permutations made possible by each of the four extremes to be balanced. First, then, we could match a universal morality with an ambitious political vision. This is both familiar territory for political philosophy and what Bernard Williams began referring to as 'moralism' in his later work. Second, we could pair a universal morality with an unambitious political vision. Williams himself, for example, both preferred liberalism to its alternatives and thought that it was only possible in certain political circumstances.[1] Third, we could combine a contextualist morality with bold political ambitions, as exemplified by Charles Larmore's conception of political liberalism.[2] And fourth, we could produce a contextualist morality without any great political ambitions at all, as captured by the recent work of Raymond Geuss.[3] We could then proceed, judging from these four possibilities, with idealistic universalism, with cautious universalism, with ambitious contextualism, or with pessimistic contextualism.

But each of these pairings, as we know, is a pairing of extremes, and not at all the kind of balance that we are after. Instead, as noted in our introduction, and as explored by the chapters that followed it, what we want to know is just how a political morality that is both universalistic *and* context-sensitive might combine with just the *right* kind of realism. And this means, as noted throughout our volume, that we shall need to draw both on what history tells us about morality and on what it tells us about politics. But what would an approach of this kind involve? Well, at the very least, it seems to me, almost any approach of this kind would have to tell us to aim for the best political state of affairs possible in whatever circumstances we find ourselves. So far so simple, and for an example of this we might consider Mill's controversial claim that whilst liberty might be best for advanced societies, others might be better suited to the rule of despots. Yet the question now becomes, how are we to know just what are the best political states of affairs that could be achieved in various circumstances? This question, I think, finally brings our problem into focus, because once we try to answer it, we soon

---

[1] For discussion of how these two beliefs combine in Williams's work, see my earlier chapter in this volume, as well as the chapters by Kelly and Honig and Stears.

[2] See my earlier chapter in this volume for further discussion of Larmore's argument.

[3] For further discussion of Geuss's work, see again the chapters by Kelly and Honig and Stears.

realise that what we shall need to do if we are to be able to identify the sought-after double-balance is somehow be able to rank different political goals – in whatever political context we are attending to – in order then to see just which amongst those currently possible should be our target. This challenge I call the ranking problem.

Note here that this is not the task demanded of us by at least one version of the ideal/nonideal theory distinction, according to which we are to separate out considerations of what a just society would be from considerations of how it could be legitimately achieved.[4] Even putting aside the two obvious doubts this distinction encounters – that there might be more than one just society, and that the task of achieving it normally takes place under conditions of awful political uncertainty[5] – there still remains what is in this context the central problem: that in situations where we cannot achieve perfect justice, we shall have to have some measure of what counts as better or worse approximations to it. If one is simply given a multi-featured picture of perfection (a vision which tells us that justice involves a, b, c, and d, etc.) and then presented with rules governing our attempts to realise it, what is one to do when faced with what inevitably will be our choice – a selection of one out of several possible but imperfect worlds (a choice, say, between a world where we have a+c and a world where we have c+d)? We commonly claim, for instance, that liberal democracy is what the world needs, but what if we have to choose between its two constituent parts? In a choice between liberty and democracy, which way should we go?[6]

---

[4] My use of 'nonideal' here follows Rawls's employment of the term in *The Law of Peoples* (Cambridge, MA: Harvard University Press, 1999), 89. For a recent discussion of this usage, as well as commentary on the wider literature, see A. J. Simmons, 'Ideal and nonideal theory', *Philosophy and Public Affairs*, 38: 1 (2010). I shall have more to say on other aspects of the ideal/nonideal theory distinction later in this chapter.

[5] For discussion of the relevance of both pluralism and uncertainty to realist political theory, see J. Floyd, 'Should political philosophy be more realistic?', *Res Publica*, 16: 3 (2010).

[6] In response to one obvious objection, we can put aside here the cavalcade of arguments made over the last thirty years to the effect either that true democracy requires liberty as a constitutive element, or that true liberty requires democracy as a constitutive element, because even if some of them are right, we will still sometimes have to choose between imperfect democracy and imperfect liberty. However much the two might be constitutively or even causally related, I know of no argument that claims they are completely identical.

Solving this problem will require political philosophy to do something that it is not at all able to do at present – provide some sort of an estimate of the relative value of each of the various political achievements that we could achieve. And why is this? Because if of the ten positive changes we might be able to achieve in the present context, only three are possible at once, we shall need to know just which three are most worthy of our efforts. This problem can be illustrated as follows. Imagine here that you have to assign relative values to the following six potential achievements: (1) the standard of consent-based legitimacy proposed by A. J. Simmons, according to which no state is legitimate unless all those under its coercive thumb have consented to its rule; (2) the standard of 'justice as fairness' proposed by John Rawls, according to which equal basic liberties are to be met, followed by a strong degree of equality opportunity, and finally by a level of economic inequality that works to the favour of the worst-off; (3) the standard of 'political equality' proposed by Thomas Christiano – or perhaps the standard of 'equality of political resources' proposed by Elizabeth Anderson – according to which certain rights and resources have to be provided to all individuals to ensure that they are able to function as full and equal citizens; (4) the standard of 'legitimate authority' proposed by Joseph Raz, according to which sovereign political institutions generate obligations for us just so long as they make better collective decisions on our behalf than would be reached in their absence; (5) the standard of 'basic needs', according to which only our most basic capabilities are ensured, regardless of the type of government that rules us; (6) the simple and Hobbesian standard of peace, according to which any regime is legitimate, just so long as it ensures freedom from violence on the part of its subjects. So, our task now will be to assign relative values to these possible achievements.

Some caveats first. Clearly I could have chosen other possibilities, and also spelled out each of them in finer detail, but that is by the by; what matters here is the basic exercise required of these six, which is to consider just which of them we should aim for under realistic political circumstances. In order to flesh out this problem we can begin by handing out our relative values as follows: standard (1) is worth 10, (2) is worth 9, (3) is worth 7, (4) is worth 5, (5) is worth 3 and (6) is worth 2. These would be roughly the kinds of score needed in order for us to weight and therefore properly rank our options. But in order to undertake such a weighting we would also need something else, because what we would also need to know is just how much political effort would be required in order to realise each potential achievement.

There are two ways of thinking about this. First, we might think about the different probabilities of achieving each of them. We might assign these as follows: a 1% chance of achieving (1); a 5% chance of achieving (2); an 8% chance of achieving (3); a 20% chance of achieving (4); a 90% chance of achieving (5); and, again, a 90% chance of achieving (6). Multiplying the probabilities by the value of the achievements would then give us the following scores: 10 for (1); 45 for (2); 56 for (3); 100 for (4); 450 for (5); and 180 for (6). Doing things this way would lead us to conclude that (5) is our most obvious priority, but again, this still hardly captures what we are after, if only because it begs the question of why we should not simply try to achieve all six of them at once. Instead, we shall need to think again about what any truly realistic conception of politics requires, and imagine this time, more sensibly, that we have only a finite amount of political capital to spend. For our second attempt at ranking, then, let us say that we have ten units of this capital, with each unit capable of buying us one value-point, as assigned above. What should we do with this capital? Here we might choose to try and achieve (1), because if we really do have ten units, then this is the best way of maximising them. And in turn, if we had eight units, we might rather choose to aim for both (4) and (5) at once, and so on and so forth – the idea is simple enough, without having to list all possible scenarios, as defined by a full range of possibilities, a full range of probabilities, a full set of relative values and a full range of political capital allocations.

My suggestion then, in short, is that regardless of the particular list of goals we think needs achieving in political life, and regardless of whether we call that list 'justice', 'democracy', or 'legitimacy', etc., we are going to have to do some hard thinking about (1) the probability of achieving each political goal, (2) the amount of political capital required to at least attempt each achievement, and (3) the relative value of each such goal when achieved. Of course, given that issues (1) and (2) are much more the preserve of social scientists, political philosophers will perhaps do best to leave much of the work here to them, but nonetheless, this still leaves us with (3), which is a concept at present neglected within political philosophy, and which, if it continues to be so, will always leave our subject open to accusations both of crass universalism and of naive utopianism.

But let's pause here for a minute, and just remind ourselves once more, and this time from a different angle, of the potential relevance to political philosophy of these extremely contrived calculations, and in particular of their relevance to the attempts made throughout this book to sketch out a balanced conception of this subject, understood here as one which aspires to be both universalistic and context-sensitive in its morality and realistic in its political prescriptions. The relevance is this. At present, although political philosophers are highly likely to say, for example, that guaranteeing free speech is 'valuable', that ensuring basic capabilities is 'valuable' and that helping the global poor is 'valuable', this will not be good enough if at least some of the preceding discussion, and also much of the discussion in the preceding chapters, holds true (and again, calling each of them a duty won't help us, if not all duties can be performed). What we really need to know, in a nutshell, is just which of these things should be prioritised if not all of them can be achieved in one go, or indeed, if not all of these achievements could be achieved and maintained at the same time. This is the problem to which the concept of 'relative value' is offered as (at least the beginning of) a solution.

Relative value, as distinct from …

The pair of theoretical items that I have been discussing here – the ranking problem, and the concept of relative value – have, as noted, been developed out of the materials of the preceding chapters of this book, but it is worth noting here how several aspects of both intersect with a number of recent arguments made concerning the relationship between philosophy and political practice.

Consider a recent argument made by Adam Swift.[7] In discussing the ideal/nonideal theory distinction, and in defending the relevance of philosophical argument in nonideal circumstances, Swift seems to have come to a similar conclusion to my own, although for different reasons. Swift talks in his paper of the need to 'evaluate and rank options',[8] and even explicitly of making judgements concerning 'the relative importance or value … of different values'.[9] I am less sure though of his suggestion as to how we might move closer to being able

---

[7] A. Swift, 'The value of philosophy in nonideal circumstances', *Social Theory and Practice*, 34: 3 (2008).
[8] *Ibid.* 364.   [9] *Ibid.* 369.

to make such judgements, or how much he thinks such judgements are, as it were, simply a 'matter of judgement'. He claims, I think quite rightly, that the 'considerations that philosophers adduce to explain what it is about their "ideal" that makes it such are likely also to be relevant to ... comparative evaluation',[10] but is that likely to be enough?

My worry is that even if we do dig a little deeper in order to uncover the reasons given for a particular proposed ideal, what we shall find is simply an argument to the effect that the proposed ideal is 'the right one', and still little guidance as to what would constitute better or worse approximations to it. And, as I have tried to explain here, we are likely to remain in the dark both (a) if the ideal proposed is a compound item such as justice – for then we shall not know the relative value of those features which, in combination, constitute its nature – and (b) if the ideal proposed is simply one small part of the 'right' political order – for then we shall not know how it ought to be traded off with other parts. It is very easy, for instance, to give an excellent case for republican liberty without being able to say which aspects of it matter most if not all can be realised at once, just as it is very easy to give an excellent case in favour of one particular conception of freedom of speech without thereby being able to say if and when that freedom should be traded off against the needs of national security.

A second overlap occurs with Amartya Sen's recent argument to the effect that we should aim for a comparative rather than a transcendental approach to justice.[11] Certainly there is some similarity between our two cases, but whereas I believe political philosophers should do as much as they can to recommend particular rankings of feasible political options, Sen ultimately opts for the procedural fix of leaving those decisions to a suitably designed deliberative-democratic system. I share with David Estlund, though, the belief that this faith of deliberative-democratic theorists in the magic of democratic institutions is more than a little ironic.[12] How on earth are democratic publics supposed to reason their way to answers concerning such things when (at least deliberative democratic) political philosophers profess themselves completely unable to do so?

---

[10] *Ibid.* 372.

[11] A. Sen, *The Idea of Justice* (London: Allen Lane, 2009), esp. 96–105.

[12] D. Estlund, *Democratic Authority: A Philosophical Framework* (Princeton, NJ: Princeton University Press, 2008), 30.

I also agree with Estlund that procedural solutions to these kinds of trade-offs always end up instantiating just the kind of procedure-independent outcome values they hope to avoid.[13] I disagree with him, however, on the question of how responsive to the 'real world' political philosophy ought to be. He says at one point that 'It would be irresponsible to set small and narrow goals without good reason to think that bigger and better things really cannot or will not be achieved'.[14] Perhaps it would be, but consider also something he says much earlier on in his book: 'If close resemblance [to an ideal deliberation] were possible that would be fine, but if not there is a problem of "second best".'[15] One of my key points here has been that if all of our current political possibilities are anything short of the very closest resemblance, we are going to be left bewildered as to what 'second-best' would be.

Consider as a final overlap, and thus a final means of detailing my thesis by distinguishing it from others, a recent argument made by A. J. Simmons in defence of what he takes to be Rawls's 'full' position on the ideal/nonideal theory relationship. There are two points worth making here. The first is that, as noted above, when Rawls presents the ideal/nonideal theory distinction as a distinction between the question of what justice is and the question of how it could be legitimately achieved, that distinction has little to do with our concerns. As Simmons has shown though, and this is my second point, when one digs a little deeper, it soon turns out that there is more to Rawls's thinking on this topic than might initially appear to be the case. Whether or not one's political efforts are themselves morally permissible, it emerges, is just one question that we should be asking ourselves, for what really matters, when we are forced to choose between different morally permissible courses of action, is the question of which one would get us closest to perfect justice. But note the ambiguity in 'closest' here, because for Simmons what really matters is whether or not we have got nearer to the achievement of perfect justice as a matter of long-term political strategy, not whether or not the current policy removes as much injustice as might be possible *right now*. You might, as he admits, have to take one step backwards now in order to take two steps forward later,[16] because what ultimately matters about any given policy is whether it 'puts us in an improved position to reach [our] ultimate goal',[17] not whether or not it makes things as good as they could possibly be in the immediate future.

[13] *Ibid.* 66–8.   [14] *Ibid.* 271.   [15] *Ibid.* 19.   [16] *Ibid.* 23.   [17] *Ibid.* 22.

Relative value and assorted historical lessons

This position, which Simmons describes as 'transitional' rather than 'comparative', is not in my view the correct one.[18] The purpose of nonideal theory here, remember, is to guide us in our actual political choices, so the question we have to ask is whether this transitional version of it is capable of doing that. The answer is that it is not, in at least the vast majority of circumstances. It is not normally possible to even introduce a twenty-year political plan, let alone implement it, so to base one's attempts at justice – when 'one' is only ever one politician amongst others, with even dictators having to be mindful of their rivals and potential replacements – on such grand ambitions will normally be more a matter of three steps backward than one back and two forward. As stressed throughout the latter half of this book, the nature of 'real politics' is such as to prohibit us from almost ever being able to introduce what we consider 'ideal', which is why approximations to this ideal matter so much. Given our political limitations, we have inevitably to try and aim for whatever concrete improvements we can manage in the here and now, regardless of whether or not each improvement would make sense as part of a one-hundred-stage plan for the achievement of perfect justice. And, given that limitation, we will then unavoidably have to ask about what, comparatively speaking, would be the best combination of such improvements that we could manage – a task which will require hard thinking about the relative value of different possible political achievements.[19]

---

[18] *Ibid.* 22.

[19] It is worth noting that Simmons does at one point acknowledge that sometimes we will be so restricted in our choices, and so unable to accurately predict and control long-term politics, that we will simply have to settle for whatever comparative gains we can find (*ibid.* 24). I disagree with him, though, not just about how rare such occasions will be – I would suggest they are the rule rather than the exception – but also about what we ought to do when they arise. For him, the idea seems to be to 'intuitively' weight things like the relative 'grievousness' of the injustice we are addressing, together with the likely success of the policy we are proposing to address it with, whilst drawing where we can on the kinds of lexical priority rules Rawls provides us with. To rely on intuitive weighting, though, is just as wishful a move as the reliance on democratic wisdom, especially when one considers just how little guidance those lexical priority rules really provide. As noted below, it is unclear how to weigh severe deviations from lesser aspects of justice (say the different principle) against mild deviations from higher ones (say equal liberty), just as it is unclear how to weigh any of these considerations against matters that seem here altogether outside of justice, such as national security or the natural environment.

My argument here, then, is explicitly about the task of political philosophers (rather than electorates) developing arguments (rather than intuitions or judgements) that directly address the relative value of different political goals (rather than just their strategic worth as part of a long-term quest for perfection). Think here, as an illustration of my complaint, of Rawls's first account of Justice as Fairness in the original draft of *Theory of Justice*. Given that there will always be a strictly limited amount of resources that we could devote to the task of ensuring equal liberty – after all, one can always spend more in order to ensure personal freedom from harm – how are we ever to know when we should then move on to equality of opportunity? And in turn, given that there is always more that we could do to ensure equality of opportunity, how are we ever to move on to the difference principle? After all, do we really not think that a tiny amount of individual liberty might be worth sacrificing for significant gains in the latter two? Rawls, clearly, did not think this was an insurmountable difficulty, and has clearly at least partially surmounted it by inserting later, instead of the 'most extensive basic liberty' principle, the meeting of suitably defined 'basic liberties'.[20] But again, this remains something of a fudge, because even if we do shorten the list of all possible political goods, we will still inevitably have to make some sort of a prioritisation amongst them, given the political realities that confront us – and how are we to know how to do that, without having at least some sense of the relative worth of each of them?

Relative value and the double-balance

At this point I think a further clarification is called for. Some readers, patient up until this point, might now be wringing their hands at the lack of a proper explanation of how this new concept is supposed to connect both to our quest for a balance between idealism and pessimism

---

[20] For discussion both of this problem and of Rawls's solution to it, see P. Van Parijs, 'Difference principles', in S. Freeman (ed.), *The Cambridge Companion to Rawls* (Cambridge: Cambridge University Press, 2003), esp. 224ff. On the move towards a refined account of the basic liberties, see J. Gray, *Two Faces of Liberalism* (New York: The New Press, 2000), 69–105. And note, to say that this move towards a refined account of basic liberties functions as a partial solution to the problem is not the same thing as saying that this is why Rawls introduced the change – particularly when one considers his desire to respond to H. L. A. Hart's challenge that indeterminacy also occurs when different liberties clash with each other.

and to our balance between universalism and contextualism. As regards the first balance, the explanation will be clear enough in the light of what has been said so far: if we are to be realistic in our political philosophy, we shall need to know what goals to prioritise when not all goals can be achieved, and, if that is so, then we shall need to have some sense of the relative value of different goals – but what of the second balance? Well, it seems reasonable here to postulate that, whatever balance we strike between universalism and contextualism in political morality, that balance will involve both a few select universal political demands and a few moral principles which dictate to us that certain *political* principles ought to vary according to the local moral culture. So, for instance, we might say both that universal tolerance of religious practice would reflect the value of virtually any religion to an individual life, *and* that certain variations in educational or economic policy are perfectly legitimate, just so long as they are the outcome of a democratic procedure. It also seems reasonable to claim that in both cases we would have to employ not just a distinction between universal moral demands and local political principles, but also a subordinate connection between the two, and indeed, it is hard to see how there could not be. It has always been a telling objection against relativism to note that the claim 'political morality should vary according to culture' is itself a universal moral principle.

If we grant these two points, though, where does that leave us? It leaves us with the following problem: if we are to demand that certain moral values are instantiated in all political contexts, and also that some political principles have only to be met in a few, how are we to decide which of either set ought to be prioritised, if only a few can be realised at any one time? So, the ranking problem returns, and with it the need for an attempt to work out the relative value of all of these potential political achievements, universal and contextual alike. Relative value is required both in order to be realistic – because when we cannot do everything, we need to know what matters most – and in order to strike a balance between universalism and contextualism – because even if certain aspects of political morality do vary according to cultural context, we will need to know how those aspects ought to be weighed up in relation both to each other and to more universal requirements. For instance, it might be more important to end slavery than to ensure peace, but also more important to ensure peace than to preserve the right to wear religious dress in the workplace. Or, in another context, we might say that it is more important to maintain peace and tolerance than to achieve democracy. And note that this problem applies regardless of one's proposed method for the justification of either universal or context-dependent political principles. Even if I was right to say in my earlier chapter that we ought to draw more upon patterns of behaviour and less upon patterns of thinking in our search for such things, there still remains the problem of how to rank whatever principles one thinks one has managed to justify.

One final concession is required. Although I have offered up relative value as at least a partial solution to the problem under discussion, I realise that it might just as easily be described as, itself, yet another problem. Throughout all of this discussion I have said a great deal about needing a concept of relative value, and almost nothing about how to deliver one. So, on what grounds might we be able to say that democracy is more important than freedom? Or that freedom is more important than security? Unfortunately, properly answering that question stands well beyond the scope of this afterword, although it is perhaps useful to pick out at least one possible point of departure. This is the thought that, at the least, we would want to know just how these various possible goals support or undermine each other when pursued or achieved. For instance, it might well be the case that it is easier to achieve basic needs in the absence of war, easier to achieve a worthwhile democracy once basic needs have been met, easier to achieve political equality from within a reasonable democracy, easier to achieve justice as fairness under conditions of political equality, and easier to secure the consent of one's fellow citizens in the presence of justice as fairness. But note that this is not to slide back into 'transitional' nonideal theory as defended by Simmons: if peace is both (1) intrinsically valuable and (2) instrumentally valuable in terms of its facilitating of basic needs, then we shall need to know (3) the relative intrinsic values of both peace *and* basic needs in order to establish the complete relative value of peace.

But still, consideration of these sorts of connections could be at least one part of trying to move past a situation in which, at present, political philosophers simply plump for 'valuable', 'not valuable', and occasionally 'more valuable'/'less valuable' as labels for those potential achievements they discuss (a situation that is even more disabling for avowed moral pluralists, and those who subscribe to varying levels of incommensurability). After all, if we do want to practise a political philosophy that is at least vaguely capable of providing guidance for action, and if we do not want to be implausible monists, burying our heads in the sand whilst telling ourselves that all things that are good upon reflection are also achievable all at once, we shall have to do better than we have so far done – or at least as well as we used to do, for consider here just how much easier this problem would have seemed in the heyday of utilitarianism. For classical utilitarians the question of what ought to be done in any given context is reducible to the question of what scores highest on the measure of expected utility, and, although it would hardly be wise to revert to the kind of conception of the good adopted by that kind of thinking, it would certainly be good for political philosophy if at least a little of that political determinacy could be regained. Although different estimations of relative value are, of course, going to be fundamentally affected by what one takes to be ideal (and thus what position one takes on the respective natures of justice, democratic authority, rights, etc.), what has to be remembered is that the theory which generates that ideal, if it is to demand our practical allegiance, has to be able to tell us something of how to make these relative value calculations.

All we can really say at this point, then, is that if political philosophy is to get its double-balance right, it will have at some point to think about the problem of relative value. At present it is all too easy to divide moralists from realists by distinguishing those who think that there exists one universal and achievable conception of justice from those who think that the need for order renders all such notions completely irrelevant. Politics, however, fits neither extreme, and as the chapters by Lane, Sabl, and Honig and Stears make clear, the reality is that we are sometimes able to achieve great things in political life, and sometimes forced to resort to brute measures to no more enlightened end than our own survival. Clearly we can always achieve something in politics, but given that that something will sometimes be very large, and sometimes only very small, what we are going to have to try and do is work out in each case just what that something should be, a task which would require, ultimately, having at least some minimal sense of the relative value of those various possible achievements we currently have in our sights.

Nor will it be enough to simply say that these things are a matter for political judgement, or that circumstances vary too much from political context to political context for us to say anything useful in the abstract. Consider here that if one makes the statement 'whether we should prioritise freedom or order depends on the circumstances', one necessarily implies that there is some point at which a certain amount of freedom should be judged equal to a certain measure of order, and thus in turn that one can assign relative values to these things (a parallel is that if one makes the statement 'the question of whether a given conception of justice is valid depends upon the morality of the local culture', one necessarily implies that there is some universal moral rule which tells us how to translate local norms into political principles). We have a choice, then, between either leaving these puzzles of relative value entirely to politicians and the electorate (both of whom will have their reasoning distorted by the electoral process, however much democratic theorists might wish to idealise their mystical ability to make 'trade-offs'), or trying to develop at least some minimal criteria for their resolution ourselves. And yes, perhaps this will prove quite impossible, but surely we have to at least try, because the simple fact is this: if political philosophers cannot manage to say something meaningful about the relative value of their various proposed political goals, then who could?

Further thoughts and assorted historical lessons

What more though might be said here about the significance of history for political philosophy, beyond these notions of double-balance and relative value? In what remains of this afterword I should like to draw out four lessons from the preceding chapters.

Lesson 1 – fool's gold

The first lesson, I would suggest, is that we need to be cautious about making the same type of mistake that has been made, according to several of our authors, in earlier works arguing for the significance of history for political philosophy. This is the mistake of rashly introducing arguments from outside of political philosophy; of importing, unexamined, what later turns out to be fool's gold. The most obvious example of such an error suggested in these pages is Kelly's 'Collingwoodian paradigm'. If it really is true that the non-objectivism and historicism combined in this view have been applied too uncritically by some to political philosophy, then what this should urge upon us is the need to be more careful in the future when importing new forms of thinking into our subject. This will be particularly important for Kelly himself, who recommends to us a Gademerian hermeneutic approach to both philosophy and history, but also for Haddock, who advances the claims of the philosophical literature on normative judgements. It will also be important in the light of my own suggestion that political philosophers pay more attention to empirical patterns of political behaviour. Adopting from outside political philosophy claims that are themselves contentious in the subjects from which they are being borrowed – political science in my own case, philosophy in Kelly and Haddock's – is clearly something that has to be done with the greatest of care.

Lesson 2 – the limits of theory

A second and related lesson can be drawn, though rather more indirectly, from the chapters by Lane, Sabl, and Honig and Stears. The risk here, it seems to me, is that in saying that we need to find a balance between progressive and conservative political goals, and between radical and conservative ways of achieving them, perhaps we take on too much in trying to make this balance, in the canonical fashion, entirely a matter of *theory*. So, when saying that sometimes we will have to be bold and sometimes cautious, sometimes ruthless and sometimes delicate, perhaps we attempt what cannot be achieved when we say that some or other new theory could tell us exactly how this balance ought to be struck. Consider here, by way of an analogy, a gripe that Kelly has with Quentin Skinner's notion of the 'fallacy of coherence'.[21] The fallacy occurs when interpreters of the history of political thought try to find an inner, unifying system to a thinker's thought that just might not be there. It might just be the case, that is, that a thinker was inconsistent, or simply that not all of their arguments derive from the same basic foundations. Kelly's difficulty with this fallacy is that it is not at all clear just how and when this occurs, but to this Skinner could well reply, 'well, that is just a matter of expert judgement, and not something that can be detailed in the abstract for each and every possible case'. This problem then returns again, albeit in a different form, in Graham's chapter when he talks of the seamless line that runs from simply translating a text to, in effect, arguing with it. Once again we shall want to ask: how is one to know where to draw this line? Once again we might want to answer – this is simply a matter of judgement.

---

[21] For commentary on this fallacy, see Kelly's chapter in this volume.

The relevance of this analogy to our problem is simple enough. If it does happen to be true that political philosophy is currently unable to cope with those changes in political circumstance and possibility revealed to us by history, and also that any form of our subject worth practising *would* need to cope in order to be *realistic* about the ever-changing nature of political affairs, perhaps we need to consider the possibility that 'not being able to cope' with these things might be a function, not so much of bad or incomplete theory, but rather of the nature of theory itself. Maybe it is just impossible to theoretically specify these things to the desired degree in advance. Perhaps we shall simply have to say that, *at some point*, knowing when to act and when to hold off, knowing when to advance and when to consolidate, is a matter for good political *judgement*, rather than good political *theory* (a point of which I am doubtful, at least when applied to choices of principles rather than actions, but which, if true to at least some extent, would have an obvious bearing on my earlier discussion of 'relative value' as an aspect of striking the double-balance described). Of course, we might then be able to say something interesting about the various considerations good judges would take into account, and about those skills and virtues we would want such judges to exemplify, and even then to learn from history just what those skills and virtues might be,[22] but still, there would remain a crucial difference between doing that and providing a theoretical guidebook regarding each and every political decision that ought to be made. One is even tempted to say that there might now be a third balance to be struck in our subject – that between theory and judgement.

Both this and the previous lesson can be further clarified by thinking briefly here about Skinner's well-known remark that we should do our own thinking for ourselves.[23] This statement can be interpreted in at least two ways: we can say that it means that we should not let others think *for* us (and certainly this is closer to Skinner's intended meaning) or that it means that we should not do politico-philosophical thinking ourselves on *behalf* of others. The first, then, warns against political philosophers having their methods and assumptions dictated to too

---

[22] There is already a strong line of thinking running in this direction in Lane's chapter in this volume.

[23] Q. Skinner, *Visions of Politics, Vol. I: Regarding Method* (Cambridge: Cambridge University Press, 2002), 88.

much by grand philosophical figures from the past. Being a footnote to Plato or Kant might well mean more than that one is a mere philosophical foot soldier – it might also mean that one is on a hiding to nothing, at least as far as political philosophy is concerned. This error, as noted above, is relevant to many of our chapters, but perhaps especially to my own, which tells us both that we have accepted too much from our philosophical ancestors (and in particular a view of normative enquiry I call 'mentalism') *and* that we should try to help ourselves by borrowing from contemporary political science. Even assuming that I am right about the first, we would still need to be cautious about the second.

But consider now our second interpretation of Skinner's remark. This version would warn political philosophers against trying too hard to specify what ought to be done by political actors far removed from their own circumstances. They should not, perhaps, be telling us how to act in *any and all* conceivable situations. So, whilst the first interpretation tells us not to be too dictated to by theoretical outsiders – ancestors from the past, or doyens from other disciplines – the second tells us not to prescribe too tightly to others what it is that they ought to be doing. Or, alternatively put, whereas the first tells us not to inherit or import our theories and assumptions too lightly, the second tells us not to prescribe too tightly, *in theory*, just what it is that political actors ought always to undertake. We might recall here Georges Santayana's famous remark that those who forget history are condemned to repeat it. My hope with both of these lessons is that we can learn from those mistakes pinpointed in our gathered chapters in order to then become familiar with the general *types* of error that they represent, and thus in turn make it easier to avoid them ourselves further down the line.

Lesson 3 – political philosophy versus history as a guide to political philosophy versus the rest

There is, however, something rather more positive that can be taken from both of these lessons. This is the thought that we should use the arguments developed in these chapters to think anew about political philosophy's relationships with all sorts of further subjects, and not just history. Here it seems important, following in particular the chapters by Graham and Hampsher-Monk, to recognise that the dividing lines between different subjects are often both fluid *and* real. That is, whilst there are certain crucial differences between, say, political action and political philosophy, it will also always be the case that there is a philosophical or at least theoretical component to the first, just as there is a performative-political component to the second. Hampsher-Monk's chapter in particular helps us to realise that both political philosophy and the history of political thought contain, all at once, historical, philosophical, and political elements. For example, we cannot make any historical claim regarding either political or intellectual history without relying, however tacitly, on some or other philosophy of history, regardless of whether we have examined that philosophy or not.

We should also recognise here that when asking what we can learn about political philosophy's general relationship with other subjects from these studies of its relationship with history in particular, the history of political thought can itself be a highly useful resource. My own chapter, for instance, uses history both to reveal the acceptance of 'mentalism' in political philosophy, and the fact that, in the past, our subject was much more open to the weaving of empirical, historical observations into its normative arguments (as exemplified by Aristotle, Machiavelli, and Montesquieu). And of course, it was not just political science and political philosophy that used to be closer. When asking, for example, what the significance of psychology might be for political philosophy, we may well choose to begin by reflecting on a Plato or a Bentham. But again, to return to the earlier point, at the same time as we look to draw on the history of political thought for guidance regarding how other subjects may be brought to bear on our concerns, we shall still all the while have to be wary of importing too easily and uncritically. The lesson sketched out a moment ago is just as true when it comes to the importation of non-philosophical arguments as it is with philosophical ones. Just as Haddock is correct to write that 'thinking in unfamiliar ways can alert us to dimensions of our own experience that might previously have been ignored' (a very Skinnerian point), he is also right to point out – along with Lane, Kelly, Graham and Hampsher-Monk – that the application of the study of the history of political thought to political philosophy has itself been, not just a problematic exercise, but also a *philosophical* one. We shall always have to be as familiar as possible with those subjects from which we borrow, in order to then apply them wisely in our own pursuits. A tricky task, certainly, but also a necessary one, at least if the history of such borrowings is to be treated, as it surely should be, as any kind of a guide to future endeavours.

Lesson 4 – the uncertainty of progress

All of which takes us to our last and shortest lesson, which is that we should be cautious about assigning value in advance to all of these various lines of enquiry opened up by our gathered chapters, particularly once it is recognised that they involve just the sorts of philosophical borrowing and inter-disciplinary connections discussed above. And if history is any guide here, we are just as likely to forget this point as we are to recognise it as common sense, despite the fact that all it amounts to is the simple claim that we just cannot know in advance how well our new intellectual enterprises are going to go. Taking this thought seriously, though, means recognising that the questions of how *far* this book has managed to move things forward, and of how *fruitful* its proposed endeavours are going to be, are ultimately going to be matters for intellectual history, rather than the subject to which it is intended as a contribution – political philosophy. This is not, of course, to say that these ideas are merely a matter of audience opinion – that their worth is subjective in some poor and no doubt highly contradictory way. My point is simply that we cannot know how useful such arguments are going to be until others have tried to make use of them, and also until others have had time and space to consider and critically reflect upon themselves. We shall just have to wait and see where these arguments go, which means in part waiting and seeing where others try to take them. As Glaucon recognised, we shall not have the measure of a certain view of justice until Socrates has had his say about it; or as Mill insisted, we cannot know the strength of any idea unless it is subject to just the kind of critical scrutiny that free speech permits.

And so, as much as I have been happy to advance the claim that this volume makes an original and important contribution to our understanding of history's significance to political philosophy, and as much as I have been happy to present it as an important response to the accusation discussed in our introduction – that political philosophy is currently practised in too ahistorical a fashion – I do also recognise, in the light of what history tells us of such things, that whether or not it will amount to a significant step forward for our subject is not for us to decide. All we can ultimately say is 'only time will tell', by which I mean, let future theory give its own historical verdict. Graham makes the point in his chapter that whether or not an author succeeds in writing for posterity is, ultimately, a matter for posterity, and not the author herself. I accept this historical lesson: as much as it has been our intention in this volume to make a fruitful contribution to political philosophy, I recognise that it is not for us, but rather for history, to say whether or not we have succeeded.

Index

Lightning Source UK Ltd.
Milton Keynes UK
UKHW020642230522
403373UK00015B/414